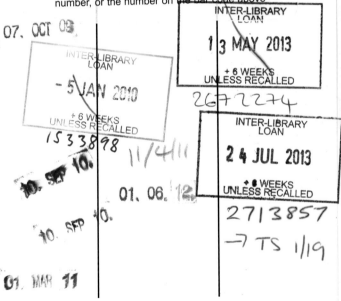

First edition 2004 Revised edition 2007/8
Edited by Raymond J Warren
Self published by the author, Raymond J Warren

Book layout by David Darling
Cover Artwork Gavin Landzaat
Cover design by Raymond J Warren
Historic research by Raymond J Warren
Illustration presentation by Raymond J Warren

Printed by
Creditson Industrial Co.,Limited
Building 5,Gemodle Garden,Shenzhen,China
Ph.+86 755 33360189

Aboriginals and Torres Strait Islanders are forewarned that images and names of tribal people
long deceased, have been used in this historic work.

FRONT COVER ILLUSTRATION: "A ghostly ship now holds her, embraced in memory's arms"
REAR COVER ILLUSTRATION: 'Homeward bound'

WILDFLOWER CONTENTS

INTRODUCTION

Among the hundreds, if not thousands of stories recorded about shipwrecks and castaways, there is one that has defied history researchers for over 160 years. This is the story of Barbara Crawford Thompson, a young Scottish emigrant who was cast away among headhunters near the northern tip of Australia in November 1844. Three scientists who were commissioned aboard the ship H.M.S. 'Rattlesnake', a British warship commanded by Captain Owen Stanley, first diarised her story.

Since that time several Authors have told her story by following the writings of these learned men and at times romanticising her tale in novel fashion. The problem is that something appeared to be missing, the whole story was just too vague and was certainly incomplete. While doing a brief at the State Library of Queensland on the Barbara Thompson drama, the Author came upon what he believes are answers to many of the missing sections of her story.

Barbara Crawford Thompson had claimed that she eloped from her home in Sydney at age sixteen with a man named William Thompson. She claimed that she lived at the Brisbane Penal Colony for eighteen months before Thompson took her on a whale oil salvage operation into the South Pacific.

In November 1844, two months after setting sail from Brisbane, the little cutter they had embarked on was wrecked on Horn Island near Cape York. She alone was rescued by natives from nearby Prince of Wales Island and remained with the headhunters for five long years.

After her rescue in October 1849, several unanswered questions remained and it is believed that this was because her family and/or the government at the time wanted the whole saga to remain a mystery. Since then, only some of her dramatic tale has been offered up for public scrutiny. Officially, Barbara gave little information about herself and even less on the man in her life. She told her questioners only that she had migrated from Scotland in 1836 aboard the ship 'John Barry, that she had eloped and that her man had drowned at Horn Island.

It is obvious to the Author, that there had been a cover up of details in the Barbara Crawford Thompson story and it is easy to show why such a cover up was initiated. Both the Australian officials and the Crawford family appear to have been in agreement in wanting the truth well hidden away.

To avoid historic tedium, this work alternates both in novel and historic form. The reader will find one or two contentious issues but better to air and discuss than to ignore. The only real contention is in where Barbara has told the truth and where she has not. It must be remembered that she was cast away from a very young age and some of her memories may have become exaggerated. There is also the loyalty problem. Barbara may have been protecting her memory of Thompson while being questioned by the men of the 'Rattlesnake'.

All references to natives of the Torres Strait and Cape York have been taken direct from the writings of Sir Oswald Brierly, Thomas Huxley and John MacGillivray, the writings of whom, have been a major source of information.

NB: *It must be understood that at the time of these events, Queensland as a state did not exist, Brisbane was still part of old New South Wales.*
Author.

Dedication

For my mother Norah Warren nee Newton,
Born Ashington, Northumberland, England 17/11/1908,
Died Broken Hill N.S.W 21/6/1958.

It was her love of a good tale that first brought Barbara Crawford Thompson to my attention.

and also
for Glenys Hatch of Perth, Western Australia and Sherrin Blum of Shepparton Victoria
whose contact with me in October 2007, made the enormous amount of
research for this book worthwhile.

"WILDFLOWER"

In a strange and rugged garden, they found her growing wild,
A sadly tarnished beauty, by all the fates reviled.
On savage shores she nestled, 'neath burning sunlit skies,
Where fire and storm came raging, to almost close her eyes.

'Midst wild winds and crashing wave, her Will had slipped away,
Only strength born of youth helped her live that day.
At terror's girth she gamely stood to struggle on alone,
Abandoned there by careless lust, a flower not yet grown

With fierce ones she did bide, for white wings from the past,
For somewhere deep within she knew, such pain could never last.
Though fire scorched and battered, she grew there ever strong,
No torment, nor a tortured heart, could take away her song.

Still she grew in every way, with wisdom to the fore,
Until they came to take her home, a wild thing no more.
A ghostly ship now holds her, embraced in memory's arms,
Whilst errant hearts are stolen, by the wildflowers charms

Raymond J Warren

FOREWORD

The Barbara Crawford Thompson story has received little investigation since she was rescued from among the headhunters of Prince of Wales Island in the Torres Strait late in 1844. What has been known about her life and times has been handed down to us by rescuers and by Captain Owen Stanley's biographer, Adelaide Lubbock.

The Author believes that he has brought to light several previously undiscovered items relating to her story, especially the true identity of her 'husband', William Thompson and most certainly her age. Prior to this work, her family and the man who took her away from them were virtually unknown.

The truth about her age when she 'eloped' is shown here for the first time, as is her family life before she ran away to Brisbane. Did Barbara have siblings, how old was she when she disappeared from her home? Did her parents report her missing or seek help from the officials in Sydney and what was her life before she left her home? What happened after she returned to civilization and what manner of official investigation was done to find the cause of her ordeal? Finally, did she have mixed race children while stranded at Cape York and why did the men of the 'Rattlesnake' ask her several times if she would not prefer to stay with the natives of the Torres Strait?

When found, Barbara was so black as to be unrecognizable from among the northern natives, her hair was matted and she had suffered several burns to her body. She limped from a knee injury and was almost blind in one eye from conjunctivitis. Her loyalty to the memory of William Thompson whom she said had drowned at the wreck site remained strong and it appeared that she was happier to speak of her time with the natives, rather than to dwell on her life with Thompson. Records from that time suggest that the scientist involved in her rescue were also far more interested in her life with the natives, than in what caused her to be a lone white woman on Prince of Wales Island.

That Barbara Crawford was never asked the obvious questions about the man in her life seems incredible. Having studied the reports given by scientists Brierly, MacGillivray and Huxley, one cannot understand what caused her rescuers to skip over such vital information. Nor can one understand why, according to our available records, Dr Thomson of HMS 'Rattlesnake' appears to have not mentioned Barbara in his medical reports.

Did the scientists question Barbara thoroughly on how she came to be in such a tragic predicament? Perhaps they felt sorrow for her loss and the terrible ordeal she had faced and declined to question her too much on such a sad subject. Or perhaps they did get to the whole truth with Barbara requesting that her story be kept as private and quiet as possible. The reports left to us by her rescuers are vague and are certainly not complete, it will become obvious to the reader that much of the tale has been left well alone.

Barbara Crawford spent nine weeks aboard the 'Rattlesnake' at Cape York. It is probable that the whole story did come out in that period but was never been officially recorded. The Victorian moral code may also be a reason for her dramatic story having been stifled.

Recent research discoveries answering almost all of the above questions have perhaps brought finality to an apparently unsolved history. Now for the first time in 160 years, much of the truth behind her story can be shown. The tragic voyage to Australia, how she left home with a stranger named William Thompson, her transportation to Brisbane, her age, her family life and many other unanswered questions can now be divulged. The reader will become immersed in her story and will, like the Author, come to understand why Barbara Crawford Thompson has received little honour for her suffering.

The Author presents the never-told side of Barbara Crawford Thompson' s story, so that history may be served.

Author.

WILDFLOWER ILLUSTRATIONS

Aboriginal, Torres Strait Islanders and New Guinea nationals are forewarned that illustrations of native persons long dead are included within these pages.

THE VOYAGERS

Dundee March 1837

The sun, though still low in the sky, had already begun its spring warming of the craggy mounts and green hills Scotland. The rugged beauty of the highlands, majestically at their best during this time of year, stood like ancient sentinels watching over the land. The rugged mountains stood fortress like, fighting valiantly for exposure to the sun as it occasionally burst through the grey rain-filled clouds that jostled and chased one another, across the windswept skies. The clouds, seemingly flustered, had little time for congregation until forced upwards and almost to a halt, over the steep and rocky landscape. There, long trails of drizzly mist slipstreamed away from the ramparts, bringing a strange almost eerie atmosphere to the darkening sky. Snow still lay in patches along the lower highlands, its chill quickly turning cheeks and noses red, on those who braved the outdoors. Late into the afternoon, grey black-tinged coal smoke rose slowly away from scattered chimneys as daylight dimmed toward evening.

Spring evenings were special for the young Mrs. Jane Crawford. As a young wife and mother, she loved watching the skies throughout the lengthening sunsets. On evenings such as this, she marveled at the thunderheads growing larger as they rose upward upon reaching the ramparts. Then would come the familiar crack and rumble, as the enormous clouds were forced together, struggling like leaden-suited giants striving to overcome each other. The rumbles were preceded by wondrous gold and iridescent blue and white lightning that paved a brilliant pathway for the growling thunder reverberating down and across the lush dark green and white misty valleys.

Jane and her husband Charles had met and married in Aberdeen where he had begun his working life as a blacksmith. In line with the traditions of their people, they married while both were still very young. During fifteen years of marriage, the Crawford's had raised seven children and now had an eighth child on the way. Almost unbelievably, Charles was still only thirty years old and Jane, just one year younger.

The Crawford Family

When first married, the Crawford's moved from Aberdeen to Dundee, so Charles could be close to the new shipyards. Work as a blacksmith had its drawbacks though, for many Scotsmen followed the trade, especially at the large shipping ports of Glasgow, Edinburgh and now Dundee. Shipbuilding had entered a new and vital phase. This prompted Charles to also try his hand at Tinsmithing. Jane as homemaker took care of the house and the children, teaching them how to read and write and although poor and struggling, Charles and Jane Crawford still managed to find room for their growing family.

Charles, [born in 1807] took Jane in marriage on March 29, 1821, when he was fourteen and Jane thirteen years old; both were of the Presbyterian faith. By 1837 the Crawford children numbered seven and in order were. Alexander, [14] born 1823, Charles Junior, [12] born 1825, Mary, [10] born 1827, Ann, aged [8] born 1829, Barbara, aged [6] born late 1830 or early 1831, Jane, [4] born 1833 and Andrew, [2] born 1835. Jane was only a few weeks away from the birth of her eighth child when the family departed Scotland in March 1837. The ages listed above are from the manifest of the ship 'John Barry' that departed Scotland on July 13th 1837.

While working at the port of Dundee, Charles heard sailors talking after their return from southern latitudes. They spoke of wonderful lands discovered in the South Pacific, lands that were now being populated by free men and convicts from all over the British empire. They brought news of how good land was being offered as a temptation to free settlers. This was enough for the Crawford's to begin planning for a new life in Australia. A place where their children would have much more space to live and grow. With the aid of assisted passage, there was nothing to stop a poor Scots family moving from one British port to another. Charles worked a trade that would never fail to attract custom, especially in a new country that would surely need his services. Within weeks, Charles Crawford and his family had made their shipping arrangements and passage was secured. Advertisements for the London Line of ships boasted of a sturdy vessel, the 'John Barry' of 520 tons, it was this vessel the Crawford's selected as their transport to Australia.

The 'John Barry', when first seen by the Crawford's, was a 23 year-old wood ship built at Whitby in

1814. She had begun her life as a convict transport and as the years progressed, she was used alternately as passenger ship, convict transport and cargo vessel. She had four previous voyages transporting convicts to Australia and had proved a trustworthy vessel with a good master. The 'John Barry' always maintained a respectable health record, rarely losing even one or at most, two passengers on a voyage. At a time when shipboard deaths were commonplace on any given voyage, she had maintained this good record, which also included her convict passages.

Going Aboard

As sailing time drew near, the family moved their luggage to the docks. There they found people dithering and fussing about, rushing here and there like ants round a nest. Charles went searching for and found a steward and few minutes later, they were delivered down into the bowels of the ship. Though dark and smelling richly of the sea, the ship seemed large and roomy, although this proved to be false notion once all the passengers were aboard. The steward directed the family to their berth, which had already been erected, while the children struggled gamely to carry favoured items aboard. They stood in sulky silence before the small apartment they would call home for the next few months. All were amazed at the tiny space they had been given, wondering just how and where they would find a place for themselves and their accoutrements. Still, the excitement of the approaching voyage raised their spirits and within a few moments, they were back to their chattering best.

Jane sent her family up on deck for peace of mind and then puzzled where she might stow the few clothes for each of them that she had brought to the berth. She gazed quizzically at the tiny space and sighed resignedly, realizing that privacy, would be a much-sought-after luxury aboard this ship. Reaching into her small carry bag, she brought out the new hand-sewn dress her mother had given her. It was a mothers parting-gift to a daughter and Jane stood with her knees pressed against a bunk, holding the treasure against her face while savoring its fresh linen smell. She stood silent, yet pensive, wishing solemnly that she could take her parents to Australia with the rest of the family. Australia seemed so far away from all that she knew and loved but with typical Scottish stoicism, she put her sadness aside and went on arranging the compartment. A few moments later, Jane felt rather than heard the presence of her husband as he silently entered her space. Charles had gone back ashore to harass the sailors into stowing the family sea chests safely and when he entered the compartment, she almost leant back in anticipation of his arms. He stood close behind her, gently placing his hands on her hips and resting his cheek against her hair. Jane grabbed possessively at his wrists, drawing his rough hands around onto her abdomen. She placed her hands over his for a moment, feeling its warmth through her gingham dress. She sighed as she lay her head against his shoulder and treasured this rare moment of uninterrupted attention. She was finally, happily alone with her husband. A tiny smile gathered at the corners of her mouth and she closed her eyes in satisfaction.

Jane was already seven months pregnant with their eighth child and she was not looking forward to travel. She hoped fervently that the voyage would not be too rough. Suddenly she opened her eyes and exclaimed;'Can ye noo feel the bairn pushing aboot Charlie, can ye noo?'

'Aye lass, aye, the bairns raight healtha '. Charles beamed happily but Jane knew that he was now a little tense about the move to Australia. Her husband seemed to feel her concern for shipboard childbirth and he stared at her knowingly before suddenly asking if she had noticed the number of pregnant women coming aboard. Jane nodded with a girlish smile as she again went back to stowing their supplies and clothing. As sailing time grew near, the scene on the Dundee dock became excited and confused. People struggled to the dock with boxes, trunks and numerous other items. This soon had the children guessing as to whether the ship would sink at the dock or when they got to sea.

When Jane finally had the berth arranged and their personal items stowed, each person in the family had their allotted area to care for. The family berth measured 3 meters long by 2.5 meters wide by only 1.7 meters high. There were only two built in bunks that stretched along the inner hull but five hammocks hung and swung rhythmically at one end of the berth. Items for use while at sea were stowed under bunks and material goods, on the few lipped shelves that ran along one end of the berth. Larger cases and trunks were stowed in the ships hold and once there, were no longer easily accessed and for most, were beyond reach until the ship arrived at its destination. Sleeping arrangements seemed harsh at first but would eventually prove comfortable enough. The bunks were small and had sideboards to keep one from falling out when the ship was in heavy seas. Mother Jane and little Andrew shared one bunk Charles had his own until the new baby arrived, at which time Andrew would sleep with his father. Alexander, Charles JR, Mary and Ann each had hammocks to themselves but Barbara and Jane, had to share the last hammock between them.

On the wharf, people kept coming and going from ship to shore, where stood the several small shops that ran along the waterfront. Most were buying small items such as cotton and thread for mending and cloth for patching, or the new one-penny magazines to read en-route. The compact and sturdy little ship was eventually loaded and after a passenger check, was given her clearance. Then, with the help of the tide and a new steam tugboat with its funnel standing tall like a stovepipe hat, the ship was slowly towed out toward the open sea and the voyage to Australia.

Many young married couples were gathered on deck to watch as the green hills of Scotland slowly disappeared from view. A lingering sad feeling followed them as they left the aulde country behind and sailed away down the English coast, perhaps forever.

Bound for Australia

All too soon the 'John Barry' passed by the ports of Newcastle in Northumberland and then Whitby in Captain Cook's Yorkshire, before it came to anchor in the Thames. After exchanging mails and taking aboard the ships matron, they were again placed under the control of a little paddle steamer. Although these tiny steam vessels, with their long slender funnels, were relatively new to shipping, they were much stronger and safer than the manhandled longboats previously used for towing ships out.

The voyagers were again treated to a change from protected waters to the bumpy choppy waves of the open sea. The less hardy types were soon back leaning over the taffrail and as usual, were ridding themselves of their previous meal. The steam tug had a good man at the wheel and the hawser was kept taut until the 'John Barry' was cast off on her own. The crew of the little steamer gave the ship a round of cheers for good luck as they turned their head for home.

The 'John Barry', sailed slowly away into the English Channel. After some hours struggling with failing winds, they arrived near Lands End where the breeze suddenly died away, leaving the ship with hardly any movement. Sailing became exhaustingly slow and the day drifted by with the ship tacking first this way and then that, searching for even the slightest air.

Woman in the mist

This first evening in the Channel, brought with it typical chilly English fog that drifted in from the cold northern regions. As the last rays of sunlight filtered through the thickening mist, the small thin figure of a young woman, with crocheted shawl pulled close around her, quietly ventured out on deck. The helmsman noticed her as she came into view. Perhaps she was trying to get away from the muffled cacophony of sound coming from below. The crying children and raucous parents always sent one or two of the women scurrying up on deck in an effort calm down and settle themselves for a while.

Jane Crawford made her way toward the big mainmast and wrapped her right arm as far as it would reach around it. She rested the side of her head against its cold wooden strength and silently marveled at the power she felt within. She had always wanted to stand beneath the tall masts of an ocean going ship, to feel the strength that stood against the strongest winds and helped drive the full riggers across the oceans. She listened to the 'flump, flump' of the huge sails as they twisted and turned, half-filling and then emptying again, while vainly trying to drive the ship forward ahead of the wafting breeze. Jane wondered with what voice the ship would speak and she listened to the creak of the yardarm, as its sound radiated down the mast. She held on to the bole as tightly as she could and mouthed a fervent silent prayer for the safety of her family. The noise from below had faded and the fog bank slowly caught and enveloped the ship as it drifted onward through the mist. The breeze now seemed so light, that it appeared to barely give the vessel headway.

3

The evening darkened suddenly and the misty fog draped itself around the ship like a thick grey shroud. Jane pulled the shawl a little tighter round her shoulders and peered skyward at the rigging, but now she could barely make out the truck. The helmsman's mate rang the ships bell, 'clang clang, clang clang', the metallic tones became muffled hollow echoes, as the ship sailed slowly and silently onward. The rolling fog now completely enveloped the ship, while those still on deck, felt the chill of its cold ghostly fingers. The helmsman watched the shadowy figure of the woman as she stood quietly beside the mast. He wondered what she was thinking but his attention was drawn back to the helm at the sounding of the bell.

A warm tear trickled slowly down Jane Crawford's cheek as she thought of her childhood and friends. The ship moved slowly onward, slicing cleanly through the glassy black seas. Jane turned from the mast and moved quickly back the way she had come. Placing one hand lightly on the elaborately carved doors, she turned, taking one last look at the rolling swirling fog, before disappearing below. The ghostly echo of the bell, now the only sound above the seething swish of the sea as the ship slipped silently away into the mist.

Surname	Christian Name	Native Place or town or county	Age	Married Single	Religion	Education Read or Write	Trade or occupation	Relations or friends in the colony	Where ashore or on shore	Health etc
Crawford	Charles	Aberdeen	30	Married	Prot	Read & Write	Blacksmith	None	ashore	Healthy
	Jane	do	29		Prot Single	do			do	
Crawford	Alexander	Dundee	14		Prot	Read				
	Charles	do	12			do				
	Henry		10			do				
	Ann		8			do				
	Barbara		6							
	Jane		4							
	Andrew		2							
		Born on board	b							
Dunchar	George	Buck. profession	46	Married	Presby	can & Write	Farmer	one	ashore	Healthy
	John	Dundee do	39	do		do				
	Jane		10			do				
	Ann		14			do				
Dewar	Jane	Perthshire	28	Married	Prot	Read & write	Mason	None	do	healthy
	Isabella	Aberdeen	22						do	do
Doig	Alexander	Aberdeen	24	Married	Presby	Read & write	Joiner	None	ashore	Healthy
	Jane		21	do	do	do			do	do
Donald	George		28	Married	Presby	Read & write	Mason	None	ashore	Healthy
	Jane		26	do	do	do				Consumption
	Thomas		3							
	George		1							died 13 June
Donaldson	James	Dundee	38	Married	Presby	Read & write	Mason	None	ashore	Healthy
	Margaret	Forfarshire	34						do	do
	Elizabeth	Dundee	17						do	
	William		14						do	
	James	do	13						do	
	Isabella	do	11						do	

The passengers register for the ship 'John Barry' 1837 note, the age of Barbara Crawford and the others in her family

4

FEAR ON THE 'JOHN BARRY'

The 'John Barry' made many voyages to Australia in its 23 years on the worlds oceans. She was used alternately as passenger ship, cargo carrier and convict transport. Her master, Captain Robson, turned her head for Tenerife as he always did on the voyage out. The 1837 voyage was no different from any other working trip. They had the usual 320 passengers to deliver to Sydney town and the crew went about their chores in the same manner as on any voyage.

The fog finally lifted three hours after sunrise and after clearing the Channel, a fresh following wind arrived to drive the vessel on toward their first port of call. Now they made good and speedy headway as they sailed southeast for Tenerife. Although the general health and well being of the passengers was fair to good at the time of sailing, the number of infants aboard caused some concern. Sickness among the little ones might eventuate and was even anticipated. The ships Surgeon worried that there might be a death or two among the very young before the coast of Australia was sighted.

Leaving the Aulde Country

Six days into the voyage, on March 31, 1837, the sixteen-month-old son, of William and Mary Finlay, took ill with the croup and died. The boy had been sick for less than a week, his parents, at first, thinking it was just a seasonal cold. They were understandably shocked at the death of their baby and wanted a funeral to take place as soon as possible. The following day, Surgeon Daniel Thompson, had the carpenter make a tiny coffin in which the parents tenderly placed their child in preparation for his burial at sea. The family and their few new friends they had made aboard ship gathered for the funeral. Many other passengers were superstitious and fearfully shunned the burial. Doctor Thompson read verses from the bible and ended the tragedy by committing the child sadly to the deep. As they offered the coffin to the waves, Mary Finlay began sobbing deeply, her shoulders heaved as the great pain of loss fought its way out. She clutched her husband and pressed her face hard against his arm, her bonnet shielding her face as she cried. William Finlay had lost his baby son Joseph and although in pain at the tragedy, could only try to comfort his terribly distressed wife.

Jane Crawford watched the touching ceremony with fear churning inside her; she clasped both hands to her swollen stomach and tried to tell her unborn that all would be well. Then at once, the funeral was over, a small splash and the ship continued onward as the sea accepted the little coffin with an almost disdainful hiss. The coffin floated for just a few moments as if not wanting to leave them. It bobbed up and down over the choppy swell until it began to list on one corner. Then the pull of the weights nailed to the bottom of the little coffin quickly took it down. As if this were a signal to the mourners, the funerary group turned away and separated. Finlay assisted his almost faint wife back to toward their berth and they disappeared below. The death of the infant made everyone feel a little more vulnerable and other parents began to take sudden interest in the general health of their own children.

The rations

The Crawford family had received the bulk of their ship-supplied rations in Dundee. They had also taken it upon themselves to buy a few home remedies and other 'much needed' items before they left that port. The shipping company supplied the passengers with rations that should see them through the entire voyage. The ships cook supplemented the rations with bread and biscuits supplied each time they were made. Passenger rations included knives, forks, spoons and bunk mattresses [two mattresses for the Crawford family], some blankets, 5 Hammocks, drinking mugs, plates and twelve pounds of soap.

Rations of food were given out per person but children one year and under received no rations and it became the duty of the parent, to make sure that the child was fed. Children over one year but under twelve, received half rations and those over twelve, received full adult rations. All passengers, including the Crawfords, had received a coupon stating the quantity of supplies provided for the voyage by the shipping company.

FOOD RATIONS PER PERSON PER FORTNIGHT ON THE SHIP 'JOHN BARRY' 1837:

Biscuits: 5 pounds per adult	**Butter:** half pound per adult
Meat: 5 pounds per adult	**Potatoes:** four pounds per adult
Raisins: 1 pound per adult	**Flour:** four pounds per adult
Pepper: Half ounce per adult	**Mustard:** One pound per adult
Oatmeal: 2 pounds per adult	**Rice:** one pound per adult
Pickles: half pint per adult	**Peas:** two pounds per adult
Lime juice: twelve ounces per adult	**Water:** sixty pints per adult

Their rations, issued fortnightly, were available for the duration of the voyage or until they ran out. Items such as cheeses and other types of dried meat or fruit could be purchased before leaving the port and many passengers did so as a supplement to their rations. There was also much personal trading done among the passengers, some exchanged foods they did not like, or want.

Passing the time

Although the days were warming up, it was still cold at night. The passengers were able to pass the daylight hours pleasantly on deck. Time was spent playing games; talking, reading and doing the thousand and one things people manage to do while crowded into a small space. Jane loved to sit well forward in good weather and feel the thump of the waves jarring the timbers beneath her. The smell of the salt air made her feel fresh and alive and the strength of the ship pitted against the power of the sea excited her deepest feelings. Only the chilly evenings drove her below. There were more than 320 persons aboard so it was always a pleasure to be on deck in the fresh sea air, especially when most of the children and many adults were suffering from seasickness.

As the ship approached the equatorial regions, the adult couples remained on deck late into the evenings. Dances were held regularly and various games and jokes were played as the ship sailed onward in those wonderful moderate breezes that sometimes make sailing such an enjoyable event. People came to know each other and small parties gathered like tribal groups. Although dances were very communal, card and parlor games were usually confined to those who had become close friends. When sickness or even death came to one of a group. It was as if a family member had been affected; everyone had strong fears of illness or death at sea.

Fever

On April 11, a second toddler died. The death of two-year-old Margaret Thompson was attributed to childhood diarrhea, her parents James and Ann Thompson were distraught. By April 20, more families were in mourning, the Williamsons, Frazers and the Johnsons each lost a child to diarrhea or some form of bronchitis. Panic set in on those who had very young children and the doctor was kept busy with visits from parents who thought their children were showing symptoms.

The doldrums were reached and the winds dropped right off. They had suddenly become marooned on a wooden island and the heat of day soon began to take a toll. During the last few weeks of April, three more infants died, all from the same type of illness. Surgeon Daniel Thompson did not know exactly what the sickness was, but he did note that it was striking the little children hardest. The adults were not yet showing signs of having anything more than a few sniffles or a cold. Surgeon Thompson did not know it but a very serious situation was arising. On May 5, the first adult passenger, an engineer, died of fever only one week after becoming ill. It was then that the possibility of an epidemic began to dawn on Doctor Thompson.

The 'John Barry' was fast becoming a fever ship but the exact type of fever was still eluding the surgeon. The captain therefore made a decision not to put in anywhere for they would be confined to the ship in quarantine anyway, whereas they might as well be sailing. Provisions were in good supply and if they had the fever aboard, they would not really be welcome at any port. The passengers were not eating very much as the sickness had understandably ruined many appetites. Captain Robson ordered the surgeon to tell all parents with very young children to avoid communal activity. The little hospital [just a small berth] was already full and families were warned to keep to themselves as much as possible. Many did not want to venture out of their berths and kept their children in the unhealthy air of the confined spaces below.

Jane Crawford in her pregnant state, began to show the strain of it all, she kept herself busy washing dishes and boiling the family drinking water. She followed the doctors advice and maintained the personal hygiene of the children. She even used heated seawater to wash every nook and cranny in their small compartment. In pregnant fear, she constantly kept the area clean, wiping over bunks and bulkhead wherever she could get at them. Ships suddenly affected with disease usually found it was caused by contact with rats, a sick seaman or by an unclean hold in the vessel. The 'John Barry' had taken convicts to Sydney the previous year and may have taken on a rat carrying 'Jail Fever'.

Many convict ships had developed bad reputations during the early 19th century but the 'John Barry' had an exemplary record. Whether she transported free passengers or convicts, she always carried about the same number of persons and never really experienced severe bouts of fever or numerous deaths. The tragedy that was now unfolding, was a very new experience for the ship and her crew.

One reason for this epidemic may have been that some of the poorer families had been living aboard ship for some weeks before sailing. Perhaps one of them had contracted the disease or maybe a sailor brought it aboard. Whatever the reason, the illness seems to have arrived at its peak while the ship was in the tropical heat of the equatorial regions. It was here that the greatest number of deaths occurred and it is reasonable to think that the tropics may have exacerbated its effect. Investigations must have been made into the death toll when the ship anchored in Sydney but it appears that little was done and even less was said about the terrible voyage. Only one or two small articles appeared in the Sydney Herald newspaper regarding the deaths and the subsequent quarantine of the 'John Barry' at Spring Cove.

The burials

Jane Crawford had ordered her seven children to spend as much time in the fresh air as possible and tried vainly to keep them away from other children until the fever ran its course. Children began to die at the rate of one every two days and soon the carpenter could no longer keep up with the demand for coffins, resorting to the use of sail canvas with weights sewn into them. Surgeon Thompson attended all burials but the services grew shorter and shorter until it became just a matter of a prayer and putting the body over the side, leaving the parents to grieve alone. The McLaren family lost 12 month old Jane on the 25th of April, the Smiths lost 20 month old Margaret on the 27th of April and the McBeaths lost their 11 month old son William on the 2nd of May. Death visited the ship day after day. The Acheson family, the Spence family, the Lamond family, the Thomsons, the Watts, the Allisons, the Frazers, the Wallaces and the McGregor family all a child in that terrible month of May. To make matters worse, the ship was sailing into the heavy seas of the southern Indian ocean where she and the people aboard her were to be battered quite severely. The passengers spent much time making one another seasick and the terrible stench could not be cleared away from down below. Mrs. Heatherington [Ships Matron] died of what was thought to be Scarlet fever on 11th of May. She was the second adult to die from an illness that Doctor Thompson eventually listed as Hospital Fever. David Farquarson, a single parent, was taking his two-year-old son William, to Australia. He was understandably distressed when on May 16, the boy died of the fever.

Jane was heavy with child during that traumatic month, she tried hard to keep from giving birth but almost at the end of May, the baby was born. Although happy to see her new child, Jane was terrified that the fever would take it from her. In early June, as they reached the colder southern latitudes, only two deaths were recorded among the children. The Lamond and Donald families each lost a child; both were toddlers under one year old. Another adult [Mrs. Deuchar] died in July before the ship reached Sydney and four more children followed her to a watery grave. When the ship arrived at Spring Cove Quarantine grounds near Manly on July 13, 1837, a total of 22 children and 4 adults had died. Many more had to be hospitalized as some were very near death.

Quarantine and release

Having laid up in quarantine at Spring Cove for just over two weeks, the 'John Barry' was released on Sunday July 31, 1837. She was taken to her dock in Sydney, to make ready for the return voyage. The ship then commenced loading for the return to London and she sailed on September 9, 1837. If she suffered any illness among the crew whilst on the return voyage, records of this fact do not appear to be available in Australia.

Many of the healthy passengers were released at the same time as the ship; the Crawfords luckily were among them. Jane and Charles had battled hard to keep their children safe during the voyage and they were among the families that had escaped the raging fever. Eleven deaths occurred in the quarantine hospital after arrival at Spring Cove. These comprised 8 adults and 3 children and all were very sad family tragedies. Mrs. Isabella Hutchison died aged 25, leaving her husband Alexander with two young children to care for. Alexander Gardin died on August 4, 1837, leaving his wife Catherine to continue on alone, he was only 29 years old. Mrs. Ann Beaton died aged 31, leaving her husband James with three young children. George Clyde died of Typhus, he was a single man aged 26 years and Donald Scott died of fever aged 27. Mary Ann Hutchison followed her mother, dying on August 11, while her father was convalescing. She was just one year old. William Clark, husband of Mary and father of James, died of Typhus [jail fever] aged 29 on August 15, 1837. George Scott aged 42, died on August 20, leaving behind wife Elizabeth and five children. John Vietch aged 31 years, died on August 26; his wife Euphemia, aged 27 years gave birth to a child while he was bedridden. Her husband was desperately ill when the baby was born and he died without ever seeing the child. Theirs was the first baby born on Australian soil from among the passengers who sailed on the 'John Barry' during the voyage of 1837. This baby died suddenly while ashore at Spring Cove, on September 16, 1837. The mother also had the fever and was struggling with the painful loss of her husband. Surgeon Thompson had become confused with so many deaths happening around him. He at first believed that he was faced with an epidemic of Diarrhea or Croup. He then decided upon Dentition Fever due to the number of toddlers among the dead. When the adults also took ill and began to die, the doctor thought that Scarlet Fever had struck but he changed his opinion a few weeks later. Surgeon Thompson also called it Hospital Fever. Only when he knew beyond doubt, did he begin listing the fever by its true name, Typhus [Jail fever]. Thus ended one of the most harrowing and tragic voyages, in Australian maritime history, a voyage that should have been well documented and talked about for years. Luck had been a fickle partner for most of the passengers. Of the 320 persons on board, 20% and more became very ill en-route to their destination. Over half of those who went down with the fever died. The final toll being 26 children and 12 adults dead with 30 or more remaining ill for some weeks after the voyage.

After the 'John Barry' was released from quarantine, her healthy passengers including the entire Crawford family, were free to go ashore. This could have been dangerous as there were still deaths occurring at the quarantine grounds at Spring Cove. After all, it was only two weeks since the ship had arrived in Sydney, yet all passengers not suffering signs of illness were allowed to go on their way.

Doctor Thomson's official death report

NOMINAL RETURN OF DEATHS for THE VOYAGE OF THE SHIP 'JOHN BARRY' 1837.

Name	Age	Date of Death	Cause
Joseph Finlay	16 mths	March 31st 1837	Croup
May Thomas	2 years	April 11th	Diarrhea
William Williamson	1 year	April 14th	Diarrhea
David Frazer	2 years	April 16th	Croup
Andrew Johnston	7 mths	April 20th	Bronchitis
Jane McLaren	1 year	April 25th	Diarrhea.
Margery Smith	20 mths	April 27th	Fever
William McBeath	11 mths	May 2nd 1837	Bronchitis.
James Acheson	30 years	May 5th	Fever
John Watt	4 years	May 14th	Hydrocephalus
John Alison	1 year	May 15th	Fever.
William Ferguson	2 years	May 16th	Fever
Alexander Frazer	5 years	May 17th	Diarrhea.
Elizabeth Wallace	2 years	May 24th	Diarrhea.
Mary McGregor	8 years	May 27th	Rheumatic fever.
Catherine Lamont	8 mths	June 4th	Bronchitis.
George Donald	1 year	June 12th	Diarrhea.
Mrs Ann Deuchar	39 years	July 3rd	Typhus fever.
Thomas Johnson	4 years	July 11th	Vomiting attack.
May Spence	1 year	July 14th	Vomiting attack.
Baby Calder	3 years	July 20th	Infantile fever
James Watt	35 years	July 26th	Typhus fever.
Mrs. Hutchison	25 years	July 30th	Typhus fever
James Stewart	3 years	August 4th	Diarrhea.
Alexander Gardin	29 years	August 4th	Fever
Mrs. Beaton	31 years	August 7th	Fever.
George Clyde	26 years	August 10th	Fever.
William Clark	29 years	August 15th	Fever.
Donald Scott	27 years	August 16th	Fever.
Mary Ann Hutchinson	1 year	August 16th	Fever.
George Scott	42 years	August 20th	Fever.
John Veitch	31 years	August 26th	Fever.
Baby Vietch	4 weeks	September 16th	Fever

The above are a direct copy of the death list as recorded by the ships surgeon.

A total of 19 adults and 11 children convalesced after the horror of the voyage, deaths occurring after the 16th of September, were attributed to the hospital on shore and not to the vessel. No other voyage by the 'John Barry' recorded such a loss of life. Even when laden with convicts this ship maintained a sound health record, rarely having more than one or two deaths per voyage. When comparing the low number of deaths per voyage on convict and passenger ships of that period, the 1837 voyage of the 'John Barry' must have had many health officials scratching their heads. This loss of life was only equaled or bettered by the horrific convict voyages, thirty years earlier.

The fear of being trapped aboard a fever ship, miles from the nearest land, with their children in extreme danger, would have almost driven parents to distraction. Their fear of catching the dreaded disease can only be imagined. Charles and Jane Crawford brought their family through the disaster in what must have been a small miracle but fate had other plans in store for this family.

CONVALESCENT SICK LIST FOR PASSENGERS ON THE EMIGRANT SHIP 'JOHN BARRY'

Name	Age	Illness
David Williams	Adult	Typhus Fever.
Euphemia Nutch*	Adult	Typhus Fever.
James Thomson	Adult	Typhus Fever.
James & Jane Stewart	21 years	Typhus Fever.
James Spence	28 years	Typhus Fever.
Frances Scott	15 years	Typhus Fever.
Margaret Reid	9 years	Typhus Fever.
Mary Mudie	15 years	Typhus Fever.
James See	30 years	Typhus Fever. Husband and
Elizabeth See	30 years	Typhus Fever. Wife.
Isabella Lamond	32 years	Typhus Fever. Mother and
James Lamond	6 years	Typhus Fever. Son.
Isabel Lamont	23 years	Typhus Fever.
William Lamb	25 years	Typhus Fever.
John Donaldson	7 years	Typhus Fever.
George Deuchar	46 years	Typhus Fever. Father and
Jane Deuchar	19 years	Typhus Fever. two
Ann Deuchar	14 years	Typhus Fever. Daughters
Mary Clark*	31 years	Typhus Fever. Mother and
James Clark	12 years	Typhus Fever. Son.
Margaret Calder	1 year	Typhus Fever.
John Clark	24 years	Typhus Fever. Husband and
Elizabeth Clark	22 years	Typhus Fever. Wife.
James Bolton	31 years	Typhus Fever.
William Beaton	10 years	Typhus Fever. Brother and
Charlotte Beaton	6 years	Typhus Fever. Sister.
Agnes Ago	21 years	Typhus Fever. Mother and
John Ago*	3 months	Typhus Fever. Son.

*The last named child was born on board ship in April 1837.

*Euphemia Nutch lost her newborn a few weeks after arrival at Spring Cove. Her baby died of the fever on September 16, 1837.

*Mary Clark lost her husband William to the fever on this voyage.

If any of the above on the sick list died after September 16, 1837, it has not been recorded in the shipping manifest and was probably deemed hospital responsibility. Such was the 1837 voyage of the 'John Barry' a voyage that the Crawford family would well remember. This account of the sad voyage has been entered here as a memorial to those who sailed aboard the 'John Barry' with the Crawford family in 1837.

THE TINMAN OF OZ

Sydney, Australia, August 1837

Arrival in Sydney provided great relief for the Crawfords, especially once they had gained release from quarantine. They, along with the other passengers, were delivered to Sydney town at the end of July, a little over two weeks after the ship had moored at Spring Cove. The new arrivals bedded down at the shipping company depot, where most were billeted until work and housing could be arranged. Although a qualified Blacksmith, Charles listed himself as Tinsmith and within a short space of time, a house and land became available in the heart of Sydney.

The family cottage was to be found in Kent Street, very close to the harbour and although comfortable for any British family, it was unpopular because of its neighbouring building, the City Inn Hotel. Charles seemed happy enough though. Now he could meet many of the locals and promote his business with ease. While still thickly wooded in areas, little Sydney was a town on the move. Charles Crawford soon became known as the Tinman of Kent Street and his business, though not flourishing at first, was slowly showing promise. Jane, as homemaker, had an enormous job to do and while catering to the needs of her older children, the four youngest unfortunately suffered with their education. The move to Australia had caused Jane to put aside teaching them the rudiments of reading and writing. Barbara and little Jane were unfortunately the wrong age at the wrong time. They never learned to read and write, remaining illiterate all their young lives.

A city born

Sydney town had its beginnings only 70 years prior to the arrival of the Crawfords. From settlement, convicts, the military and a smattering of enterprising business people had populated the colony. Many ex-convicts had taken up allotments around the township and some had even taken to market gardening with great fervor. Other courageous families had been lured out as migrants to become farmers, while still others arrived as hired managers sent from England to take up bought holdings. People were constantly on the move loading their bullock drays and carts, before heading off into the interior with their flocks of sheep or cattle. Woolen factories in England, in time, came to realize that the new Australian product was far superior in quality to that which was home grown and they were already beginning to look out for wool arriving from New South Wales.

Charles considered himself lucky to find his niche, a place from which he could work, especially one that was so close to the central area of Sydney. At times, he worked on the docks where he could earn extra money and for a while everything seemed on the up. The Tinman made every effort to succeed but times were tough and it was an effort to maintain a little respectability living so near the hotel and waterfront.

The change

Five years later, during the year 1842, things had become decidedly worse for the Crawfords. Charles is said to have turned to drink, which if true, probably was the cause of the rumored slide in his business. Although a drinking problem has not been proven, the close proximity of the City Inn hotel and the stress of the times could have easily contributed to a change in his character. Charles Crawford, up until this time, had shown himself to be a model father and husband. His business operation though, did begin having difficulties and finally, in September 1843, Charles was arrested for having goods in his possession that the police thought to have been stolen.

Charles Crawford was charged, convicted and then sentenced to one year in prison with hard labor. His crime was listed as receiving stolen goods. He entered prison on September 19, 1843 and from that moment on, life became very harsh for his wife Jane and her children. She had no hope of supporting such a large family on her own. Even if her older children, Alexander [20], Charles Jnr [18], Mary [16] and Ann [14] had left home or found employment, things would still have been very difficult while caring for and supporting the four youngest children.

Sydney Harbour, circ. 1844

Alexander and Charles junior were young men and had probably gone to sea or found employment by the time Charles was sent to prison. Mary, as the oldest girl, may have taken work at the City Inn hotel, while Ann might have begun work as a domestic servant. The older girls might well have married early and Barbara [12] was also been ready for domestic work but the three youngest were still to be cared for. The Crawford family was already financially weak after arriving in Australia and it is likely that they followed the tradition of the British poor and sent their children off to work at an early age. It seems ludicrous and out of character for Charles Crawford to have done something illegal whilst having such a large family to care for, especially whilst apparently having had no previous trouble with the law. His obvious love of family and his work habits do not align themselves with such an act. Charles was already quite well known in the area and it would have been either total stupidity or great need that caused him to take such a risk.

Charles had brought his family to live in a penal colony and this surely gave him insight into the convict way of life. Road chain gangs frequently passed by the family home and the harshness of prison life was evident everywhere. Only financial desperation or perhaps a false or trumped-up charge, can be the answer to his petty crime. The charge of having stolen goods in ones possession, has been long favoured by police and others, as a means by which someone innocent of a crime could be taken out of circulation for a while. By simply planting some object at the home of the person one needed to be rid of, opened up the way for charges to be laid and the person gaoled or defamed. The decision of the court to sentence a first offender with such a large family seems out of proportion to the crime and it is likely that the prosecutor pushed hard for a gaol term rather than a bond or suspended sentence.

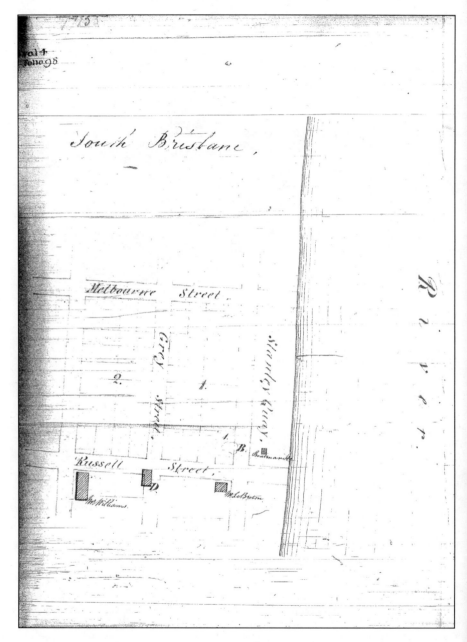

Map of Brisbane 1842 (Southside)

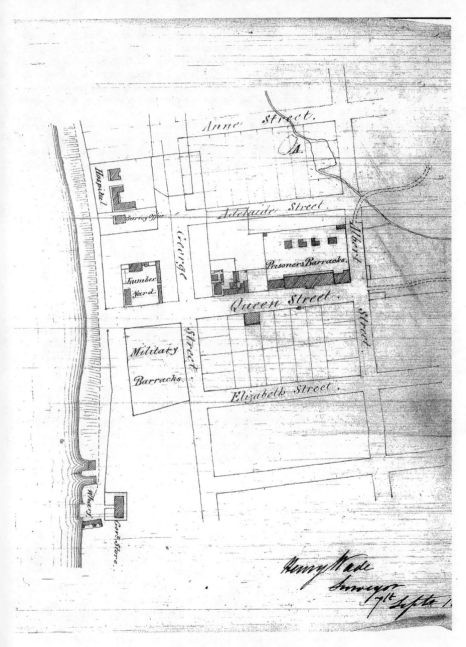

Map of Brisbane 1842 (Northside)

Finding William Thompson

Several months before Charles Crawford was charged [perhaps between July 1841 and September 1842], a stranger named William Thompson [also a Scotsman] came into contact with the Crawford family. He struck up a friendship with at least one of them. The first member [Authors opinion] of the family Thompson met, was probably the oldest daughter Mary Crawford. The meeting between Thompson and Mary probably took place at the City Inn hotel, perhaps at sometime between July 1842 and early September 1842. This rather churlish piece of guesswork [on the part of the Author] is arrived at through several connecting links in the history of the Crawfords.

The first of these is that the City Inn hotel was one of the earliest meeting places for many people in and around Sydney and its waterfront. The age of the eldest girl [almost 16 years old at the time] and the probability that she may have been employed by the hotel, combine to create the opportunity for William Thompson to make his first contact with the Crawfords. Once Thompson had met Mary Crawford, it is thought that he became infatuated with her and made a plan to lure her away from her family. Two small pieces of evidence point to Mary being the first person in the Crawford family to meet William Thompson.

The letters

First and most important, is a letter that arrived at the Sydney post office in September 1842, it was addressed to Miss Mary Crawford. This letter is believed [by the Author] to have been posted by William Thompson as an invitation for Mary to take up a position with him in Brisbane as his housekeeper. Thompson either had become infatuated with Mary Crawford or he just wanted a woman of his own background. Whatever the reason, his connection to the Crawfords grew more intense from that moment onward. Letters being held at the Post Office were recorded in the Sydney Herald newspaper. At no other time since the family had arrived in Sydney is a letter held for any member of the family, except for one other occasion, a letter arrived for Charles Crawford in May 1843. It is possible that William Thompson and Charles Crawford, met at the City Inn hotel and as countrymen, became friends, with Charles later inviting Thompson into his family home. This meeting could have taken place as far back as January 1841. Thompson [if he did make overtures to Mary] was very unsuccessful in his efforts to secure his aims.

Barbara enters the scene

It is now that we arrive at the true beginning of Barbara Crawford's dramatic story. Somehow, William Thompson was disconnected from trying to lure Mary Crawford and was able [according to later reports] to entice twelve-year-old Barbara Crawford into eloping with him. For Barbara to have eloped meant that Thompson was well known to her and this could mean that Mary may not have been part of the equation. About two months after Barbara disappeared, [May 1843] a letter arrived at Sydney Post Office for Charles Crawford. It purportedly informed him that Thompson had eloped with his daughter Barbara. This information comes direct from Barbara and although she could not read or write, she stated that a letter had been sent and if so, had to have been written by William Thompson.

Barbara Crawford did not make any other statement regarding her leaving home, except to confirm that they [Thompson and Barbara] had eloped. This could be accepted as fact had Barbara been a little older, if a child of twelve had gone missing from the family home, it would, even in those times, have been reported to the police or officials. This though, did not happen, Charles Crawford did not make any such report regarding his missing daughter or if he did, the whole affair has been hidden away by officialdom.

The fact is that in records, no report was made and this can only mean that Charles either knew that Barbara was going away with William Thompson or for some reason, he chose not to report her disappearance. Therefore, Charles Crawford must have been satisfied that Thompson was telling the truth, no matter what story he had told the family. Charles Crawford, unwittingly, had at first been convinced and as [for some reason] Mary had rejected Thompson's original offer, he [Charles] believed it only right that he should offer Barbara as substitute in Mary's place. That this may have been the case, is not an absolute proven fact because Barbara claimed she and William Thompson had eloped, rather than she had gone as a servant for his household.

The Conundrum

The real question here is, if Barbara suddenly went missing, why did Charles Crawford not go straight to the police as soon as he realised that she was gone? There were no official reports made to police or anyone authority. Nothing is listed or recorded, not even in the Sydney Herald or the Police Gazette. It is therefore very likely that Charles Crawford never did report Barbara Crawford's disappearance or if he did, it has been officially deleted from the records. One can therefore only assume, that as no official reports were made on Barbara's disappearance, she went with Thompson with her parents blessing. After all, Thompson was a countryman and probably gained the family's trust over the previous twelve or eighteen months that he had known them. For two months [March until May 1843] Charles probably believed that his daughter was fine and working as a domestic servant. It is then, [May 1843] that a letter arrived for Charles Crawford at the Sydney post office. The Crawford family received only two unexpected letters during the period 1837 to 1851. Both were registered in the Sydney Herald newspaper as awaiting pick up at the Sydney post office.

Although it cannot be proven that the letters were from William Thompson, it is likely that the first [to Miss Mary Crawford, September 1842] was an offer for her to come to Brisbane. The second letter probably did arrive from Brisbane, [May 1843] and was a statement to the Crawford parents, telling them that William Thompson and Barbara Crawford [Barbara to Brierly October 1849] had eloped. At no other time, from the family's arrival in Sydney in 1837 up to and including the year 1851, are letters recorded or listed as awaiting the family at the Sydney Post Office.

If Barbara Crawford truly did elope with William Thompson, he had to have known Barbara well enough to tempt her into running away with him. Exactly how this happened cannot be ascertained but it is possible that after getting to know the family, Thompson won Barbara's trust and affections. She may well have been overworked assisting her mother with the younger children and any change in her lifestyle might well have been welcomed. It is also possible that she might have craved adult male attention due to the size of the family.

Second thoughts

The second reason [though only minor] as to why Mary Crawford may have been Thompson's first choice is that Barbara stated that she eloped with Thompson when she was sixteen years old. This was Mary's age at the time Barbara disappeared. If Mary had been Thompson's first choice, it would have been natural for Thompson to have Barbara tell anyone and everyone, that her age was sixteen when she left home, especially if she looked the part. If it was Thompson that sent Charles Crawford a letter in May 1843, it was done believing that he [Thompson] could keep the Crawfords at bay. Perhaps he thought that by using the old 'Gretna Green' symbolic marriage to show that he had done the right thing by the girl, Charles would be forgiving and not look for the couple. It is obvious that Charles did not find them if he did try and it is also obvious that he did not wish to use official means to do so.

Although solid evidence cannot be presented regarding the two letters that arrived at the Sydney Post Office, they were the only letters ever sent to the family by this means. Barbara stated that she left her home by eloping with Thompson and that she had married in Brisbane. She did not give a date for her marriage or state how they managed to get into the penal colony without permission. Especially at a time when all persons travelling to this harsh settlement, required documents allowing them to settle in Brisbane. The only precise clue as to when Barbara departed her home, came with her statement several years later, that she left Sydney for Brisbane, eighteen months before both she and William Thompson departed Brisbane for Cape York, on September 17, 1844. She stated that their salvage party left Brisbane to find the wreck of a whaler, two weeks after Ludwig Leichhardt's expedition departed Brisbane for the Darling Downs on the third of September 1844. This gave an approximate month for her departure from Sydney, as March 1843 and this can probably be accepted as fact.

A pointer to her departure date being correct is shown in Barbara's statement that, 'her father was a respectable Tinsmith in Sydney'. Barbara could not have known that Charles Crawford had been sent to prison in September 1843. She had departed Sydney in March of that year and would not have known of his going to gaol. In fact, during her questioning at the time of her rescue, Barbara does not show that she has any knowledge of her father serving time in prison. This of course, may have been her way of ignoring such an embarrassing subject but it is far more likely that she really had no idea.

Thompson at some stage took advantage of Barbara and this probably occurred at sea on the way to Brisbane. He then took the trouble to convince Barbara that they were now eloping and that they would marry upon arrival at their new home. After settling in, Barbara perhaps wanted her family to know the situation and asked that Thompson send a letter. She could not have written a letter to her family, for she was 'quite illiterate' [Brierly and Huxley, 1849] and years later, still could not sign her name [see marriage certificate for Jane Crawford] and could not read. If a letter did arrive from Brisbane, it had to have been written by William Thompson and probably explained that he intended to make or had made Barbara his wife. Could this letter have prompted a 'Mr. Crawford', into making a trip to Brisbane aboard the vessel 'Sovereign' [Sydney Herald, May 31, 1843]? Although it cannot at this moment be proven that this man was indeed Charles Crawford, most fathers would have set out to find a missing daughter and more so if he feared she were being badly used.

On the Waterfront

The Crawford children, while growing up next to a hotel, would have watched the drunken antics of the hotel patrons and their 'adult education' would have certainly been hastened. Many of the free men in Sydney were released convicts and the area was not an ideal place to raise a young family. It would have been somewhat dangerous for the girls as they grew into young womanhood. Charles Crawford must have come close to a break down when he was arrested and convicted for receiving stolen property. They were a close family and he would have been totally shattered at leaving them on their own, when given a year in gaol for this crime. No record seems to exist showing how Jane and her three youngest children survived without income while Charles was in prison. Perhaps the two eldest boys were earning and assisted Jane in her hour of need or maybe the church lent a hand. It would be very interesting to read the original police reports and evidence submitted at the trial of Charles Crawford.

When Charles came out of prison [perhaps in September 1844] he knew that his family would never be the same again. Barbara had disappeared and was possibly in Brisbane while only his wife and little Jane, along with young Andrew and the baby [if alive] were still at home. Charles returned to his former trade but the pressure had been too much for his wife and she remained in poor health for the rest of her life.

Although it seems unlikely that a girl of such tender years would willingly elope to Brisbane with a stranger, it is now history that no matter what prompted her to go with Thompson, he did what he had set out to do. Barbara soon became infatuated with Thompson and was perhaps excited by the prospect of having her own family life. After the initial act, she may have willingly complied with all that he wished to do with her.

THE MYSTERIOUS WILLIAM THOMPSON

Brisbane, March 1843;

    Brisbane penal settlement was certainly no thriving metropolis when William Thompson and Barbara Crawford arrived there in March 1843. The township had only a few small official buildings ranged along the hillsides beside the nearby river. A wind and manually driven flourmill built by the convicts dominated the skyline [on the northern bank of the river] above the penal settlement. The lightly populated southern bank of the Brisbane River was made up of a small number of commercial buildings, aimed mainly at ship maintenance and sustenance. There were very few private citizens and most of these were pardoned or ticket-of-leave convicts. The one or two ex-convict-operated stores dominated the southside, while a naval storehouse, convict barracks and the women's factory were the main buildings on the northern side of the river. The nineteen-year-old colony of Moreton Bay must have been mysterious and exciting for Barbara Crawford. This was totally wild country compared to Sydney and the only sign of habitation came when one arrived almost on top of the few houses that could be seen from the river. Natives still went naked for the most part and the animal life was much closer at hand than in Sydney. For incoming shipping, the bar at the mouth of the Brisbane River was much too shallow to allow large ships access to the colony. All stores had to be ferried up river by lighters or by shallow draught paddle steamers. The latter vessels were able to negotiate the bar at high tide and were well used in transporting stores from Sydney. The pilot boat at Amity point was always on hand to assist smaller boats that could get over the bar, in arriving safely at the settlement. Brisbane in 1843 was still only a very small colony, made up of colonial officers and marines, male and female second offence convicts and a few men and women who had married and taken up land on completion of their sentences. Although the marines were slowly being re-assigned and the colony being readied for transfer to township, it was still a penal colony and would remain so, until the last of the convicts residing there had finished his sentence. As in Sydney, the convicts had been put to work building stone walling, storehouses and roadways. The difference was that Brisbane was a punishment settlement for second offenders. These were convicts that had committed other crimes while serving their original sentence. Therefore, the Moreton Bay colony was run much more harshly than the southern colonies.

    Life in the early days of Moreton Bay went on for these men and women, no matter what drama occurred. The settlement would have to find its way at its own pace and it did so by use of the knowledge of the earlier inhabitants. Aboriginal trackways just as in the south, quickly became small roads and the small roads would eventually become highways. Almost all the famed discoveries of the Australian explorers came from following in the footsteps of the aboriginal. Stone-built houses, at first only for the officials, slowly began their relentless march outward from the town centre. Gardens were created to keep the colony well supplied with fruit and vegetables and in the space of only thirty-five years from settlement, statehood would come to Queensland. For the present, convicts of both sexes were afraid of the Moreton Bay colony. It had gained a bad reputation due to the harsh treatment of inmates, especially whilst under the command of Lieutenant Gorman who took command during the late 1830's.

    A few sheep stations had sprung into life well to the west of Brisbane, the nearest being at Limestone some fifty miles [by river] inland. This station [Limestone station] was probably operated to supply meat and wool for the convicts. It was soon to become the small and mainly ex-convict populated township of Ipswich and like the penal settlement, used the Brisbane River as a delivery source for supplies. Limestone was also the site of later mining interests but in 1839, it was the home of Lieutenant Gorman's motley crew of convict police. From here, convict constables protected the colony from aboriginals and kept watch for runaway convicts.

Moreton Bay

    When Thompson arrived at Moreton Bay with Barbara Crawford, there were no fancy hotels or boarding houses and the entire settlement was still convict orientated. Finding suitable living quarters would prove almost impossible, unless Thompson had local connections. Moreton Bay settlement had already been registered as being officially disbanded as a penal colony at the end of 1842 but nothing had yet been done to accommodate persons arriving in the area. A new settler and his family could billet themselves in one of the shipping storehouses but this was no easy matter before the first settler ships arrived at the beginning of 1845. Although the colony was supposedly thrown open to the public, accommodation could only be handled by camping out.

If William Thompson was a newcomer to Brisbane [although the settlement was now open] his first requirement was to notify officials of his wish to enter the colony. To gain permission, he would be required to give notice as to his intentions. He was entitled to stay aboard his vessel [if he owned one] for a short period but could not stay at the colony unless his intention was to settle or to go inland as a farmer. At this early period of open settlement, Brisbane was still very much, as it had been for almost twenty years.

Official letters dating up to 1851 and beyond testify to the regimentation and restrictions of the colony and show that Brisbane did not suddenly become open slather. Regimentation was adhered to for several years after the colony was declared open, convicts who had not yet completed their sentences were still wandering about and others, were on ticket of leave or colonial pardons that applied only to the colony. Until 1845, no real effort was made to lure new settlers into Brisbane and it was mostly the inland farmers that used the town as a storage base and jumping off point. William Thompson was required to tell the officials what he intended to do while at Moreton Bay if he wished to remain. Short term visits [a day or so] were permissible but a stay of any length, even after the official 1842 disbanding, needed the proper paperwork. William Thompson though, had somehow brought a young girl, only twelve years old, into the Brisbane penal colony and managed to keep her under wraps for eighteen months without ruffling official feathers. It was only possible to do this by bringing her into the colony without permission and by keeping her out of sight. He would have been allowed to take a woman into the colony had he been a free or freed man of good intent. Obviously, there is no record of any type that proves Thompson and Barbara Crawford ever lived together in Brisbane. Thompson was successful at hiding her from official eyes or records of their time in Brisbane have been expunged from the archives.

For Thompson to bring a young female to Brisbane while it was still a penal colony, shows that he was either a resident and knew the place very well or had friends who were living there who could give the couple food and lodgings.

Finding Thompson

A search in colonial records for men with the name William Thompson, who had arrived or were living in Brisbane, had to be made if one wished to have any chance of finding him. During the 160 years since this tale unfolded, little data has been discovered in relation to Thompson and Barbara at Moreton Bay. While researching part of her story, the Author found a possibility. This came about while searching out information on the prominent convict James Davis. It was then that the Author's research of letters sent to the Colonial Secretary by officials at Brisbane commenced. Just as one was found, a second possibility entered the scene and we now had two contenders for the role of William Thompson. Both were convicts, both were named William Thompson and both had committed second offences after arrival in Sydney and were then shipped off to Moreton Bay.

Heads or Tails?

The first man, an English born Roman Catholic, received a seven-year sentence and transportation to New South Wales in 1827. He was charged with having committed a second offence in Sydney in 1831 and was given a further 18 months over and above his original sentence. This additional time [and the last of his original sentence] he served in Brisbane. His full name was William Henry Thompson and he was transported to Australia aboard the ship 'Marquis of Hastings' in 1827 to serve his sentence. His total servitude the extra 18 months ended about 1836 and it is believed that he thereafter returned to England or at least Sydney, which was considered the 'populated area' of Australia. He did not die in nor was he buried at Brisbane or Ipswich and a search of Australian death and burial records has not yet divulged his fate in this country. This man was unimpressive and not at all 'well known and much favoured,' [Barbara to Brierly and Huxley, October 1849] by the officials at Moreton Bay during his time as a convict. Nor did he come under notice for having any bush or rural experience. He remained at the Brisbane penal colony as a quiet prisoner until his sentence was served.

The second William Thompson, was [like the Crawfords] a native of Scotland. He was given a life sentence for forgery while working as land steward at his masters property in Louth, Ireland. He was a man of knowledge who could easily place himself above others by acting like the land manager that he was. This man, it will be shown, was the only one of that name who could have been the 'husband' of Barbara Crawford. Unraveling the mystery surrounding William Thompson, especially in regards to his identity and how he managed to get Barbara Crawford into the Brisbane penal colony without detection, cannot be explained, unless we examine the conditions that prevailed at the time.

The colony

Many will state that the Moreton Bay colony had been disbanded and was officially open to settlers from the end of 1842. This should have made it easy for someone to live among time-served convicts, anonymously. This was not so, for not until early 1845 did the first settler ships arrive in Brisbane, until that time, the colony was run much as before and strangers quickly came under notice on arrival.

The colony still demanded the credentials of all those arriving at Moreton Bay and those who would cause financial burden to the colony were turned away. Many convicts were still serving out their time as ticket-of-leave and colonial conditionally pardoned men. Some had purchased land and built homes for themselves but they still needed some supervision until their Crown sentences had been served. Several convicts that had escaped into the bush were forced to complete their sentences once they returned to the fold and at least two of these returned to Brisbane when they thought the colony had been disbanded in 1842.

William Thompson obviously knew his way around the Australian penal colonies and due to the regulations in place at that time, it must be accepted that he was, or had been, part of the Sydney and Moreton Bay penal establishments. Thompson did not receive official sanction to enter Brisbane with Barbara Crawford at anytime during the early 1840's. There is not one official report, letter or notification of any kind, signaling his intent to enter Brisbane or to bring a child or intended wife to the penal colony. William Thompson probably was a ticket of leave or pardoned convict, who had the freedom of travel between Sydney and Brisbane. The fact remains that Thompson did live in Brisbane with Barbara Crawford for 18 months and he did so without attracting unfavorable attention. The colonial officials in Brisbane may have relaxed a little due to their intent to disband the penal side of the colony but judging by the number of letters requesting permission to enter Brisbane at that time, the officials were allowing little to get past them. The only way travelers could arrive at the Brisbane settlement was from the sea or by the overland route through the New England Ranges. Overland travelers needed to carry supplies that would last many weeks and such a trek would not have been easy for a very young girl. Records of each outgoing traveller were noted before leaving Sydney and as Thompson and Barbara Crawford appear to have no such file, it is believed that Thompson brought his charge by sea. This could have been done on one of the convict run inter-colony traders. Larger supply vessels had their passengers recorded and published in the local newspapers of the day and the two runaways cannot be found as passengers on these vessels.

Prior to the end of 1844, all persons seeking permission to enter Brisbane, with residential intentions, had to apply to the Colonial Secretary in writing stating their intentions. If William Thompson were not a resident of Brisbane, his application for permission to enter would still be available to us. To understand what prompted Thompson to take such a young female from her home is a little difficult to ascertain. Suffice to say [at this point] that he appears to have been desperate for young female company, even at the risk of losing remissions if caught.

Thompson's type

Barbara Crawford's description of William Thompson appears to denote a man aged between 25 and 50 years old. Although she did not give his age, Thompson was too competent in his personal dealings with others to be a very young man. His ability to impress his superiors, especially those at the Moreton Bay colony, show that he was an experienced person. For history's sake, it is imperative that we discover just who William Thompson was and from whence he came. His young 'wife' Barbara Crawford Thompson has left behind a few delicate hints about her lover, perhaps enough to finally identify him.

LOUTH, IRELAND, 1828.

The land steward struggled to free himself from the two powerful Irish policemen holding his arms and the scruff of his shirt. They dragged him, protesting toward the police cart, his boots leaving skid marks in the sod as he forced his toes downward to drag against his captors. His protestations went unheeded, as the burly officers manacled and tossed him unceremoniously into the rancid-smelling vehicle.

An English gentleman farmer, dressed finely in an immaculate tweed suit, motioned with his gold handled cane to the senior officer, proffering a document that the Englishman appeared to find distasteful to the touch. He muttered a few words to the senior officer, who respectfully tipped his hat before turning back to the yelling prisoner in the wagon. The policeman stepped up into the cart as his fellow officer gee-ed the horse forward. The prisoner kept bellowing and protesting his innocence as they pulled away. Soon, the angry yelling abated into pleas for forgiveness as the forlorn prisoner reached out a hand toward his master.

Convicted

The prisoner was a sandy-haired man, born in the old shire Clackmanan, Scotland in 1792. His father and mother were perhaps house or manor servants and as a young man, their son achieved the post of Land Steward. Like many other Scotsmen, he was sent off to manage English owned property in Ireland. His birth name was Henry Shetland and at the time of his arrest in 1828, he was 36 years old and married with a young wife and two children.

Henry Shetland was charged, convicted and found guilty of the crime of forgery and it is probable, that he used his master's name to obtain goods for his own use. This brought upon him the sentence of life in the colonies. Henry Shetland was placed aboard the convict ship 'Sophia' with 179 civilian convicts and 12 court-martialed convict soldiers. The ship 'Sophia' sailed for Australia in the latter months of 1828, arriving and discharging her cargo in Sydney during January of 1829.

Indentured

Henry Shetland proved to be a capable and professional man in his work once he had adapted to the penal system. He was indentured to the Berry and Wollstonecraft Company in Sydney, where he worked quietly for his new masters. Somehow, he was lucky enough to be involved in the capture of an aboriginal killer named 'Brogher'. The aboriginal had murdered a white man [John Rivett] at Illawarra in New South Wales and a reward had been posted for his capture. How the capture was accomplished is not known but for capturing 'Brogher', Henry Shetland was given a ticket of leave, which allowed him to live as a free settler in New South Wales. As long as he did not attempt to leave the colonies he was virtually a free man in Australia. His Crown sentence was commuted from life to 7 years. The remissions were awarded in 1830 and it was thought by the officials, that Shetland might become a trusted member of the community and serve out his time usefully. Henry obviously felt he deserved more and a few months later in 1831, he was foolhardy enough to again try his hand at forgery.

Shetland was caught and convicted for a second time. For this he received a colonial life sentence, his ticket of leave was cancelled and his crown life sentence was re-instated. Henry Shetland, as a second offender, was sent to the harsh Moreton Bay penal colony, where life would be much tougher than he had known in Sydney and Illawarra. This was a bad blow for the Scotsman; he was now faced with two life sentences to serve out, in an unforgiving colony in the tropics.

For the next seven years, Henry Shetland served his time under Moreton Bay commandants who offered nothing and were not interested in his abilities. Shetland had learned a little patience and although he must have suffered mentally on receiving his new prison sentence, he was rewarded for his patience in 1838, when a new officer took command in Brisbane.

Lieutenant Gorman was a military man who found that he did not have a large number of soldiers under his command at the Moreton Bay colony. This brought about the creation of a convict police force in Brisbane, like that operating in Sydney. This would protect the settlement and the officer's wives and families. The convict police would also have the more frequent duties of rounding up runaway convicts and wild aboriginals who attacked or killed any member of the colony. Taking a few select men, Gorman promised them remissions, tickets of leave and pardons if they performed their duties well. He researched the background of each convict he thought could be employed in his new police force and Henry Shetland's capture of an aboriginal murderer in Sydney, became an instant asset for the forger.

Convict ship 'Sophia' transported William Henry Shetland Thompson to Sydney in 1828

The Convict Police

So began a new career for Henry Shetland. His work as a convict police constable earned him a remission of his sentence in the very same year that he joined the constabulary. His colonial sentence was commuted from life to seven years. Then, less than a year later in 1839, with convict chief constable George Brown, he tracked down the escaped convict Henry Daley, finding him living with natives near the Clarence River in northern New South Wales.

Henry Daley had arrived as a teenage convict per the ship 'Florentia' in 1828. He was 30 years old when finally captured and at that time, had become fluent in many of the native dialects, especially those to the south, north and west of the penal settlement at Moreton Bay.

The two arresting constables [Brown and Shetland] were sent to Sydney on September 13, 1839, where they were to apply for their reward for the capture of Daley. The tickets-of-leave given were not pardons but they did allow convicts the freedom of the Australian colonies. They could also continue in their usual work or open and run their own business.

The two excited convicts returned to Brisbane via the overland route, probably as a demonstration of that new found freedom. The route was through the New England ranges and on September 17, 1839, they departed for Brisbane, knowing that the new year would usher in many changes.

Convict ship 'Florentia' transported convict escapee Henry Daley in 1828

Not long after they had returned, Lieutenant Gorman received a message from Limestone [Ipswich] that a convict who worked in the area had cut and run. The convict, named John Pawson, had gone toward Cunningham's Gap, which is about 60 miles south west of Brisbane. He boasted that he would easily reach the settled areas of Sydney and that the police constables would never catch him. Lieutenant Gorman sent chief constable George Brown [a native of India], three aboriginal trackers and convict constables Giles, Eagan and Henry Shetland. The party went after Pawson with enough supplies, to last them four days march beyond Cunninghams Gap.

Stationed on the McIntyre

The four convicts and three aboriginals made their way through the Gap and out onto the grassy plains beyond. They followed his trail until they had gone 150 miles [250 klms] south of the mountains, out onto the lightly wooded plains beyond. There, they encountered an aboriginal carrying a canvas bag and a tomahawk. When questioned by the trackers, the native stated that settlers had already taken up land as far north of Sydney as the nearby McIntyre River where a new sheep station had already been established. A short time later, the constables arrived at McIntyre River Station, owned by Peter McIntyre. There, the superintendent in charge, Arthur Cooper, welcomed them. He arranged for the men to eat and gave them fresh stores, for which he was given a receipt by George Brown. The party then headed back toward Brisbane, having done all they possibly could to recapture the escapee Pawson. Seven miles from the station, Brown suddenly stopped to mark a tree while sending the other constables on ahead. He then set out in another direction with the aboriginal trackers. Shetland, Giles and Eagan returned a short time later to look for Brown when he did not join them as arranged. They fired the musket they were carrying in an effort to contact him but Brown had disappeared.

Suspecting some form of treachery, Shetland and the other two constables headed back to the station where they were later joined by two of the aboriginal trackers. They explained the situation to Superintendent Cooper, who then helped Shetland, Giles and Eagan to proceed toward Sydney, rather than take the chance of being ambushed perhaps by aboriginals on a return trek to Brisbane.

The sting

It is possible and even likely, that George Brown may have concocted the whole operation by having Pawson feign escape so that he could recapture him and gain further remissions. Pawson may have followed the party at a respectful distance and then shown himself to Brown when the others were not around. The three constables might have guessed that Brown had arranged to capture Pawson himself, which would have given Brown all the glory and remissions. If this was so, is not known but it is a possible answer to the trouble that arose from this trek. Perhaps after considering what Brown was up to on his own, Shetland and the others decided that they would walk away from Brown's plan. Shetland knew the route to Sydney, he had already made the trip overland when he and Brown had been sent back to Brisbane by that route after receiving their tickets of leave for the capture of Henry Daley.

Overseer Cooper, of McIntyre station, sent letters to Sydney with the three constables explaining the position to the Colonial Secretary. This prompted that gentleman, to write to Lieutenant Gorman to inform him of the circumstances. Lieutenant Gorman, on hearing that his men were at the Hyde Park Barracks, wrote and asked that they be sent back to him on the first available ship.

A few days later George Brown arrived in Brisbane [possibly with Pawson under his wing], stating that he had been deserted by the three other constables. Things now would have looked bad for Henry Shetland and the other constables but it was George Brown, who eventually got it in the neck. He could not refute the testimony of the three constables who probably told Gorman that something strange was afoot with the way Brown had acted. Although officially Brown was guilty of only following orders, it is likely that Shetland and the others told Gorman that Brown and Pawson had conspired to cheat and this suspicion was enough to cause Gorman to dismiss Brown. George Brown had returned to Brisbane once he had reached the limit of his supplies. But by leaving the others, Brown had placed himself in the minority and therefore, in jeopardy. Shetland and the others enjoyed a spell in Sydney and then were able to effectively join forces against Brown.

Lieutenant Gorman studied the situation and found that Brown could not be trusted. He wrote to the Colonial Secretary requesting Brown's removal from Moreton Bay. Gorman asked that Brown never be allowed to return to that colony. Gorman also stated that Brown 'would probably end up running with the aboriginals'. He reasoned that he believed Shetland and the other constables and stated that he thought Brown, 'who is an Indian national and the same colour as the aborigines'. As such, 'he is more likely to abscond and will easily blend in with the natives, if he does run away'.

Convict Pawson turned up and was punished but that was over-shadowed by the problems had with George Brown. If it was Brown that brought Pawson in, Gorman did not mention it. Writing to the Colonial Secretary, he explained only that Pawson had been captured and was fittingly punished for his escape. Whether convict Pawson really did try to leave the area is not known, perhaps he was part of a conspiracy by Brown, perhaps not. Whatever the truth behind the situation, Henry Shetland appears to have continued with his police work, rather than start out on his own with his ticket-of-leave. Shetland was indeed a smart man and probably had a full pardon in mind. It appears odd that no one was credited with Pawson's capture, unless Brown brought him in. Although a reward had been posted, no one appears to have claimed it. George Brown was sent down to Sydney, to await punishment for deserting his men while in the performance of their duty. The least he would have suffered would have been the loss of his ticket of leave and shipment to one of the more rugged settlements.

Learning the Bush

Henry Shetland had by this time, become well acquainted with the culture and much of the language of the natives in Moreton Bay. During his work as a police constable, he had also gained insight into the doings of the convicts at the settlement and always managed to be on hand when anything serious was happening. When John Sherry Baker [runaway convict] gave himself up to the settlement, Shetland was there to oversee his surrender. Baker was well versed in the dialect of the natives of the Lockyer valley, which runs westward from Brisbane into the Darling Downs and he also had much knowledge of the Kabi language.

A few months later, aborigines killed local Surveyor, Mr. Gilbert E. Staplylton. He was encamped some miles from Brisbane when his group was attacked. One of the men escaped and made it back to the colony where he reported the matter. The natives ransacked the Staplyton camp and when the rescue party arrived, it was all they could do to convey the remains of Staplyton back to Brisbane for burial. The murder of Surveyor Staplyton attracted much attention and on May 31st 1840, Lieutenant Gorman issued a proclamation. It stated that 'whoever captured the murderers, would be the recipient of, at the very least, a ticket of leave or even an conditional pardon'. Henry Shetland saw this as a chance to win his colonial freedom and he went after the natives. It was he who found and captured the killers. On June 22nd 1840, the natives were sent from Brisbane to Sydney for trial. John Baker was sent along to act as interpreter for the bewildered natives, while Shetland was assigned as escort for the party. It is sure that Shetland would have gleaned as much information as he could from Baker, especially concerning the local aboriginal dialects.

The Coup de Grace

In July 1840, Shetland's colonial life sentence was remitted to seven years for the capture of the three aboriginals. Again he had succeeded in gaining himself remissions but in October 1840, before he could be rewarded with certification, he again showed his heroic side while conducting a new station owner, to a property west of Brisbane. Shetland noticed a gathering of aboriginal warriors [about 700, in Shetland's report] while they were passing some gullies about 80 miles [135 klms] west of Brisbane. According to station owner, Mr. Gilbert Elliott, the natives were 'a great source of annoyance' and for the most part, the whites were in fear of their lives. Many of the natives knew Henry Shetland and they called on him to take the white men away from their territory. Shetland rode forward to where the blacks were grouped and told them that he was taking the whites clear across their territory to the land of their neighbours. This placated the natives and they allowed the men to pass unhindered. Much to the relief of the settlers, Henry had extricated his people from the predicament without a shot being fired and thenceforth, they were conveyed to their destination without further ado. This fearless act must have seemed somewhat heroic to the settlers, for Shetland was recommended for a conditional pardon at the request of his commandant and letters of praise from the landowner, George Elliott.

Henry Shetland later petitioned for a conditional pardon from Governor George Gipps and in July 1841, the pardon was awarded. Lieutenant Gorman had written to Governor Gipps highly praising Shetland for his police work and was happy with the petitions outcome. Gorman was justifiably proud of his man, for he too, received credits for Henry Shetland's brave deeds.

The discovery

It is important that we now explain how and why the convict Henry Shetland has become connected with Barbara Crawford and her fate. To do so, we must go back to when he was first arrested in Ireland. At that time, he was referred to as Henry Shetland but later, in the convict muster for the ship 'Sophia', he was also listed with an alias. The alias was the name he used as a forger and was probably the name of his original master. The alias 'William Thompson' is shown alongside Henry Shetland's name on the muster list of the 'Sophia'. Unless and until researchers accidentally stumbled [as the Author did] across the Shetland –Thompson petition for a colonial pardon in official files, the connection with Barbara Crawford could have been quite easily missed. It was only by one in several thousand chances that this William Thompson was found by the Author.

Whilst combing through thousands of letters to the Colonial secretary for any mention of Barbara Crawford, a petitioner's letter [petition for a conditional pardon by Henry Shetland alias William Thompson] gave up the name William Thompson. This William Thompson may have never been found, had it not been for the search for references to Barbara within the files. Convict Shetland's arrival date, the name of his ship and all relevant details on how he became a second offence convict at Moreton Bay were soon dredged out of a sea of blue micro-film. Finally a 'well known and much favoured' William Thompson had come into the light. The name William Thompson was never officially used by Shetland until William Henry Shetland Thompson was given that full title by Governor George Gipps in 1841. He was at first referred to in colonial letters as Henry Shetland with the side note 'or Thompson'. Later, on his petition to the Governor, he used the name William Henry Shetland Thompson, which he bore for the rest of his life.

Once a proper candidate had been found, the missing pieces fell into place, a 'much favoured and well known' man appeared out of the gloom. Finally a man fitting the description given by Barbara, who did have a solid reputation with the officials at Brisbane, had been found. The two other William Thomsons [one resident up until 1836, the another who arrived as a settler/farmer in Brisbane in late 1844] were quickly laid to rest and the only real contender for the part took his rightful place in history.

Conditional Pardon

For the many services performed in Lieutenant Gorman's service, William Henry Shetland Thompson received remissions for all but seven years of his Crown life sentence. He was given a conditional pardon, which allowed him the freedom to move about the colonies in Australia without fear of arrest and without having to report to the commandant.

What is very surprising is the fact that Thompson received no historic recognition for his bravery or for his reputation. In fact, it is almost surreal to read reports from various officials telling of the capture of aborigines that killed Surveyor Stapylton, yet W.H.S.Thompson gets no kudos in history for his deeds in the new settlement.

Thompson had faced down several hundred natives that were in no mood to have more settlers coming into their tribal hunting grounds. He had also done other meritorious deeds in the service of his captors, so why did he not receive historic recognition? Perhaps the truth is that this man was, like some of the Pharaoh's of Egypt, cut out of history by officials who disregarded his deeds due to his sins.

Thompson's final pardon was issued to him at some time between July 1st 1841 and January 1842. To receive this conditional pardon, Thompson traveled to Sydney, where he stayed at Hyde Park barracks until the papers were handed to him. The pardon made him a free man anywhere in Australia but did not allow him to travel abroad, this was a condition of his pardon. Thompson had to remain in Australia until the final seven years of his Crown sentence were served. Numerous letters proclaiming his good character were sent to the Colonial Secretary, especially by the officer in charge at Brisbane.

It is known that Thompson traveled to Sydney on several occasions between 1841 and 1843, probably in the small cutter owned by his convict police colleague, John Durkin. Durkin had earlier received a pardon and gone into business trading goods between Sydney and Brisbane. It is also believed that Thompson worked as an assistant or even partner to Durkin at this time.

The official petition of William Henry Shetland Thompson (continued next page)

The official petition of William Henry Shetland Thompson (continued next page)

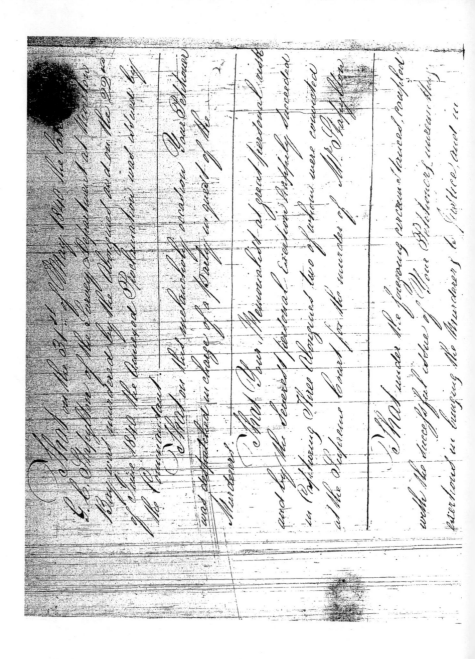

The official petition of William Henry Shetland Thompson (continued next page)

The official petition of William Henry Shetland Thompson (end of petition for a colonial pardon)

Notes on Thompson's petition by the Colonial Secretary (continued next page)

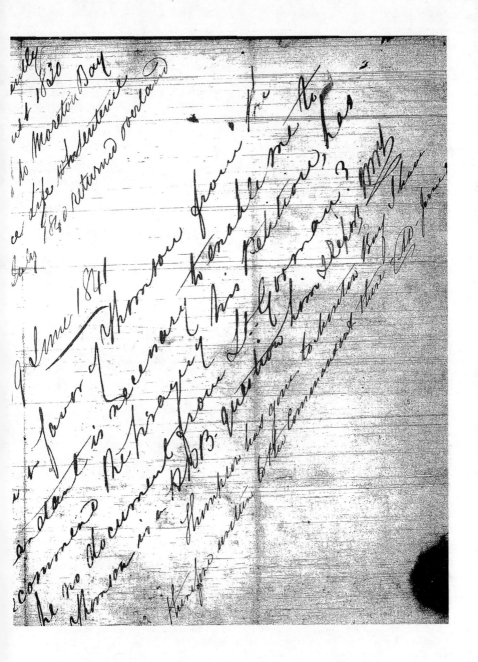

Notes on Thompson's petition by the Colonial Secretary (July 1841)

Goodbye Gorman

After a short term [1838-1841] as commandant at Moreton Bay, Lieutenant Gorman began having problems with the new surveyor. This was a man named Robert Dixon who somehow became disenchanted with Gorman and accused him [Gorman] of being corrupt. Gorman countered this accusation and accused Dixon of keeping government equipment without permission. This of course was tantamount to an accusation of stealing. It was Dixon's claim though, that eventually brought about the downfall of Lieutenant Gorman. After initial investigations were made Gorman was replaced by a new commandant [Lieutenant Simpson] in late 1841, shortly after William Thompson had received his conditional pardon.

Is he the one?

Convict police constable William Henry Shetland Thompson had all the attributes to make him the number one suspect as the man with whom Barbara Crawford supposedly eloped. His capture of convict Henry Daley, the arrest of three aboriginals involved in the murder of Surveyor Stapylton and saving Mr. Gilbert Elliott's party from natives near Toowoomba, gave him unprecedented standing with the officials in Brisbane and Sydney.

No other convict came near his popularity with the Brisbane officials and there was certainly no other 'William Thompson' residing or had resided at the Moreton Bay penal colony, who had attained such renown. Thompson also had many friends in the convict police forces, both in Brisbane and in Sydney. For Thompson to hide Barbara away at Ipswich, especially from the attentions of an irate father, would have at first been easy. Though it is possible that Charles Crawford may have come a little too close for comfort on a possible visit to Brisbane in May of 1843. One begins to suspect that Thompson and some of his convict police cronies stationed in Sydney may have created the prison term that Charles Crawford received. This might be fantasy but those that wish to cover their trail have done much stranger things. Framing Charles could have been initiated to ease the pressure on Thompson if Charles had decided to go looking for his daughter. When or if Thompson received news that Charles Crawford was in Brisbane searching for his daughter, he [Thompson] could have easily arranged for Charles to be taken out of the picture, once Charles returned to Sydney.

There is no record of Charles Crawford approaching the Brisbane officials and nothing is recorded in the local paper of the day. If a visit to Brisbane by Charles Crawford did take place, the records of this were destroyed, hidden away in archives or Charles must have done his own searching without going to the officials.

Looking for recognition

William Henry Shetland Thompson [he preferred to be known by that name in his petition] wrote to the Colonial Governor, Sir George Gipps, in 1841, to request a conditional pardon. Sir George noted the alias and that Thompson had signed himself William H.S.Thompson on his petition. George Gipps accepted the petition and the Colonial Secretary officially awarded Thompson a conditional pardon in his new name. So why has William Henry Shetland Thompson been completely overlooked in Queensland's history? Could it be that his record was expunged because of something unpardonable that he had done?

The Evidence

Now that a worthy candidate for the role of Barbara Crawford's 'husband' has been established, it is required that all known evidence be presented to substantiate our claim. The first item on the agenda is to offer proof that Henry Shetland was indeed the 'William Thompson' who transported Barbara Crawford into Australian history. The evidence, circumstantial or otherwise, must be extremely strong, especially so, now that more than 160 years have passed since these events took place.

If we hypothetically assume that an unknown free man named William Thompson arrived in Australia from England or even New Zealand. It should first be noted that Brisbane was the site of one of the harsher convict settlements and as such, it was also one of the hardest to visit. Even after official closure of the penal colony, officials demanded that letters of introduction and permission to enter, be issued by the Colonial

Secretary. The sub-tropical climate was also considered harsh by many of the Irish and English convicts transported there.

All non-residents entering the region needed a written introductory pass. This was strictly adhered to during the official penal colony years from 1826 until the beginning of 1843. From then until the end of 1850, it was still in use though slowly being done away with. This made it impossible to enter the colony unannounced, unless by a person who was already resident at or working within the colony.

For at least two years immediately after the announced disbanding of the colony [December 1842 through December 1844] the colony was still stringently regulated. Many resident convicts still had time to serve and although several of the lifers were returned to Sydney, others remained at Moreton Bay to serve out the few years they had left. Others still were on conditional pardons and even more were on ticket of leave, they were all still prisoners until their time was officially served. This meant that the military had to remain in some capacity until the last of the convicts had finished serving out their time. Proof of this arrangement is shown in the fact that Brisbane was able to receive its first two direct-from-England convict ships, in 1849 and 1850, the first ever to arrive at that port.

After the 1842 disbanding, even vessels in distress or shipwreck survivors arriving unannounced at Moreton Bay, were reported to the Police Magistrate, he would notify Lieutenant Simpson who would also notify the Colonial Secretary, by reporting the vessels arrival. The condition of those aboard the ship or boat, the condition of the vessel and the housing of the passengers or survivors ashore were also organized and then reported to Sydney. Names of the vessel's captain, crew and any passengers were also taken and the colonial secretary notified. Anyone travelling overland from Sydney was pre-warned about the conditions in Brisbane and also had to state what their intentions would be, once they had arrived. It is therefore inconceivable how anyone could migrate to Brisbane and reside there for a lengthy period without being noticed by anyone at all.

There were literally thousands of letters sent to Sydney by Brisbane officials, describing even mundane events taking place at the colony. Everything from shipwreck survivors, to the transport of a cow into the penal colony was well reported. It was from among these letters that the name William Thompson was brought into the light.

This letter, written in support of convict police constable Henry Shetland with his alias of William Thompson, rescues this name from obscurity. It also opens a few doors and we are soon presented with much more information regarding this man and his connection to the colony. His work history and even his purchase of a property at Ipswich are shown. The Sydney Herald announced land sales both in Ipswich and Brisbane about April of 1844 and listed some of those who had purchased land. William Henry Shetland Thompson is one of those listed. On searching through records on the land sale, we are given all the information needed on his purchase.

William Thompson's arrival and subsequent stay at Moreton Bay, [if he were new to the area] without the knowledge of officials, was virtually impossible. It is certain that if he arrived in Brisbane with a young female, that officials at the penal colony would have duly noted the arrival. The officials would have questioned Thompson as to his intentions, with the safety and comfort of the girl in mind.

As yet, all we have shown is that William Thompson was probably a resident of Brisbane and not a newcomer. By the time Thompson departed Brisbane in 1844, the colony was under the control of Lieutenant Simpson. When Captain Wickham arrived to police Brisbane in April 1843, the two officials would hold dual control until the military were no longer needed in the area and the civil police could wholly take over. Wickham's arrival as Police Magistrate did little to attract settlers to the area. Brisbane had earned its reputation as a harsh punishment colony based in a hot tropical climate. From then until the end of 1844, the colony remained almost as it had been from its beginning. Letters of request by new arrivals at Brisbane were still being sent to Lieutenant Simpson long after Thompson and Barbara Crawford left Moreton Bay in September 1844. Yet nothing is recorded regarding Thompson and Barbara during or prior to 1844, no mention in any newspaper or official file. This indicates that Thompson somehow managed to keep his young lady hidden while they lived and survived in Brisbane for the 18 months, [March 1843 to September 1844] as was later reported by Barbara Crawford.

Ipswich

The convict police unit, to which William Henry Shetland Thompson was assigned, was housed at Limestone station [Ipswich] where most of these men had their own shacks along the river. Here, they could fish or enjoy some solitude well away from the main penal area. Some of the convicts even had aboriginal women visit them. Officials did not inspect this area often, for it was a convict trustee village. Ex-police constable William Henry Shetland Thompson also had his shack at Limestone and it was to this place, that he brought Barbara Crawford.

Once the couple had settled in, Thompson and Barbara kept a low profile. She kept house and when he had to go into the bush on work or minor excursions, she would accompany him. Thompson, as a free man, did not have to answer to the officials in Brisbane but he did have to make a living. He could no longer accompany Durkin on his voyages to Sydney and so probably lived off the bush or by doing some form of land work for the commandant or by fishing the river and selling his catch at the settlement.

Thompson was not often required by the officials and he probably only did a little contract work for Lieutenant Simpson. His expertise as a Land Steward and knowledge of his surrounds would have allowed him at least a modest income. It is unclear if he was receiving supplies from the colony but as he was still a Crown prisoner and would remain as such, at least until 1849, it is probable that stores were allotted to him.

Barbara Crawford later stated, [Barbara to Brierly, 1849] that she had learned many of the timber types that were growing along the coast of what is now Queensland, while she lived with and assisted William Thompson. It is known that Lieutenant Gorman sent a letter to the Colonial Secretary giving the same list of timber names and the quantities available in and around Brisbane. It was probably Thompson who originally supplied that list.

How important this piece of information is to our story. Only someone living and working in the colony could have given her such detailed information about Queensland flora. How could she have gained the knowledge of at least 14 native trees unless she lived for some time in that area? Being illiterate, Barbara learned the tree types by visual record rather than by memorizing written names. Perhaps this was why she was able to run off the names of so many trees with the ease of someone well experienced in Queensland timber, five years after she had studied them.

It is possible that the officials turned their backs while a few females were somewhat surreptitiously brought into the colony after 1842 and before the end of 1844. The announced closure of the colony and the transfer of convicts back to Sydney would have caused officials to relax somewhat. It must be remembered though, that Lieutenant Gorman had been replaced and Lieutenant Simpson would have been reluctant to become involved in any form of corrupt activity. Still, the imminent arrival of free settlers would have probably caused the officials in Brisbane to be less restrictive in matters of the heart. So long as the girl made no complaint, she was considered to be in no danger, moral or otherwise.

The Cutter 'America

Thompson's friend and police colleague, John Durkin, owned a small craft [see letter to Col Sec; January 1841] which he sailed back and forth to Sydney carrying goods and supplies for the northern colony. Durkin applied for permission to run his vessel soon after he was in receipt of his own colonial pardon in early 1841. It is very likely that Thompson traveled with Durkin on more than one occasion. It is fact that the two men were friends and colleagues and as such, would have been protective of each other.

Durkin's vessel was probably that same small cutter rigged craft that Thompson renamed 'America'. It is likely that his plans for the little vessel would have meant more than voyaging back and forth to Sydney. It is possible that he and perhaps Durkin, made plans to sail first to China and then take ship to America, his renaming of the small craft hints at this final destination.

It is interesting to note that one particular author writing on this subject, states that the cutter 'America' was previously known as the 'Ada'. If this were true, it would have probably been the name of John Durkin's vessel before Thompson changed it to 'America'. The reasoning behind this is because at that time there were so few vessels in Brisbane and each of them was well known. Only Durkin's 'small craft' is not officially named and unless Thompson purchased one of the well-known cutters [there were three in Brisbane] Durkin's boat becomes the only other possibility.

Other than the three boats spoken of, there is no mention of any other cutter arriving or being based in Brisbane at this time. Durkin's boat is the only one that is nameless in official reports. How the author came by his information on the 'Ada', is not known but there are obviously 'more things in heaven and earth Horatio'.

As there are no reports of Thompson or his cutter in official records, the suggestion that he arrived in Brisbane as a free first time visitor by boat or ship can be dismissed. Thompson would have been able to bring Barbara Crawford into Brisbane surreptitiously on John Durkin's cutter. He could easily enter the area without challenge as he had done several times before.

They did not need clearance and had no need to go near the officials. The pilot station at Amity Point recognised Durkin's boat and as both Durkin and Thompson were trusted members of the colony, reports were not considered necessary. When Thompson was told of the wreck of a whaling ship, it is possible that Durkin sold his boat to William Thompson. Perhaps Durkin finished his sentence and decided to go back to England or perhaps went to live in Sydney. If this were the case, Thompson still had many other convict friends on whom he could rely.

William Henry Shetland Thompson quickly made himself and Barbara quite comfortable at Limestone; he was well protected by his fellow convict police, who probably did not know where Barbara had come from or how old she was. The soon-to-be town of Ipswich, was somewhat like the American 'hole-in-the-wall gang' fortress, where convicts could enjoy a little privacy. The exception being that the men involved, were trustee convicts working as an official convict police unit.

Leaving Sydney town, March, 1843

Barbara watched as the heads of Sydney's great harbour disappeared into the distance. She smiled with excitement while the little boat continued to bounce its way north along the New South Wales coast. The great excitement she felt at entering the strange unknown was a little disconcerting but she was comfortable in the knowledge that she would be cleaning house for a countryman and family friend.

William Thompson had ingratiated himself with her mother and father and they had come to trust him completely during the approximately fourteen months they had known him. Thompson had made several voyages to Sydney from his home in the far north and each time he arrived he would visit them and the hotel next door. His interest at first seemed to linger on Barbara's sister Mary and eventually, he asked Mary if she would like to work for him in Brisbane. Mary Crawford was excited by this prospect, the whole family gathered around to hear Thompson's tales of the wild bushland and his home in Brisbane. Thompson later wrote to Mary from Brisbane in September of 1842 but by this time Mary had changed her mind about leaving home.

Charles Crawford would have been apologetic when Thompson arrived in Sydney in late February of 1843. He had believed that Mary would accept Thompson's offer and now felt ashamed that she had apparently moved on. Thompson was casual about the loss of his arrangement and shrugged his shoulders resignedly; there was nothing else for it but to look elsewhere for a housemaid.

Charles though, with finances going badly, had been seeking housework for young Barbara and now that she had turned twelve years old, he could see nothing wrong with her taking Mary's place. Even though it was only three months after her twelfth birthday. So he suggested that Thompson take Barbara with him instead. The proviso on this arrangement would be that Barbara could come home on visits whenever Thompson came to Sydney. Thompson had been a friend now for 18 months and was a regular twice-a-year visitor to Sydney, he was well liked by the family and more importantly Barbara trusted him, just as she trusted her father. Thompson was canny enough not to accept this offer too quickly and said that he would think on it overnight as he would be leaving with the tide the following day. Thompson told Charles to have her things packed and ready in case he thought Barbara would be acceptable as his new housekeeper. The next morning William Thompson, with apparent disinterest, called for Barbara and told Charles that he would bring her back to see them within the next few months and that he would report on her progress.

The awakening

After an exciting day at sea, night settled over the little boat and Barbara moved to the below deck where a straw bed had been made up in a snug little area behind some rope coils and goods being sent north. She used the small cloth satchel her mother had given her, as a pillow and lay down to let sleep claim her.

Some hours later, Barbara struggled upward into semi-consciousness, she felt herself being bumped and pushed sideways on the straw and heard William telling her to move over. She did not understand what was occurring in her dream-like state. That someplace that lingered between deep sleep and half awareness. Barbara's crowded family life bade her accept the order to move over and she sleepily did as she was told.

Again she was brought almost awake as she felt hands moving over her underdress but childlike, did not resist when that garment was removed. Again she drifted down to deep sleep and again she was pulled back toward consciousness. The persistent hands continued over her now almost naked body, removing the last of her clothing. Still she could not bring herself into the real world and it was not until she found herself with Thompson's weight pressing down upon her, that her mind came swiftly upward into a fearful awakening. She felt him positioning himself and then felt a sudden sharp pain that brought her fully aware. Her lower stomach now felt like fire yet she could not cry out, her mouth opened but no sound came out. She felt new pain and strange sensations but the painful shock of his entry took away any thought of trying to understand what was happening. She knew what was being done but except for the pain, did not fully realise the situation.

She could hear William telling her not to worry that it would be all over in just a minute. She tried to make a reply but still nothing could escape her mouth. William went on doing what he wanted and now the worst of the pain had dissipated, she lay with legs akimbo waiting for it to end. She bit her lip and clenched her teeth and tears of shock rolled silent down her cheeks. Finally, Thompson rolled off and away from her. Within minutes he, without recrimination or even an 'are you alright', fell asleep, while Barbara listened to his steady slumbering breath for what seemed like hours.

When she knew William was well asleep, she quietly and with childish innocence, repaired herself and returned to the netherworld from which she had been so rudely awakened. She understood what had happened and her mind kept telling her that 'she was married now, she was owned body and soul' by the man who now lay sleeping beside her.

The Northern Colony

Barbara was kept below deck and away from prying eyes on arrival at the Brisbane settlement. She was not allowed to come up from below at all while the cutter was progressing up the Brisbane River to Limestone.

Durkin's boat made it simple to bring the twelve-year-old to her new home but she had to be hidden until they reached his hut. Thompson was smart enough to tell Barbara that she should now consider that they were husband and wife. He would write to her parents to inform them of the changes he had made to their agreement, he would let Charles know that they had eloped.

Barbara by this time, had accepted her fate, she had been taken several times during the voyage but did not complain, the way of the times stated that she was now virtually married. In fact, William was now teaching her many things about her body and pleasure had begun to take the place of pain.

She knew that the events aboard the cutter had changed her life forever, that she belonged to William Thompson and in the culture of her people, was now his wife. Her mental age would determine what next would happen in her life. She had calmly accepted the new arrangements without the realisation that anything was wrong. William had taken her to wife and that was the way of it, she was resigned to this and soon came to love the man who had been first to take her.

The search

Barbara Crawford's true age at the time she 'eloped', has become a determining factor in her drama. According to all other written history, Barbara was 16 when she left home and presumably almost 21 when brought back to civilisation.

The truth has now been found and it can be revealed that she was actually six years old when her family arrived in Australia in July 1837. Proving that she was 12 years old when she departed Sydney in March 1843. She therefore turned 12 at some time late in 1842 or early 1843, with November 1842 being the most likely month for her previous birthday.

William Thompson stopped going backwards and forwards to Sydney with Durkin from that time onward, he knew that Charles Crawford would be trying to find them and it was better for him to stay in Ipswich with Barbara. John Durkin may have decided at that time also, to quit the sea and go back to England or retire to Sydney. He disappears soon after and if he did sell his boat, he would have surely had enough for his ticket money home.

The cutter

Barbara Crawford after her rescue stated that he [Thompson] had purchased the cutter 'America' in Brisbane where he renamed it. It is with this reasoning that we believe John Durkin was the man who sold the 'small craft' to Thompson. He of course would use it for his fateful voyage twelve months later.

Of the three cutters in Brisbane at the time of our drama, one was a vessel named 'John'. It was owned by the ex-convict, John Williams and it was skippered by another ex-convict, John Chambers. Williams owned a small store in South Brisbane and to service his store, he applied for and was granted permission to bring the cutter to Brisbane for use as a storage vessel.

The cutter 'America' aground on Majii Reef (Line drawing by the Author)

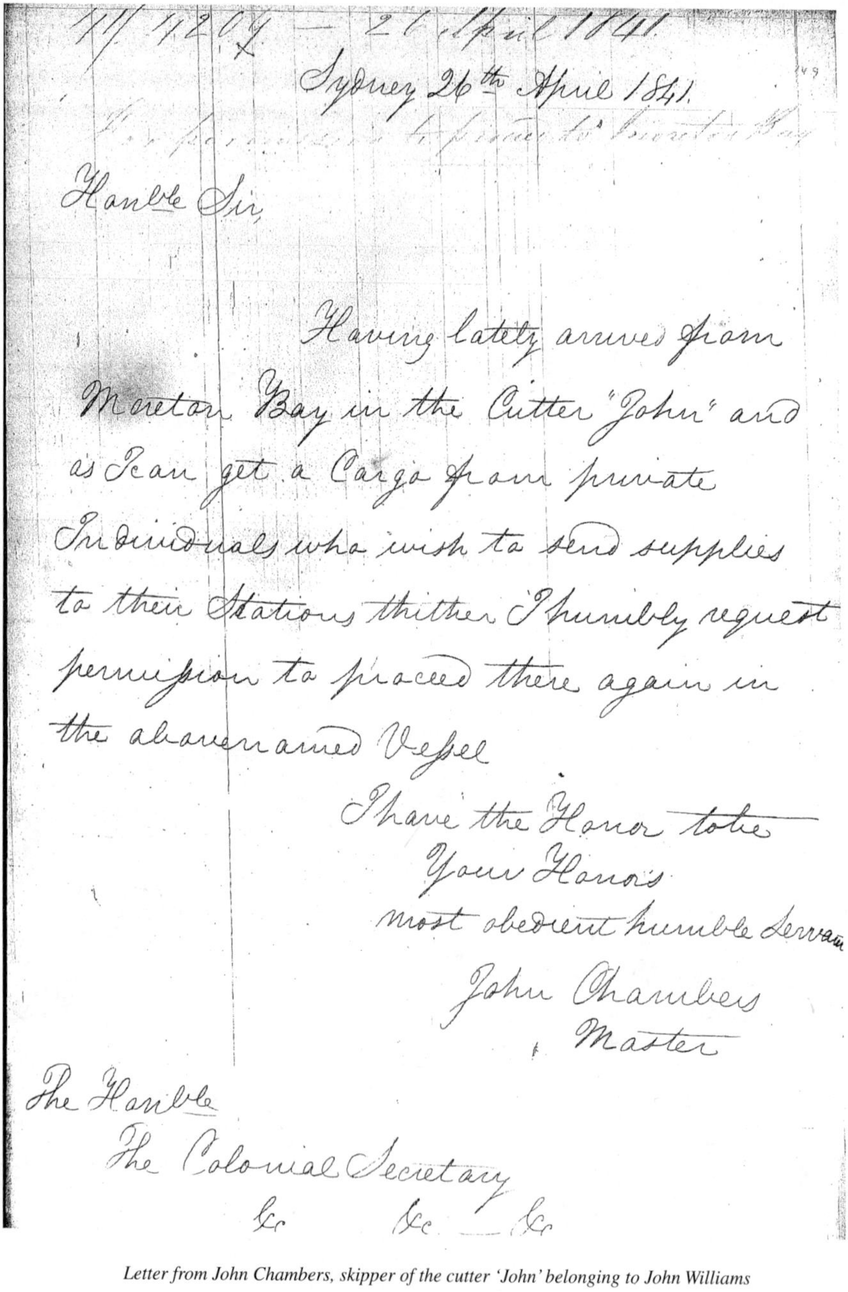

11/4207 — 26 April 1841

Sydney 26th April 1841.

For permission to proceed to Moreton Bay

Honble Sir,

Having lately arrived from Moreton Bay in the Cutter "John" and as I can get a Cargo from private Individuals who wish to send supplies to their Stations thither I humbly request permission to proceed there again in the abovenamed Vessel

I have the Honor to be
Your Honor's
most obedient humble Servant
John Chambers
Master

The Honble
The Colonial Secretary
&c &c &c

Letter from John Chambers, skipper of the cutter 'John' belonging to John Williams

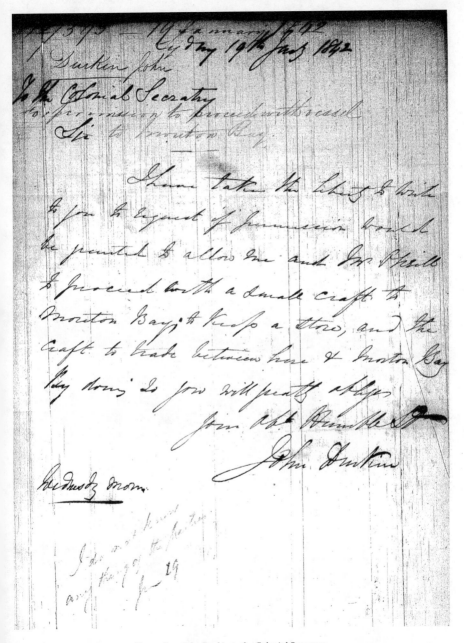

Letter from John Durkin to the Colonial Secretary.

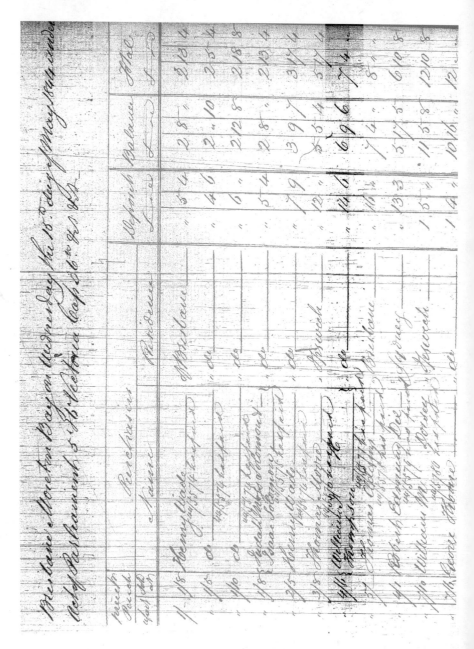

Land purchase certification by William Thompson at Ipswich (Almost all on the list were released convicts)

Such was the severe shortage of small craft in Brisbane during this period, that many letters are found requesting that boats of any size or shape be purchased and sent to the little colony. One of the three small cutters in Brisbane, most certainly became 'America', with preference being for the Durkin boat. There were so few boats arriving at or stationed in the Moreton Bay colony that purchase or sale of any vessel during this period should have been well documented. The 'America' was a decked vessel with single mast and tiller. Below deck, she had a storage area and perhaps a couple of bunks. Thompson would have needed at least one other man to help make any sea voyage that was planned. Strange as it may seem, absolute proof of the cutter and its origins are not easy to trace and it is probable that later researchers will uncover more archival evidence.

Settling in

By March 1843, William Thompson was a free man. Except of course, for the approximately five years that was left of his crown sentence to serve. This though, could be served out on his conditional pardon, which gave him the freedom of the colonies.

Thompson's attributes were manifold. He had mastered bushcraft and knew the aboriginal track ways between Sydney and Brisbane. He also had a very good understanding of aboriginal habits and some of the dialects spoken around southeast and mid-south western Queensland. Whilst living at Ipswich with Barbara, Thompson made application to purchase the land on which his shack stood. On Wednesday 15th of May 1844, Thompson made a down payment of 14 shillings and sixpence on an allotment of 32 perches at Ipswich. The full price of the land was 7 pounds 10 shillings, he and all other land buyers at that first Moreton Bay land sale, were given one month to pay off the balance and this was effectively done.

In November 1844, Thompson's deed of ownership for the land on which he had lived since becoming a police constable in 1838 was issued and recorded in the Sydney Herald newspaper. He probably had every intention of staying at Ipswich with Barbara but when a much more lucrative situation arose, he was not able 'resist the temptation'.

About Limestone

Ipswich [Limestone] was a small settlement situated on a station near the Brisbane river, about 30 land miles from Brisbane. It was populated in its early days by men and women who were free or almost free of the convict system. The convicts were mostly men but a few women, who were also on their way out of the system, began living as wives to the trustee convicts and another settlement was created. At least a dozen and perhaps more convict police constables lived among them. They maintained their own small shacks alongside Brisbane river while the freed men farmed and toiled to supply the Brisbane settlement.

On the trail

In 1844, the explorer Ludwig Leichhardt wrote to the Colonial Secretary, requesting that convicts of good character, who were experienced on the land, be allowed to accompany him on his inland expeditions. Like most explorers, Leichhardt required men who knew the aboriginal trails and mountain gaps that led out onto the Great Plains and the central areas of Australia. To gain such an invitation, a man would have a proven bush record and a good knowledge of the aborigine and their lands.

Limestone was home base for several such men but none could compare to William Henry Shetland Thompson. Ludwig Leighhardt must have been referred to Thompson because Barbara later stated that the explorer had invited her William to accompany the September 2, 1844 overland expedition to Port Essington from Brisbane. This invitation must have been made sometime between July and September of 1844 because Thompson had already met the crewmen from a wrecked whaler and they had convinced him to undertake a salvage operation for whale oil that was ready and waiting in casks for the taker.

Thompson refused Leighhardt's offer, stating that he was going to Port Essington by boat and that he would inform the inhabitants of Leichhardt's coming. This statement by Thompson to Leichhardt was probably a lie. Thompson had no real intention of going to Port Essington. This was an obvious ruse to avoid telling anyone about the salvage operation that he [Thompson] was planning. Thompson probably told all who needed to know, that he intended to set up a trade situation between Brisbane and the northern port.

In the short time since Police Magistrate Captain Wickham had arrived in the colony, [April 1843] until Thompson and Barbara left the area in September 1844, Thompson was able to become 'well liked and much favoured' [Huxley] by the new official. Perhaps this was due partly to Lieutenants Gorman and Simpson's reports. They would have conveyed Thompson's good record on to Captain Wickham and he would have told Leichhardt about the deeds done by Thompson as a police constable.

Thompson had gained his reputation in the bush, well before Captain Wickham arrived in Brisbane. He had already secreted Barbara Crawford at Ipswich a few weeks prior to Wickham's arrival. Thompson was now a free man and did nothing to bring himself under notice or to give himself a more remarkable reputation before leaving Brisbane, in September 1844.

This almost confirms the fact that Wickham had to rely on Thompson's file for any information he required, rather than having personal dealings with the ex-convict. In fact, Captain Wickham probably met William Thompson on very few occasions. Thompson had been released from his colonial sentence and had a pardon that allowed him to live an almost normal life, provided he did not try to return to England.

He was a conditional pardon holder, with only about four or five years of his crown sentence to serve and with Brisbane closing down as a penal settlement, Thompson now felt relatively safe taking a wife, without bothering to report his intention. Thompson was well known by those in Brisbane, his heroic deeds and his reputation preceded him into all sections of Brisbane's official administration. He knew that if he kept a low profile, things would go well.

One thing that tends to alter the trend of things regarding Thompson and his wish to leave the colony is that he had now bought land in Ipswich, this was not the doing of a man wanting to return to England. Could it be that he had decided to settle with Barbara or was the threat of her father finding them too strong and this became the driving force behind his wish to leave Moreton Bay?

William Henry Shetland Thompson's first real penalty for his crime against the Crawford's was that he could not accept Ludwig Leichhardt's offer. His ties to Barbara and other arrangements that he had already made would cost him remission off his Crown sentence, which indeed may have ended his servitude altogether. It must have angered him that by taking or eloping with Barbara Crawford, he had again made a costly mistake.

The Wedding

Barbara stated that she married William Thompson in Brisbane yet there are no marriage records with any church group, minister or padre. There was no application for marriage through the Colonial Secretary's office and no mention of it anywhere, not even in the Brisbane Town News.

As both Thompson and Barbara were Scottish and Presbyterian, an official marriage would have been done by banns. Perhaps they used the traditional old Scottish way of tying the knot. This was done as per this report, given in the Sydney Gazette of September 1836, headed,

'Marriage in Gretna Green in the style of 1771'.

'There a young couple may be instantly joined in wedlock by a fisherman, a joiner, a blacksmith and etc, the cost, from two guineas to a dram of whisky'. Thompson could have read this article or perhaps he well knew the tradition, he was able to read and the Sydney Gazette was a must for the Brisbane convict police. As an aside, some rather interesting coincidences occur at different times, especially regarding dates in the life of William Thompson. This man was convicted of forgery on July 28, 1828. He was convicted a second time in Sydney, this time, on July 8, 1831. He was then given his conditional pardon on July 1, 1841. To cap the matter off, Barbara Crawford and her family arrived in Australia during July 1837.

Another coincidence in this story occurred when the British warship HMS 'Rattlesnake' arrived in company with an emigrant ship one week after the 'John Barry' brought the Crawfords to Australia. The 'Rattlesnake' was to play a huge part in the life of Barbara Crawford. The name of the passenger vessel that arrived in company with the 'Rattlesnake' was the ship 'William'.

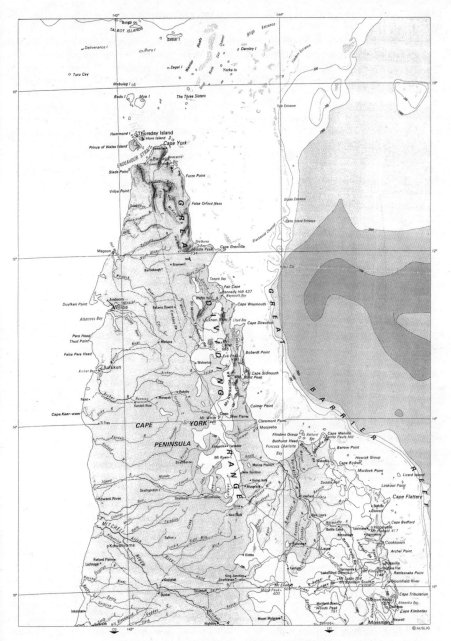

Map of Far North Queensland including the Torres Strait

MORETON BAY AND ITS BEGININGS

The large river that runs into Moreton Bay on that which is now the present day Queensland coast had long hidden itself from the open sea behind Stradbroke and Moreton islands. The explorer and cartographer, Matthew Flinders, had already guessed that there might be a river in the area from the amount of brown silt to be seen in the ocean. Then one day in 1823, three ticket-of-leave convicts from Sydney named Pamphlett, Parsons and Finnegan, were cast away on Moreton Island and the mystery of the missing river was solved.

When rescued six months later, Thomas Pamphlett claimed that they were on their way from Sydney southward to the Wollongong area, when a storm drove them out to sea. After many weeks, they were able to reach Moreton Island where local aborigines adopted them and they survived until they were accidently rescued.

John Oxley, who was on a mission to explore the area, found two of the men still being looked after by the natives, while the third was attempting to walk to Sydney. Oxley promptly used Thomas Pamphlett to guide him up the river for some fifty miles and was impressed by the timber and land capabilities he found there. The Oxley party found that the river was large enough to support a new settlement and plans were later made for shipment of twenty convicts to Moreton Bay, with instructions to create a new colony.

Edenglassie

Attempts were soon got underway to create settlements at Redcliffe and later at Cleveland but water supply and shipping facilities were unsolvable problems in those areas. So the new settlement was built along the Brisbane River about 10 or so mile inland, the little colony was at first named Edenglassie but was later changed to Brisbane, in honour of the Governor of the time.

At first the colony consisted of about twenty male convicts and a few officers commanded by Henry Miller from 1824. He was later replaced by Patrick Logan, who was replaced by Foster Fyans and after him Lieutenant Gorman took over in 1838. This commandant was later relieved of duty and replaced by Lieutenant Simpson who commanded the penal colony from 1841 until about 1845 or thereafter, when it partially ceased operation in that capacity.

Although Brisbane was declared a township in 1834, freed men or ticket-of-leave convicts were not allowed to settle within fifty river miles of the newly formed town. This law proved to be almost unmanageable and convicts were soon settling closer to Brisbane. They did keep to a modest distance so that the officials would not begin enforcing the law but their shacks were usually well within the fifty-mile ban.

By 1840, the little colony had built solid barracks for both convicts and military. It also had a small hospital and a woman's factory. The officials were situated in their own encampments, which had originally been military tents but later became stone or timber built permanent homes. These were erected by a slow but steadily growing number of convicts. Official buildings were made from locally quarried stone dug out of the surrounding hillsides and a few of the old buildings still stand as witness to the hard work of long-suffering felons.

Early settlers to Queensland [still known as New South Wales until 1859] did not use Brisbane as a 'jumping off point' when going to the western or northwestern inland areas. They traveled overland from Sydney, across the Great Dividing Range and out onto grassy plains, before turning north toward the Darling Downs and onward. The miles traveled by bullock dray while driving their herds of sheep ahead of them were long and tiresome but the reward of having their own land on which to work, was an irresistible urge that kept new settlers arriving.

The convict settlement at Brisbane was officially closed at the end of 1842 and disbanding began, albeit slowly, from the beginning of 1843. Settlers going to Moreton Bay were almost non-existent until the first migrant ships arrived in 1845.

Settler farmers were interested only in using Brisbane as a base before heading off inland almost as soon as they were ashore. Some farmers did purchase land along the river so that they could build storage sheds for incoming and outgoing goods.

The European population at Brisbane and Moreton Bay numbered only several hundred by the time the penal colony was shut down. It was not until the settlers arrived, that these numbers were swollen somewhat and a slow progression onward to the modern world was begun.

Convict ships as such, did not travel direct to Brisbane from England and it was probably a shortage of labour that caused the first and only 'direct from England' convict ships, to arrive at Moreton Bay in 1849 and 1850. Although the penal settlement had officially closed, the officials were still in place and were quite able to arrange for the last of these convicts to be allotted their schedules. The two ships that transported them were the 'Mt Stewart Elphingstone' in 1849 and the 'Bangalore' in 1850. By the time Brisbane became part of the new state of Queensland in 1859, the new convicts had either completed their sentences or been shipped to other areas.

Brisbane was a much more sedate and quiet village when William Thompson arrived with 12 year old Barbara Crawford. In March 1843, it contained only a very few buildings and most of these were official government premises. Hotels did not exist as we know them today and living quarters were pre-arranged before a woman could be brought to the colony. If new arrivals owned their own boat, they could take up a mooring on the river but they could not remain in the area unless they applied to the Colonial Secretary stating their reasons. Even released convict women living in Sydney, who had husbands serving time in Brisbane, could not easily gain permits to enter the Moreton Bay penal colony.

Prior to 1843, the settlement was strictly penal and living quarters were few. This difficulty with housing continued until the end of 1844 and even long after that time. The few women applying to live in Brisbane before 1843 were usually rejected and settlers were warned of the privations that would be suffered in the region. Convict women on release in Brisbane, took husbands from among the ticket of leave or pardoned convict males. This practice began after the women's factory had started its operations.

Many wives of convicts transported to Australia, developed a cunning practice whilst feeling the need to be with their menfolk. The hapless ladies would commit a petty crime which would earn them a sentence and transportation to Australia. Some of these ladies waited up to six or seven years from the time their husbands were taken from them, before they arranged their own transportation. They simply waited until their children were old enough to fend for themselves, before taking the plunge. The women began by committing a petty crime and on being sentenced, stated that their menfolk were in Sydney, Hobart, Melbourne or Brisbane and begged that they might be able to join their husbands.

Others could not wait until their children were grown and as soon as the husband was shipped out, the wife committed a minor crime and when given her sentence, she applied to take her children. This in some cases meant that four, five or even six other souls were transported for the one petty crime. Once in Australia, the women could ask to be put near their husbands and as the idea was to populate the territories, these requests were usually granted. Where originally the husband alone was sentenced, the whole family would then become Australians. Many people living in Australia today would be surprised to find that at least one of their grandparents was transported to Australia aboard a convict ship, without ever having committed a crime.

Women of Brisbane

Trustee convicts living outside the penal settlement of Brisbane, were able to apply for permission to have their wives join them from Sydney or have freed convict women come live with them. Once the men had proven their reliability, this arrangement was deemed acceptable for Limestone but Brisbane was strictly penal and as housing was limited, a couple could only be brought together when the circumstances were right.

From its beginning until it was opened to the public, the only women living in Brisbane, were officers wives, convict maids, servants or female second offence convicts at the women's factory. Once they had built their homes, freed convict farmers and trustee convicts could apply to have wives join them or even marry a convict woman who had earned release or served her time. In general, wives were not permitted to join their husbands at a second offender's colony, unless the convict had served out his time.

The Whip

During the final years of the Brisbane penal colony, Lieutenant Gorman controlled the prisoners and officers under him with an iron fist. His treatment of those who were not 'on side' was particularly harsh. At one stage, his official scourger [whip man] had to be taken out of his living quarters in the barracks in fear of his life. Gorman always had this man lay on the cat with gusto and this made them both very unpopular in the colony. The whipman was removed to a small shack in the government garden [Botanical gardens] where he lived a much less stressful life. Lieutenant Gorman knew how to run a convict settlement and although it is obvious that he did several things that were unbecoming, he did keep the settlement safe from attack.

It was not until the death of the Surveyor Stapylton, that Lieutenant Gorman's reign became threatened. A new surveyor, Robert Dixon, was sent to replace Stapylton and this man proved to be a man of principle. Dixon discovered that Gorman was corrupt and fronted him on the subject, only to be accused of causing trouble in the colony. Gorman went so far as to accuse Dixon of having government materials in his possession which he was not supposed to have. This was tantamount to an accusation of theft.

The commandant even used some of his men to witness against Dixon but soon found that the surveyor also had friends, men who had grown to hate Gorman during the period he ruled the settlement. Finally, about 1841, Lieutenant Gorman was relieved of his duty and Lieutenant Simpson took over command.

Much of the delay, in transferring the settlement into the care of civil officials, was due to Gorman and his tactics while he ruled the area. Gorman had been like a god to the police constables. Most of them had been given remissions of sentence, tickets of leave or conditional pardons. Payment for this was their loyalty and protection for Gorman and his family.

Land for Sale

Many applications were sent to the Colonial Secretary, begging permission to use the Brisbane River for the shipment of wool and supplies. The officials though, wanted the area cleared of convicts before this could be effected, so that a regular township could be formed.

So it was that Government land sales in the Brisbane area did not begin until early 1843. Sales were very slow and it was mostly the officials, freed convicts or the smart inland farmers who were applying for blocks of town land. Even Captain Wickham bought land in numerous areas around the settlement, yet many blocks did not sell at all during the first offers.

By 1844, everything in Brisbane was moving at a snail's pace but with the announcement that migrants would arrive at the end of that year; the little town began to function. Shops, hotels and other business enterprises were created from convict buildings such as the women's factory, which was sold in 1843, for use as a hotel.

Although the convict settlement was partially dismantled, it was still necessary to state a purpose for being there. Letters to the Colonial Secretary for this era, number in the thousands. Most were requests begging permission to buy this property or to obtain that building along the riverfront for warehousing or shipping depots.

While all this was going on, convicts with long prison terms still to serve, were slowly being sent back to Hyde Park Barracks in Sydney. Others were given their tickets of leave or pardons while the rest had to bide while their time was served out. This brings forth the question, why were two convict ships sent to Brisbane in 1849/50? The answer probably rests with the need for tradesmen, shepherds and farm hands at that time. It is likely that most of these men were petty criminals who were virtual trustee's from the moment they arrived, Brisbane though, was still able to cater for a few convicts, as much of the penal colony was still in place when these vessels arrived.

From Penal colony to Township

A few freed convicts were able to purchase land in the new settlements at Brisbane and Ipswich. Many convicts on release had already taken up residence at Ipswich and on the south side of the river at Brisbane. Other convicts like Auctioneer and Real Estate agent Thomas Dowse, found it easy to make the jump from convict to businessman and landholder within a few short months of the closure of the penal colony.

Dowse was only 14 years old, when he was transported to Australia aboard the ship 'Florentia'. He was placed under the control of the Harbour Master at Moreton Bay after being sent to that colony for a small second crime [probably attempted escape] which he committed in Sydney. Dowse made up for his youthful problems and worked hard, he quickly learned to write with a professional hand and upon closure of the penal colony, also came to realise the value of land.

At age 28, Dowse requested a conditional pardon from the Colonial Secretary, stating that he had married a young lady who was native to the colony and they now had two children. His mother had also arrived from England to live with him since the colony had been closed. As Dowse now had a great deal of responsibility to his women, his newspaper and real estate business, his request for a pardon was rewarded.

There was only one hotel in Brisbane in 1842 but an application had been submitted the following year, to allow for a second hotel. The applicant was a man named David Bows, he became well known to everyone in the new free township once his establishment opened.

Bows made his application to the Colonial Secretary with the now empty women's factory in mind, as a site for use as an inn. After his application was accepted, he named the establishment the Victoria Hotel and it opened for business in 1844.

As can be seen on the map of Brisbane for 1842, there was little housing on the north side of the river, with the convict quarters and hospital dominating. There was only one or two small residences being used by the prison officials within the town center, most were housed further out, away from the convict area. Other homes had been built for the military officials who ran the convict settlement, many of whom held small farmlets on the outskirts of town.

The south side of the river was already being set as the working class side of town. Even before settlers arrived, this was where the more industrial type of enterprise, the dry docks and timber yards, were established.

This then, was Brisbane of the 1840's, to where Thompson brought his prize and lived quietly for 18 months, in a strongly regimented society of second offender convicts and harshly strict officials.

Culture Shocks

To give readers some idea of the conditions faced by the new settlers, convicts and aborigines alike, it is necessary to list a few of the goings-on between the two cultures, especially during the period with which we are dealing.

Aborigine tribes inhabiting the coastal areas of New South Wales and what is now Queensland, had many contacts with seamen from Europe and the Orient, well before Cook arrived on the scene. After Moreton Bay began its 20 years as a convict settlement, contacts between the two cultures along the northeast seaboard became much more frequent.

Beforehand, tribal groups took in shipwrecked sailors and castaways whom the natives believed were returning relatives coming back from the dead. Only when a survivor could not be 'recognised' did the natives attack, kill or completely ignore castaways or convict runaways. This phenomena, occurred almost everywhere around the Australian coast.

Sea voyagers from China, Indonesia, Portugal, Spain, Holland and England ran foul of reefs and heavy seas, to be cast up on wild shores where they had to adapt to tribal life or die. Some were killed and eaten because they bore no resemblance to a dead relative, while others made simple mistakes that would cost them their lives.

If and when adopted, the strangers became part of the native way of life and after the first settlers arrived, many remarked on the occasional yellow skin [mixed race] natives seen here and there in the bush. Death for a white usually resulted from a tribe not 'recognising' the castaway, perhaps believing that he or she belonged to an enemy tribe.

Castaways sometimes lived out their lives with native tribes without hope of rescue. This must have been a terrible culture shock for shipwrecked European men and women, especially when they realised that they would be leading the life of a tribal native forever. Thankfully for many whites, the natives for the most part, found some pride in having a spirit [ghost relative] living among them and on frequent occasions, many of these people were saved. The natives often bragged to other tribes and sub-groups about their good fortune in having such a prize and after settlement, this sometimes this led to the castaway being found.

Years later, when the aboriginals came to understand that the whites were just another tribal group trying to dislodge them from their hunting grounds, trouble began. Records of atrocities occurring on both sides are rife. Many natives were killed just to make some matron feel safe in her farmhouse, while others did not like naked 'savages' wandering around what had become white man's property.

The natives, in turn, wanted the material possessions owned by the whites. Shepherds were the first to suffer at the hands of envious warriors. They administered death by spearing or clubbing to any spirit who did not share their possessions or the sheep they herded. Soon white women and children became the victims of native attacks. When tribal groups began turning up at farms requesting flour and biscuits, supplies were not always forthcoming and so the killings began. Attacks on whites increased drastically in the 1830's. Over 120 farmers, shepherds and townspeople were speared or clubbed to death in greater New South Wales during that period. In turn tribes were attacked by vengeful whites that cared not if those they attacked were mostly women and children.

It should be understood that the Australian natives lived in a feudal society and when whites suddenly appeared as a competing nation, inter-tribal fighting was extended to them. This was just as it had been for all neighbouring tribes. The sad case for the aboriginals was that they lived and fought only as small tribal groups. For them, their own tribal areas were all important, they could not match the armies of white men, who exacted vicious retribution upon them. A sample of the sufferings endured both by settlers and the local native inhabitants in Queensland's colonial history are briefly recorded here.

Most often killed on the white side, were shepherds and farmers but white women and children also suffered attack. On occasions, women were left alone at home while the men traveled great distances to their work. Unlike their black female cousins, white women were rarely raped in the early days; they were usually clubbed to death alongside their children. Rape appears to have not been on the agenda for the first generation of aborigines to meet up with whites. This ended once white men began having their way with native women. Even during the twentieth century, young native girls were rarely seen at native functions being attended by white men.

The natives could not fight against the guns of the whites men without sustaining losses that had no comparison to even the most terrible spear fight. Apart from one or two pitched battles, the aborigines usually waited until the odds were a little better. They contented themselves with spearing shepherds in their huts or farmers travelling through a tribal area. This created hatred among white farmers and it was not long before the well organised among them began to arrange 'Snipe' or 'Dingo' hunts in areas in which the natives had proved troublesome. These genocidal activities have proven embarrassing to quite a few notable people in our modern day society.

Britain issued orders from the earliest days that natives were to be shown the same treatment as whites when it came to what it called criminal acts. The English had acted with some arrogance in placing the natives under their laws. The aboriginals had their own laws and had no idea what the whites were trying to say when a native was suddenly arrested and placed in chains for killing a white. The law was supposed to be equal for all but this of course did not work, the killing of shepherds and farmers was so widespread and the native killers so hard to find. It was only a matter of time before groups of white farmers began exact payment.

At Hornet Bank Station in western Queensland, eleven women and children were hacked and clubbed to death while the men were away. Refusal of flour was the reason given for the killings. A boy of just twelve years survived to tell of the attack and this sparked a terrible massacre of natives in the area.

Over two hundred men women and children were hunted down and killed. The whites went on a rampage, killing many that were not and could not have been at the station at the time of the murders. Such was the anger at the killings, that it has been said that the only survivor was offered open season on any native he saw during the rest of his life.

Natives living near Kilcoy in Southeast Queensland were given flour laced with Arsenic; this killed some 70 women, little children and the elderly of that small sub group of the Kabi tribe. The poisoning was allegedly ordered by a prominent landowner. He is accused of having two of his shepherd's carry out this horrific criminal act. The landowners family, are still deeply affected by this accusation, for many years they have vigorously denied that their forebear was involved, placing blame solely on the shepherds.

Considering the difficulty and financial ability two shepherds [possibly convicts] would have had in buying or obtaining the deadly poison, it is more likely, that the Arsenic was given to them by their master. After lacing the flour with the poison, they distributed it among the natives and the rest is history.

Runaway retribution

Escaped convicts living with the Kabi, including David Bracewell, James Davis and Samuel Derrington, were said to be among the Kabi natives who later captured the two shepherds. Suffice to say that the revenge taken upon these men was fierce but whoever supplied them with the Arsenic probably never received his just reward.

A white girl [four years old] was shown no mercy when taken from her home at Limestone by two rogue natives. Two native women witnessed her death at the hands of the aboriginal men who decided that they hated all white interlopers. The native women were just as shocked as any human would be by this senseless killing and they quickly reported the matter which resulted in the capture of the two men. This seems to be the case with all races; even our so-called 'civilised society' has this type of murderous animalistic human among us.

White farmers found they could not get aborigines to work the land, failing to understand that the natives were hunters and gatherers. Aboriginals had no interest in agriculture; they could not be coerced into working sheep or cattle for the farmers. This created the impression that the natives were useless and lazy but they had survived for thousands of years in a climate that went from one extreme to the other. They lived the land as the land required and they survived even the harshest times. Sheep and cattle belonging to the whites soon had the natives hunting the much easier-to-kill animals. The white farmers quickly became incensed; they wanted the natives to stick to kangaroo meat and their natural diet.

Aborigines have lived among the kangaroo and emu for many thousands of years; they have learned to hunt and gather in the same way that other mammals survive in Australia. The men hunted in hot areas in the cool of mornings and/or evenings. The women and children handled the gathering of small animals, vegetable matter and insects. Australian natives knew no other lifestyle; they could not be expected to change overnight. The work world of the Australian native never took him 'out in the noonday sun', after all, 'only mad dogs and Englishmen' have that renown.

The natives to the far north in Australia were little different from their southern brothers. They also treated whites in the same manner, initially thinking they were spirits and then later, treating them as human interlopers. The Torres Strait natives kept several whites as spirit relatives but in general, those who became shipwrecked in the Strait, usually became trophies for the headhunters.

The loss of native lands to European encroachment in Australia and its surrounding islands, is a sequence of events no different to any other in the history of mankind. The Norman Conquest of England, the Spanish take-over of South America, the European strangulation of the North American Indian tribes and many other conquests too numerous to mention, are all part of human history. The true Englishman is still bound to his village while the aristocracy owns the greater proportion of his land.

The destruction of the North and South American tribal cultures, with the loss of numerous lives and even whole tribal groups, ended with many native peoples deprived of their rightful lands. Almost every tribal group on earth, white, black or brindle has at one time or another lost their homeland to a more powerful people.

Sadly, many wonderful cultures have been integrated into others, disappearing forever as they were dispossessed, so too were the rightful owners of Terra Australis dispossessed. In the like manner of all other lands of conquest, Australia cannot and will never, return to the days of yore, it is time that all who live around her shores become one with their country.

Cannibalism

True cannibalism and headhunting among the natives of Australia did exist and it appears to have been practiced fully mainly along the northern coast. This has been vigorously denied by some but there are just too many qualified reports, proving its existence during and prior to colonisation.

Inland, many tribesmen contented themselves with the kidney fat or liver of a vanquished foe. In the far northern areas of Australia, cannibalism of the same standard as in New Guinea was in vogue when the first white men arrived on these shores.

Chinese seamen and miners did not like contact with the northern mainland aboriginals or the Torres Strait islanders. The Chinese were quickly killed and in many cases in northern Australia, hung up in trees by their pigtails [plaited hair] to cure. The natives, when asked why they did this, commented that the Chinese were much better eating than whites [probably due to the Chinese vegetable diet] and therefore, were hung out to cure. It must also be acknowledged here, that cannibalism was never restricted to blacks throughout the history of man, this practice has applied to almost all races.

During the colonial period, several vessels sailing in the far north lost their entire complement of passengers and crew to headhunters and this created a massive fear of Torres Strait and New Guinea natives. When Barbara Crawford was discovered living among the savage islands, she was considered not only wonderful intelligence for the area but all were amazed at her survival.

WHALERS AND THE BRISBANE TOWN NEWS

Brisbane, 1844.

It is now vitally important that we discover the name of the wrecked whaling ship, the cargo of which William Thompson had planned to salvage. Thompson was informed of the wreck of a whaler by some of its crew. Five of them managed to make it back to Brisbane from Chesterfield and Bampton Reefs.

These reefs and small islets are located about 800 klms east of Bowen, perhaps 1000 klms to the northeast of Brisbane, the whaler, according to the informant, was upright and still had its cargo intact. Barbara Crawford Thompson later stated that it was at this time that Thompson purchased the cutter and began to make ready. She also said that an old man from the whaler was the one who would guide them to the wreck site.

Thompson immediately set about organising a crew of four other men. Could it be that the other four were from the whaler? Barbara had to accompany them on the operation because there way no way she could be left behind. The name of the whaling ship which Thompson and his party would attempt to salvage has eluded those who have previously researched this story. Now, for the first time in 160 years, the name of the vessel can accurately be shown.

Whalers Two

During the latter months of 1844, South Pacific coral reefs received two whaling ships into their craggy clutches. The first, a vessel named 'Clarence', was an Australian built wooden brig of 255 tons under the command of Captain McCardell. Her crew, were probably all convicts or ex-convicts, released on ticket-of-leave or time served.

The 'Clarence' was wrecked presumably on Bampton reef about 800 klms east of Bowen in North Queensland on the 10th of June 1844. The second whaler was an American ship, the 'Thale', commanded by an American named Captain Coffin. This vessel was of about 500 tons and it became wrecked on Minerva reef near Tonga during August 1844. Although the wrecks were many sea miles apart, they were basically in the same region. The wrecks though, happened almost two months apart, the 'Clarence' on June 10,1844 and the 'Thale' in late August 1844.

Strangely, both vessels had surviving sailors rowing safely into Brisbane in their whaleboats. The Australian brig 'Clarence' [the first to be wrecked] had five survivors arrive in Brisbane on July 7, 1844. The crew from the 'Thale' arrived mid to late September.

Newspaper reports by Thomas Dowse in his newspaper, the Brisbane Town News, were posted on the arrival of both whaler crews in Brisbane.

Report per the Brisbane Town News, July 1844, on the wreck of the 'Clarence', from the journal of crewman Richard Rule:

'June 10, 1844, the 'Clarence' was running alongside Brampton [Bampton?] shoal when 'upon coming to the end of it, the vessel struck a reef of rocks. She was well hung up and so it seemed, there was nothing that could be done to extricate her'.

Lady luck though, can do strange things and amazingly, at high tide, the ship refloated herself giving her crew quite a surprise. Unfortunately, the sailors were unable to stop her from going ashore again. This time she was well stuck and the captain ordered the men to cut down the masts in an effort to keep the vessel stable. That way, any later efforts to salvage the oil cargo might well be met with success.

Five of her crew sailed one of the whaleboats to and down the coast to Brisbane, where they arrived on July 7, 1844. This voyage had taken twenty-six days. The men aboard the whaleboat were Richard Rule, John Owens, Samson Sensui, Thomas White and William Clarence.

Nothing is reported regarding the captain and the rest of the crew, they probably sailed for Batavia in one of the other boats. Richard Rule commanded the whaleboat that eventually made it into Moreton Bay. On arrival, Rule submitted his journal regarding the wreck and subsequent voyage in the whaleboat.

A letter was sent to the Colonial Secretary from Brisbane by the Police Magistrates office requesting support for the men of the 'Clarence' as they had no stores or supplies and no means to sustain themselves.

The shipwrecked men were generously given a four-day supply of food, to 'tide' them over, while they awaited transport out of the area.

When the American whaler 'Thale' was wrecked some weeks later, it was much further away, nearer to Tonga. Publisher Thomas Dowse wrote in the October issue of the Brisbane Town News that 'Captain Coffin of the 'Thale' was given a celebration at Bows Victoria Hotel' prior to he and his men going to Sydney on October 14th 1844.

The brig 'Clarence' was an Australian built whaling ship

The old seaman

During the period July through to the 17th of September when Thompson and his group left Brisbane, he [Thompson] had made contact with at least some of the survivors of the 'Clarence'. Thompson was obviously convinced by one of the crew, that a salvage party could retrieve the whale oil from the wreck before anyone from Sydney could get at it.

The identity of this man is anybody's guess although it is very likely that Barbara did give his name to her eventual rescuers. As there were really only four men to choose from, [Richard Rule can probably be disregarded, as he was probably required in Sydney to report on the matter] it really does not matter who the old man was. Barbara only gave evidence to the fact that he was an 'old seaman' and did not mention if there was more than one of the whaler's crew in the salvage party.

At this point, it should be clear that it is highly improbable that any other whaling ship, apart from the 'Clarence', could be the vessel that Thompson and his crew were attempting to salvage. Both wrecked whalers are mentioned here, simply because they were wrecked within weeks of each other, with a whaleboat from each vessel, rowing into Brisbane and safety.

It is also interesting to note that any reference in official files, to William Henry Shetland Thompson or John Durkin, stop before this point. After July 1842, nothing more is recorded in the hundreds of letters still being sent to the Colonial Secretary. No requests, no official data regarding the cutter or its voyages are reported and certainly, nothing is reported on Thompson's salvage party, everything goes deathly quiet.

The Americans

The 'Thale' wreck was a different kettle of fish; it was sunk well outside Thompson's planned search area and was not recorded as having its cargo intact. The cutter 'America' departed Brisbane on the 17th, of September 1844, about the same time as the Americans were rowing into Brisbane and it is doubtful if Thompson ever made contact with or even met them.

Captain Coffin and his remaining crew, left Brisbane for Sydney in October 1844, this was almost a month after Thompson had left the settlement in search of the 'Clarence'. Dowse stated that the American captain was pleased with his treatment in Brisbane and that he [Captain Coffin] would inform his whaling friends of Brisbane's great hospitality. He wished the little colony all the best and that is last to be heard of the captain and crew of the 'Thale'.

Contact

At some time during the ten weeks, July 7, 1844 to September 17, 1844, a crewman from the 'Clarence' contacted Thompson and they quietly began making plans for a salvage operation on the wreck. Thompson perhaps convinced his friend John Durkin, to either sell his cutter to Thompson or at least become a partner, so they could use the vessel to transport them to the wreck site.

Where Thompson got the four men that accompanied him can only be conjecture. Perhaps four of the whaler's crew went with him but this would have spelt danger for Thompson, he would never leave himself one out against four that were already shipmates. One convict Thompson definitely contacted, was James Davis, a convict who escaped the Brisbane settlement to live with the Kabi Kabi tribe of aboriginals near present day Maryborough. Davis survived among them for about 14 years, returning to Brisbane in 1842. James Davis was undoubtedly the best man at Moreton Bay in regard to native intelligence. He knew the country to the north almost as far [700 klms] as the present day city of Rockhampton.

Davis was fluent in the language of the widespread Kabi people and he had at least one young mixed race son living with them. He also knew how to make sign with native tribes that could not speak any dialects that he knew.

His return to civilisation from among the aboriginals, came just after William Henry Shetland Thompson retired from his police work in 1841 or early 1842 and it is sure that he would have had many discussions with a convict he had been unable to capture. Although James Davis did not accompany the group [he was still serving out his sentence] to the wreck site, his knowledge of the Kabi way of life was passed on to Thompson. This was in case the wreck of the whaler was within the range of the Kabi people or if Thompson at some time found it necessary to be on Kabi tribal land.

Once an agreement was made between Thompson and the crewman or men from the 'Clarence', a crew was found for the cutter. How many men actually made up this crew, cannot be proven but there are two separate reports regarding their numbers. Barbara tells us that only five men including her 'husband' were aboard the vessel [Barbara to Oswald Brierly, 1849]. The other report came from Thomas Dowse of the Brisbane Town News, November 1845. He states that 'about six or eight men went north with William Thompson'. These he may have believed, were Thompson, Durkin and one other ex-convict, with perhaps the five sailors from the 'Clarence'.

Of the two differing reports regarding crew numbers, Barbara Crawford's statements should be regarded as the more reliable. She spent two months at sea with the men, until they had all perished in one way or another, surely she would have remembered who sailed with her.

While the cutter 'America' was being made ready for its voyage to the 'Clarence', Thompson made plans but just what was on his mind is not known. It may be that his plans were to head for Port Essington and from that place, go to China and eventually on to America.

The Port Essington Expedition

Barbara Crawford related after her rescue, how Thompson, when asked to join Leichhardt on the explorers expedition overland to Port Essington, jokingly told Leichhardt, that he was 'going to Port Essington by sea and would let the people at that port know of Leichhardt's coming'.

Thompson may well have had it in mind to sell any oil they salvaged at Port Essington. One thing is sure; Thompson would not have wanted his plans for the salvage operation to be leaked out. The whale oil was his opening to money, freedom and perhaps a new life in America.

Before leaving Brisbane, Thompson had purchased what stores they could afford. Water casks were filled and other requirements purchased or purloined from one source or another and the group made ready to sail. The salvage party, had only limited funds for an expedition to the wreck and the seaman [or men] from the 'Clarence' were not financial at all. Fishing line and other materials to assisting procuring food from both land and sea must have also been placed aboard.

Supplies were needed if the group were to remain at sea for any length of time. Thompson did know about food supplies that had been left on Booby Island in the Torres Strait for shipwrecked sailors and there may also have been some stores still aboard the wrecked whaler.

From 1835, vessels had begun using Booby island as a sort of post office. Ships would call in and leave mail in a cave near the landing site, this was where the cache of supplies were secreted and periodically upgraded.

Other than finding stores on the whaler or on Booby Island, the men would have to hunt and fish if they found themselves running low on their own supplies. Thompson and Durkin both knew bushcraft and should easily have been able to find enough food to survive.

The First Australian Regatta

An aside is found in an interesting report, from the December 1844 issue of the Brisbane Town News. The report states that the two whaleboats from the 'Clarence' and the 'Thale' were used as entertainment at a Brisbane River regatta about Christmas time, 1844. The 'Clarence' was a colonial built brigantine whereas the 'Thale' was an American built ship. The whaleboat races spoke for the difference between the two vessels. The regatta was easily won by the American whaleboat, even when they changed crews to race the six miles back to the starting point. The whaleboats provided much enjoyment during the regatta but they would have been much more appreciated many miles to the north where Thompson and his group were in troubled waters.

The odd voyage of the schooner 'Elizabeth'

Shortly before Thompson and his crew headed north, Richard Rule presumably sailed off to Sydney, where he reported to the owners of the 'Clarence'. He told them 'that the vessel was wrecked but that the cargo was still salvageable'. This prompted the owners to send the schooner 'Elizabeth' from Sydney to the area almost immediately. Three times the 'Elizabeth' made the attempt but she was beaten back by bad weather twice [August 1844 and November 1844]. She was finally able to reach the vicinity of the wreck site in March 1845.

Stangely, it was then that the 'Elizabeth', also struck trouble. Captain Riley took his longboat in one direction while the mate and the rest of the crew went on searching with the schooner. The search took place after the two parties had arranged to meet again, at an agreed time and place. The 'Elizabeth' never arrived and Captain Riley could only assume that the vessel was lost. He and his five crewmen sailed in a longboat, first to Hervey Bay and then on to Brisbane. From there, they caught a steamer to Sydney. It seems very odd that the captain gave over his ship to the mate while he went with some of the crew in a whaleboat.

A question mark hangs suspiciously over this attempted salvage by the 'Elizabeth'. Did the crew on the schooner find what was left of the oil and then leave the others behind while making off to ports unknown, perhaps even to America?

The crew of the 'Elizabeth' were more than likely trustee convicts, they would have rejoiced at having the schooner free and clear without its captain. Truth seems to have been much stranger than fiction, especially where the wrecks of two whalers and two missing salvage vessels were concerned. Four vessels were now wrecked or missing and so far, crews from three of them had rowed into Brisbane, lamenting their losses, could history again repeat itself?

Arrival at the wreck site

After leaving Brisbane for the wreck of the 'Clarence' in September 1844, the cutter 'America' sailed quietly along without incident. On reaching the area in which the wreck was stranded about two or three weeks later, they began the search in earnest. Two more weeks went by and at about this time Thompson and the old man began to argue. Barbara states that the two men argued because the wreck could not be found. This may be so but it is hard to believe that the wreck could be missed in such a small area. Two weeks searching and not finding a fairly large ship that has run aground does not seem plausible.

Finally, after much ado about something, Thompson marooned the old man on a small island. It is possible the 'old man' from the 'Clarence', may have disagreed with the ultimate objectives of Thompson and the others or perhaps Thompson became disenchanted for one reason or another.

Whatever the case, there was now one less mouth to feed. It should also be noted that marooning a man far off the beaten track would have been tantamount to murder. This would have surely been the act of men who had little compassion and plenty of greed. A short time later two more men were drowned when the cutter's dinghy was swamped while loaded down, with firewood?

Barbara also related this event to her rescuers, telling how Thompson and two of the crew had gone off to fetch firewood. On their return, the dinghy, being somewhat low in the water, was swamped, throwing the three men into the water. Barbara went on to say [with some pride at Thompson's ability] how the two crewmen were left struggling, while Thompson, with deft strokes strongly swam back to the cutter. The two crewmen were left in the water and could only struggle and flop about until they finally drowned, apparently no attempt was made to save them

This part of Barbara Crawford's testimony does not read well, firewood in the tropics can only mean that they had food to cook. They were at sea and aboard a wooden boat, so why they required a large amount of firewood is open to conjecture. It is possible that they had made camp on one of the unwooded atolls. Why would they do this if nearby there was a wooded island on which they could make camp? It seems much more probable that they were loading casks of oil and these were what caused the dinghy to be swamped.

It is doubtful though possible, that the cutter carried a small wood stove but this does not explain why they would require a dinghy to be so heavily laden with firewood that it was swamped. There are some wooded islands in the search area but the weather at that time of year is hardly freezing even though the nights can be cool. This though, does not tell us why the group did not make camp where firewood was readily available.

It should now be noted, that wherever the cutter went from that time forth, the crew would have to swim ashore in places where the cutter could not dock. Without the dinghy to assist in loading and unloading, the whole operation would have become much harder. This is probably one of the main factors as to why they left the area and headed for the Torres Strait. There are a few contentious issues arrived at in this section of the drama, the first and foremost being, where exactly was the wreck site?

By rule of thumb

Richard Rule, in his journal written while ailing from the wreck to Brisbane, gave the site as being 18.47 Latitude x 150 Longitude. Most give the site as being Chesterfield and Bampton reefs, which are 800 klms east of Bowen, Queensland.

According to Barbara Crawford, the wreck site was not found before they left for Cape York. The problem for us then is, why in an area so far from the mainland, could the wreck not be found? According to Richard Rule, the vessel was upright and in a position ashore where salvage would indeed be possible. Wrecks such as this can sit ashore for years until they eventually rot away.

The Chesterfield group of coral islets, number only eleven and the entire ground area is only 100 hectares [250 acres] combined. Finding the wreck sitting up atop the reef with its masts missing, should have been no problem at all. In reality, it is far more likely that the cutter was overloaded with oil casks causing the dinghy to be swamped. When this happened, there was no way to go ashore except by docking or swimming and getting more casks would have been out of the question unless they built a raft. This may have been the main reason why Thompson decided to head for Booby Island, its stores and perhaps ship repair materials. Could it be that this was where the 'old man' was left behind [marooned] to perhaps guard the site?

The 'Fly'

Barbara Crawford stated that the little cutter 'America' then sailed on to Cape York where they anchored overnight. It seems probable that Thompson's intention was to secure stores he knew had been taken to Booby Island by Captain Blackwood of HMS 'Fly'. Booby Island was now less than a day away from where 'America' had anchored.

The 'Fly' had gone in company with the cutter 'Prince George', some time previously to the Torres Strait. The intention was to leave supplies for any that were shipwrecked in the area. Much was made of that event when HMS 'Fly' departed Brisbane. The dramatic wreck of the 'Charles Eaton' in the Strait had caused a sensation in the colonies and it was recommended that something be done regarding the lack of food on uninhabited Torres Strait islands.

A newspaper report

Convict Thomas Dowse, Auctioneer, Land agent and later Brisbane Town Clerk, was the publisher of a small colonial newspaper, the 'Brisbane Town News' at Moreton Bay. It is from his newspaper that we are able to glean a great deal of information regarding the whaling ships and their involvement in the Barbara Crawford Thompson story.

His reports on the American whaler 'Thale', are more or less comments on a dinner in honour of the Americans and their departure for Sydney aboard the steamer 'Sovereign'. Dowse does not give a time for the wreck of the 'Thale' and only records it as having struck on Minerva Reef near Tonga.

The 'Clarence', being the first shipwreck Dowse had reported on, was given much better coverage in his newspaper. William Thompson though, must have kept his salvage attempt on the 'Clarence' very quiet, because Thomas Dowse reported nothing of the departure of the cutter 'America' from Brisbane on September 17, 1844. He also knew nothing of a party having been formed to salvage the oil from the 'Clarence'.

His first reports [November 1845] on the 'America' and the salvage party, are mysterious because there was no way he could have received information on Thompson or his group. It is obvious that the cutter left Brisbane in secrecy for none but Thompson's close friends knew of the voyage. Thompson made no official application for salvage rights, nor in fact, did anyone else from Brisbane.

Thompson knew that time was short and that a salvage vessel from Sydney would soon be headed for the area. Thereafter, the cutter 'America' sailed from Brisbane on or about September 17th 1844 or about [Barbara to Brierly October 1849] two weeks after Leichhardt and his expedition left Brisbane for the Darling Downs on the 3rd of September 1844.

More than a year [14 months] went by before news broke that the cutter and all aboard her, with the exception of the girl, had been lost. This news report was released by the young Thomas Dowse and how he came by this information, is another part of the story that is open to conjecture.

Report per Brisbane Town News, November 13, 1845.

'A small decked boat, cutter rigged, left this place about three months since, with a party of six or eight men and one woman, wife of the owner of the craft, named Thomson. [Dowse's spelling] To proceed to the wreck of a vessel, reputed to be stranded in Hervey Bay by the people who, some months since came up in a boat from the Brampton Shoals. Where they had been left through their vessel, the 'Elizabeth', schooner [Captain Riley] having been blown off '. The above report is a jumbled mix of two occurrences. It relates the name of the schooner that left Sydney on or about 23, March 1845, in an effort to salvage the whale oil from the wreck. Dowse believed that 'Elizabeth' was the whaling vessel that Thompson and his party had gone after. Thomas Dowse at this point is confused, he does not know which vessel or about what people he is reporting. His confusion though, does not last very long, he is quickly brought back into line by his informant and his reporting gains an understanding of the situation. Dowse at first believes that the schooner 'Elizabeth' is the whaler which Thompson and his party had gone to salvage. Someone then obviously tells him that Thompson left Brisbane in September 1844, one year earlier.

Dowse soon corrects the error and reports that the ship carrying the cargo Thompson wanted to salvage had been wrecked in July 1844, sixteen months earlier. He knows that the schooner 'Elizabeth' had disappeared at sea three months before but somehow he confuses the event. Perhaps it was because the crew from the 'Elizabeth' were the most recent to row into Brisbane, that Thomas Dowse made his mistake.

This error is one that would not have been made if Dowse had known the story himself but his informant had told him that the cutter 'America' departed shortly after the survivors of a wreck had rowed into Brisbane. Dowse naturally thought of the schooner 'Elizabeth', this being the latest vessel from which survivors had arrived in Brisbane. This proves that Dowse had absolutely no idea of the departure of Thompson's salvage party in September 1844.

Now to the second report by Thomas Dowse dated November 14th 1845:

'The party in the cutter ['America'] it is reported, through information received by the blacks, landed on the coast to the northward. Whether near the wreck, I cannot ascertain, and were there attacked by savages and the whole party massacred, with the exception of the woman, who, it is said, is kept among the tribe. The party in the boat were not provided with arms and ammunition and 'well knew' the dangerous disposition of the blacks along the coast. Still, from their treacherous nature and the 'long period' the vessel has been away, I fear there is some foundation in the report.'

It can be noted here that Dowse now accepts that the cutter had been gone for quite some time but he again misquotes his informant by stating that 'the whole party were massacred by the natives, except for the woman'. It is also hard to understand how Dowse could know that 'the party were unarmed', unless his informant had personal knowledge, or was quoting from scripted information. Dowse in his third newspaper report states,   •

November 14, 1845; [the paper ran monthly with follow on reports]

'Northern blacks came to the settlement [Brisbane] and reported that William Thomson [Dowse's spelling] had drowned, the rest of the men, six or eight in number, had been killed by natives. The woman is still alive, is kept almost nude and is subject to disgusting treatment'. **End Report.**

It is hard to comprehend how this information was being supplied. How could the northern natives know Thompson's name? Why, or more precisely how could they state that he alone had drowned, while the rest of the crew had been massacred by the natives. How could they then describe the condition of the woman, a subject that would have left them [the aborigines] open to fierce retribution?

Natives so far north of Brisbane did not understand the white language well enough to give such a report. There was no such visit to Brisbane by natives from the Torres Strait this would have been an inconceivable event for the time. Dowse, it appears, was talking about blacks from the Hervey Bay region, which were known as the Kati Kabi. Aborigines from a community so remote from Brisbane as was the Torres Strait, could never have relayed such information by land or sea and we shall discuss this problem shortly.

Whoever Dowse's informant was, he could not have been getting his information from natives that lived in the Torres Strait. If someone in Brisbane were fabricating the reports, why would such a risk be taken, especially if the reporter were unsure of the reality?

From here, the Dowse reports grow intense. No matter how, or more importantly 'if ' the natives were able to relay these messages, the reports, are 98% correct. The position in which Barbara Crawford had been placed was as the reports stated. William Thompson's manner of dying had been correctly reported and last but certainly not least, he had been named.

Dowse now began appealing to everyone's imagination in an effort to stir up a public outcry and thereby gain enough funds for a search to be made for the missing woman. It is painfully obvious that

Dowse was being fed this information and that his informant kept correcting him on small but important errors. Wild natives did not and could not have supplied these reports, they could not have named Thompson, nor would they have reported that all the crew, except Thompson, were killed by natives or that Thompson alone had drowned. They most certainly would never have strutted into town and told Dowse that natives were holding the woman in a 'nude condition and were doing disgusting things to her'. If natives had seen or known of the wreck, they certainly would not have known the names of those aboard the craft.

William Thompson had taken great pains to ensure that very few people knew of his intentions regarding the salvage operation. Only the convict James Davis and perhaps one or two other convicts knew the truth regarding the salvage operation. Of the truth so far, we are certain, the cutter was lost on Horn Island and Barbara Crawford was cast away among headhunters. Thompson was reported as drowned in Dowse's paper in November 1845 and Barbara confirmed this report four years later. It is also certain that Thomas Dowse had a mole feeding him these reports, a mole that knew the relevant details in the dramatic events that were now revealing themselves. The only part of the report that does not agree with the facts, is the way in which the crew died. This section of the report may have been planted to make the story a little more dramatic.

When Barbara Crawford stated years later, that William Thompson had been invited to join the overland expedition to Port Essington headed by Ludwig Leichhardt, she gave a definite clue to Thompson's real identity. Leichhardt was adept at using locals who knew the inland areas around his departure points. On his fatal expedition in 1848, he applied for permission to take the well-known convict Thomas Hand with him when his expedition left Brisbane. He was duly given permission to take Hand and a few other convicts. It is known that Leichhardt, in 1844, had been interested in William Thompson in the same way and for the same purpose.

Numerous other explorers and would-be explorers were itching and clamoring for the chance to join Leichhard's expedition on its long walk from Brisbane to Port Essington. William Thompson though, refused the offer and this cost him dearly. A full remission of his Crown sentence being the probable reward. Unfortunately he had over-burdened himself with Barbara and could no longer send her back to her family for fear of retribution and perhaps another prison sentence. Thomas Dowse thenceforth began a literary crusade aimed at the governor. In November 1845, his reports become more fervent as each new article is printed. Why was he so concerned about Barbara's plight and who or what, was causing Dowse to write so strongly about the missing woman.

The drowning of William Thompson is a most annoying factor in his [Dowse's] reports. Why not death as was suggested happened to the crew, by savages, why drowning? Why were the reports almost identical to the statements made by Barbara Crawford some five years later? Whoever was passing on the information knew far too much to be a tribal native. The reports had to have come from someone very closely connected to Thompson and to Barbara Crawford. It is also feasible, though not likely, that someone was making up the reports, perhaps in an effort to gain a remission or a reward.

To add another twist to the mystery, we shall deviate back to the beginning of February 1845, when Dowse places two very interesting reports in his paper. Just four months after Thompson took the cutter north and only 8-10 weeks after his supposed drowning; Thomas Dowse gives the first of these reports.

February 11th, 1845;

'Four large casks of whale oil were found at Moreton Island near Brisbane. They had been opened and emptied, probably by local natives, there was only about ten gallons of oil left inside. The barrels are thought to have come from the American ship 'Thale' which was wrecked at Minerva reef about August 1844'.

This implied a very strange drift on ocean currents, one that had failed to deliver coconuts or other south sea produce to the Australian coastline over thousands of years. Oddly, the following day, Dowse wrote a seemingly unrelated [?] and insignificant report, for the small size of his paper;

'February 12th 1845, an outrigger canoe of the type used by natives of the Coral sea region, was found half buried in sand, on Moreton Island. The canoe was of 'South Sea islander workmanship'. It is thought that due to tides that, 'the canoe, like the oil barrels, had also made its way down the coast to find its rest on Moreton Island'. If one looks at Moreton island in the present day, it seems miraculous that the canoe or the oil casks were found at all. With hardly any population in that area, someone from the penal colony managed to be wandering about on this large island and after stumbling over a half-buried canoe then proceeded to find the empty oil casks. Whoever found the canoe and oil casks then rushed to tell Thomas Dowse about the amazing discovery, which even for those times, would have been a rather mundane subject.

Could it be that the cutter 'America' had to sail for Booby Island empty? Did they leave the old man behind intentionally, knowing that they would return with tools and stores? When the cutter was lost, did Thompson and his mate manage to sail a big native canoe back to the wreck of the whaler and retrieve four barrels of oil?

South sea islander outrigger canoe very much like the one Thompson may have used which was discovered half buried on Moreton Island

THE SEARCH FOR OIL

September 17, 1844

Barbara sat near the bow of the little cutter with her bare feet dangling over the side as it sailed quietly away from their mooring at Limestone. She quite liked the name 'America' that had been given the boat by her husband and although it was a little crowded with five men and herself, she did not fear the lack of privacy. She was very proud of her new home and spent a few evenings on deck at the Limestone mooring, watching the oil lantern light reflect on the river.

Sleeping aboard the tiny cutter was much more exciting than the stringy bark slab hut they shared at Limestone. The hut was in a good position not far from the river but Barbara did not like the spiders and other bugs that spent their lives crawling in and around the strands of bark that hung from the rafters. At least here on the boat, nothing crawled over her body during the night, only the mosquito's biting and the high pitched 'zzeeee-it', caused her any annoyance.

It was just after dark when the cutter slipped its mooring, silently and unhurriedly drifting away in the river flow. The little craft soon left behind the steep-sided gullies of Ipswich through which the river made its way down toward the sea. All too soon they were sailing smoothly out into its wider reaches and the hours passed quickly. Dawn had begun to lighten the eastern horizon as they neared the settlement at Brisbane and a cool early morning breeze drove them onward to the river mouth.

The cutter crossed the river bar without incident and just after sunup, Thompson waved to the little pilot boat, already out-and-about from Amity Point Pilot Station. The pilot knew the little cutter well; he saw nothing at all unusual in Durkin's boat heading off to sea.

Barbara awoke lying flat on her back on the bundle of bedding she and Thompson shared below deck. She rolled onto her side and struggled to her feet before quickly climbing up on deck. She could not believe that she had overslept, putting it down to the sea air and her own excitement.

By midday, they were slowly bobbing their way past the red cliffs, some 20 miles north of the Brisbane River mouth. Barbara lay on deck watching as small fish rushed away from the prow, driving first this way and then that. Perhaps they thought the cutter was some great leviathan, ready to swallow them up.

She was proud of her William and liked to watch him as he worked. He could do anything and the people who knew him, treated him like a hero. She was happy that he wanted her to be with him, he was strong and like her father knew so much. William Thompson was a tall man for the times, just one inch and a half under six feet. Barbara liked the way the men looked to him for guidance as they sailed off toward the tropic regions. Toward sundown on the first day out, the cutter passed some very oddly shaped volcanic hills that Captain Cook had named the 'Glass House' mountains. The range ran along the coast just a few miles inland and Barbara thought that the largest of the hills looked like a man hunched down in a sitting position, watching them as they sailed by in the cutter.

The sun, setting behind these hills was the most beautiful sight Barbara could remember. The eerily strange shape of the ancient volcanic cores gave them a mysterious and haunting look in that wild landscape and though Barbara was happy with William, she felt an immense and sudden loneliness well up from deep within her. Soon the evening was upon them and the men shortened sail for the night. Thompson [on the old seaman's recommendation] gave orders for the steersman to keep the cutter heading well to the northeast for the evening and then arranged for each of the crew to take a shift at the tiller.

The following morning, Barbara awoke to the sound of shouting and she felt the little boat surge forward. She knew the breeze had freshened and they were again under full sail and would soon be back within sight of the mainland. As they made their way along the coast, she spent her time watching the blue grey smoke that native campfires sent drifting into the air above the dusty greenish-blue canopy that hid them. Barbara adored the swish and seething sound of the salt water as it rushed past the timbers of the little boat. She loved to feel the kick the stern gave, as it first jolted one way and then, seemingly tore itself free of the water and threw itself back the other. She did not have time to relax for long though. She was always in demand, fetching water and helping to feed the men from the limited supplies they had obtained in Limestone.

The search begins

There were many excited smiles and jokes among the salvage party during the first week or so out from Brisbane. They had sailed along the coast until they reached the beginnings of the Great Barrier Reef at which point, the old man recommended that they head east by nor-east. It was to be almost another ten days before they reached the area where the whaler was said to have struck the reef. Now it was time to begin their search in earnest.

According to Barbara, as each day went by and nothing was seen of the wreck, the men began to argue, quietly at first but then with more anger as time and the rations, grew short. Tempers occasionally flared to breaking point. Finally after one very heated exchange, the old man from the whaler was left marooned on a small island. The operation was then ended either because of the loss of the dinghy or perhaps they were satisfied with what they had achieved before the dinghy was lost. Now the main concern was getting to where they could get stores safely. It was thereby decided that the little cutter would sail for the Torres Strait and Booby Island.

Amity Point pilot station, Moreton Bay. c1844

The beginning of the end

It is at this point; that we are left with a history that has been created from statements given by Barbara Crawford to her rescuers in 1849. The information she gave regarding this part of the voyage was simply that one man had been marooned and that a short time later, two others had drowned when an overloaded dinghy capsized. Another possible answer to this set of circumstances is that the old man may have been directing the salvage operation from the island on which the wreck had come to rest while Thompson attempted to ferry the oil out to the cutter. When the dinghy was swamped, Thompson perhaps decided to head for Booby Island to retrieve any work tools left there for shipwreck survivors. After the loss of the two crewmen, the cutter proceeded to Cape York perhaps leaving the old man to maintain the camp at Bampton Shoal. A few questions hang over Barbara's statements on the loss of the dinghy. How does one sink a wooden dinghy laden with firewood, most of which would float, so quickly that two men drown and worse, why when one of the three thrown into the water is an experienced swimmer, does he make no effort to save the others? Barbara, in her statements, did not relate this part of the story in depth. She appears to have told the story as if it had been a teaching. She does not say why the men did not try to save themselves or why they could not support themselves on the wood they were transporting.

When the surviving three arrived at Cape York, they decided to shelter in the lee of Horn Island and the cutter was safely anchored alongside Majii Reef. A storm came upon them during the night and by midday, the cutter had been wrecked and ruined, Thompson would have been in a quandary. He could no longer journey into the unknown, if it were possible for him to find a means of getting to the mainland, he was satisfied that he could escape south and return to Brisbane.

He could not do it with Barbara 'in tow'. This would have been an impossible situation, especially now that Charles Crawford was, out of gaol. Thompson had to return to the penal colony but he could not take Barbara with him. He knew that he had to find some sort of transport, if only to the mainland and then he also had to find a way to leave Barbara behind

Thompson knew all about native superstition in regard to returning 'spirits', he may have told Barbara about this as well and with this knowledge, was able to more easily deal with any natives they may have run into. Barbara would have believed she could not leave the wreck of the cutter without rescue, for she could not swim. She could only rely on Thompson to get her out of the now sticky situation. It was with her inability in mind, that Thompson told her that he would swim ashore and find food and if possible, a way to save them.

Planning the way

Thompson would have then made sure that she knew what to say to anyone that might rescue her if he did not return. She should stick to the story he gave her, no matter what happened. Thereafter, there was nothing else for Barbara to do but remain where she was and hope that Thompson would return safely to fetch her.

Thompson would have told Barbara that if he did not come back for her, it would be because he had drowned and if she were rescued she should tell whomsoever saved her, that this was the way of his passing. Although it seems outlandish, Thompson had decided that Barbara was now a liability and there was nothing to do but leave her behind. The two men knew that the natives had canoes and that with a little bargaining, they might be able to secure one. If not, they could steal one during the night and make their escape, if only to the mainland.

The loss of the men

What really happened, in regard to the death of all of the men in the salvage party, before and while the cutter was anchored off Horn Island at Cape York, is known only from Barbara's reports. Her explanation of the drowning of the two crewmen [at Bampton shoal] does not appear to be that of an eyewitness.

Her bland description of the accident is flat and only comes to life when speaking about Thompson's prowess. Although the incident is recorded through Oswald, she has no apparent hysteric or horror tone in her report relating the event. Her description is more a boast of how good Thompson was at swimming. Barbara stated that while he easily swam to safety, the two crewmen struggled in the water until they drowned.

When questioned about the wreck of the cutter, she does not describe Thompson's death or the death of the last surviving crewman at Horn Island at all and simply states that they drowned. It appears obvious that she did not see their fate. It is possible that Barbara is not being entirely truthful at this point, Oswald perhaps decided not to include her narrative regarding what really happened to William Thompson.

If Thompson did procure a canoe, he probably told her that it was unsafe and rather than risk her life, he may have told her that he would proceed to Brisbane and set a rescue in motion. He would then come back quickly for her, if he did not return, it was because he and the crewman had drowned in such an unsafe craft.

Believe it or not

The boating tragedies that were happening at this stage of the salvage attempt, show that Thompson and whoever remained with him were either terribly inefficient sailors or something truly strange was unfolding. The swamping of the dinghy through overloading should never have happened. It seems doubtful that it was loaded with timber and the drowning of the crew appears to be an accident that did not overly worry Thompson.

'America'

The days of the cutter 'America' ended when she was driven up onto the reef at Nurapai [Horn Island] in mid to late November of 1844. The small cutter had been anchored and probably seemed secure alongside a reef [Madji reef] situated a short distance off Horn island. During the afternoon, they watched natives fishing along the same reef at a distance of about half a mile [1.8 kms]. That first night a storm arrived and the next morning things did not bode well for the cutter.

The wind and sea were up and already it was impossible to get underway in an effort to clear away from the reef. About midday, the first telltale crunch and grind of timber on rock and coral signalled the end of the cutter. She was badly holed and taking water. Finally a large tidal surge lifted the boat clear up onto the reef and she went over on her beam end with her keel facing the seas.

The cutter was so small that it was luckily washed into position atop the reef, where the seas could no longer cause the vessel further damage. The three survivors were a little uncomfortable with the cutter tilted over but at least they could survive the waves. The seas continued to pound at the vessel but did little more than grind her timbers around on top of the reef, first this way and then that, as the waters rushed and seethed around them.

The 'America' held out against the squall for its duration but the seas continued strong for several days. Oil casks were rolling about in the hold and when the waters settled, Thompson and the crewman edged four of them out and onto the reef. Food was a growing concern and hunger was gnawing away at them. Exactly how long the seas continued to batter the survivors is not known precisely but Barbara stated that they were with the cutter for about two weeks after it was wrecked.

An error in judgement by Thompson had cost him the boat. It should never have been anchored alongside the reef, where it would be vulnerable to storm or heavy seas, especially nearing the monsoon season. In Thompson's defence though, the area is dotted with islands, islets and reefs and it is hard for anyone to imagine thunderous waves in the area.

It is interesting to note, given the savage reputation of the Torres Strait Islanders, that William Thompson stopped there at all and it can only be surmised, that they were more worried about sailing in among the islands at night. They only had to round Prince of Wales Island and it was virtually clear water [and a few reefs] to Booby Island.

The wreck of the cutter ended Thompson's dream of escaping to America. He no longer had a way to leave Australia or the remaining four years of the crown sentence that still hung over his head. It is debatable that the remaining four years of his sentence were enough to cause Thompson to have the need to leave Australia. Perhaps his decisions had been made, based entirely upon his relationship with Barbara and the possible consequences that would arise should he be found with her. Without the cutter, he certainly had a problem in regard to remaining with the girl.

Dying to tell

This now brings us to the odd death of William Thompson. Barbara tells us that Thompson and the seaman that accompanied him had drowned while trying to swim to a shore that was only a few yards distant. This point is proven by the fact that natives were able to call out to Barbara over the sound of the sea. She heard and recognised but did not understand the one word they called out to her, 'Toomah' 'Toomah'. She was able to make the word out above the sound of the waves, which therefore tells us that the distance to shore could have been no more than fifty or sixty metres.

If we are to believe that William Thompson drowned, we must also relate what Barbara has already told us about this man. She stated that Thompson was an excellent swimmer and an experienced bushman. He had swum flooded rivers and creeks whilst making his way overland throughout New South Wales and what is now Queensland, some of these rivers were two or three hundred metres across and were at times, swift running.

The possibility of his death occurring in the very short swim needed to make Nurapai Island seems very unlikely. He was not stupid enough to attempt to gain the shore if the swim was impossible. The cutter was in no danger and the seas were abating. Thompson would surely have waited until he and the crewman could get ashore safely before making the swim. Without knowing exactly where the cutter lay, it is easy to make statements but the distance between the reef and three surrounding islands should not have troubled a good swimmer.

It is not wholly believable that William Thompson drowned at Cape York, it is more likely that he deserted Barbara Crawford, leaving her to an unknown fate. With the aid of a stolen or traded outrigger canoe, Thompson then made his return to Brisbane. Now that the cutter 'America' had been wrecked, he knew that their plans must go from salvage to survival, even if it meant abandoning the girl.

The Canoe

The discovery of a South Sea Island canoe on Moreton Island points to the fact that there is much more to the story than meets the eye. The canoe arrived apparently without human aid, along with four oil casks, which had all been full. Aborigines were blamed for having emptied these casks, leaving only a few gallons behind.

According to the reports, the aboriginals obviously found a use for the oil but discarded the much more useful casks. The canoe then conveniently half buried itself until one of the Moreton Bay colonists suddenly stumbled over it and the casks. The aboriginal's certainly would have commandeered a south sea island canoe had they found it first. These events are more mysterious than they sound, why did natives not take possession of the canoe at the same time as they took the oil? The overall truth is that someone, other than natives or unbelievable currents, brought the whale oil casks to Brisbane, just as someone sailed the sea-going canoe.

Thompson [in the opinion of the Author] had sailed directly to the wreck of the whaler. While loading the oil casks, an accident had lost the dinghy and two crewmen. This now caused a problem Thompson had only managed to load a few oil casks and now the two men alone and without the dinghy could not manage to load more. The men then decided to proceed northwest toward the Torres Strait, there they could get food and perhaps tool supplies.

The seaman remaining with Thompson had to have sea-going experience and a working knowledge of the Great Barrier Reef and the Torres Strait. This was certainly needed to get them through the maze of reefs that faced them further west. Thompson alone would not have dared to tackle these dangerous waters, only ignorance would have allowed him to do so.

Sailing time is also of some importance to the voyage of the 'America'. She left Brisbane on or about the 17th of September 1844 and after a voyage of approximately four weeks, she reached the wreck site. Allowing a 10 days for finding the wreck and trans-shipping some of the oil, the date would have been about the 20th of October before they lost two of the crew. Allowing another three weeks for the voyage to the Torres Strait, 'America' would have arrived at Nurapai Island about the middle of November 1844. This absolutely co-incides with Barbara Crawford's version of the time of arrival, she remarked that it was late in November or about the first of December when the natives first made contact with her.

Parting

The natives fishing and turtling on Horn Island's Majii reef were at about half a mile distant when the squall hit Nurapai. They were also troubled by the wind and heavy seas and mid-morning, retired to the safety of the island away from the beach and the wind. Their women and children had accompanied them to the island, as custom would have it, for the natives used that place to grow their fruit and vegetables.

Thompson waited a few days until the seas had calmed a little and one night, he and his mate slipped into the water and headed for the shore. They were armed with knives and axes and their intention was to steal or barter for one of the native outriggers, preferably one of the larger ones with sails and fishing platform. Such a canoe could easily take them to Brisbane and would even carry a few oil casks to a safe place. Before leaving the wreck, the two men told Barbara, 'that they would go ashore in search of food and as she could not swim, she should wait until they returned'. If it so happened that she was rescued while they were gone, Thompson told her to tell any rescuer that he and his mate drowned while swimming ashore. The wreck at this time was in no immediate danger. This is proven by the fact that Barbara was able to remain on board. It is obvious from her reports, that she was suffering no real discomfort. Barbara knew that she would now be a hindrance to the men, she could not swim and it would be better for her to take her chances with the natives or hope that a passing ship might find her.

Barbara was able to stay where she was for some time after the men left her. She stated [in her testimony to her rescuers] that she remained on board the cutter, until the natives came to take her off a day or so later. Barbara did not describe the drowning death of William Thompson. She simply stated that he drowned with the other sailor. She may have believed that this was his end because he never came back for her, how could she think otherwise.

Thompson must have thought long and hard, especially about the repercussions had he chosen to return to Brisbane with Barbara. It would be far better and less troublesome for him to quietly arrive alone at his shack in Limestone and then act as if nothing had ever happened. No one knew who was aboard when the cutter left Brisbane. If he were lucky enough to make it back and avoid detection, he could act as if he had never been away. Only a very few convicts knew that the group had left Brisbane at all.

Leaving Barbara behind on the boat would avoid having to dispose of her in any other way and if she were rescued, she would relate the story given her by Thompson. If she believed him to be dead, no one else would ever think of him as still being alive.

The question regarding the purloining of the canoe, also needs to be resolved, although Thompson was deserting Barbara, he may have worried about what the natives might do to her. One would hope that he made amiable contact with the natives who had been fishing at Horn Island. Thompson could have then tried to arrange for her to be saved among the villagers by promising to bring back more axes and other items as gifts, once he had traded for a canoe.

The Wild White Man of the Strait

The natives of that period would certainly have been easy to approach. Weenie [Wini] the king of Badu was the most feared man in the region and was a white ['spirit'] man. Thompson [to the natives] was also considered a spirit. Although not 'recognised', he would have been shown respect because of the reputation of Weenie.

Thompson knew how to act with aboriginals and would have schooled Barbara on how to behave, if she were at any time taken by natives. Trading with the natives would have also been easy, metal objects were much sought after and an axe would have bought even the largest canoe. When the islanders made preparation to take Barbara off the wreck, one of them [Tomagugu] called to her using the native attempt at the white word 'Tomorrow'. The word sounded to her as 'Toomarh' or 'Toombah'. This word could have been used at Thompson's request; he would simply hand sign a sleep posture, telling them to take her off the wreck tomorrow. The natives then told Barbara that they would come for her 'Toomah' by which time Thompson would have been able to clear the area. At no other time does Barbara mention this word as being used by the natives. It was not listed as being part of the local language and it seems apparent that it was used only on this occasion.

Survival

Thompson no longer had Barbara to worry about, he was free and for the moment, few people had any idea that he had left the colony. Officially he was still at Limestone or sailing about with John Durkin, doing all the things a free man in the colony would do.

Having feigned his own death, it enabled him to go on his way without the fear of trouble from

Barbara's family, which would cause him to lose his remissions. He knew that the natives would either adopt her or kill her, leaving him with a guilt free lifetime ahead. Once their deaths were eventually realised, Charles Crawford would no longer be searching for them and Thompson would be totally in the clear. But until the matter was somehow cleared up, Barbara's father would probably go on looking for her and Thompson, so someone must bring the salvage operation to the notice of the officials and the press.

The missing reports

During the 19th century, everything official was usually always written down and filed. The questioning of a shipwrecked girl would and should have been precise. All records detailing the questions asked and the answers given would have been kept and eventually made their way to the government officials concerned. This would include a medical examination by a competent surgeon and official questioning by her rescuers. A full and comprehensive report on her rescue should have been entered into the ship's log and on her arrival in Sydney, another on-shore examination should have been required.

Accordingly, all three scientists that took part in questioning Barbara Crawford Thompson must have done so. Yet to all appearances, they only recorded the questions asked in their diaries, which were published at a much later date. Even worse was the fact that the officials in Sydney made no attempt to reason how and why the whole saga had happened.

If this was all that had been recorded by Oswald Brierly, his colleagues Thomas Huxley, John MacGillivray and the surgeon aboard the ship HMS 'Rattlesnake'. Then they could not have acted with the scientific acumen they were accredited with.

They were dealing with an almost nineteen-year-old girl who had been left apart from her own kind for five years, she should have been quite happy to tell her story. The first thing that her rescuer would have wanted to know, was who William Thompson and the crewmen were and from where they had emanated. It also appears that Captain Owen Stanley was also somewhat derelict in his recording of the event. The fact that the Australian officials appear to have shown little interest in where Thompson came from or in what position he had been employed while in Brisbane also seems odd.

Sarcasm aside, this was not how scientists of the day, went about their daily work, they recorded everything in very precise detail. It is almost sure, that there are many official records and notes, telling much more in the lives of William Thompson and Barbara Crawford, which for one reason or another, have been kept from the public. Even the diary of the ship's surgeon has suspiciously lost its pages for the year of 1849 yet it records all events for 1848 and 1850. The logbook of Captain Owen Stanley would also be a very precious source of information regarding Barbara Crawford's story.

Oswald Brierly also came to know Barbara Crawford very well in the four months he spent with her. While recording all she could tell him about the Kaurareg people, he made little observations in his notebooks, giving little hints at the truth. There is so much Brierly would and could have recorded about the salvage party, including the names of the men who had sailed on the cutter.

Barbara was not away from society long enough to forget the traumatic events of her early teenage years, nor the names of the men with whom her lover consorted. She was able to quote the English given names of 14 different tree types [Barbara to Brierly 1849] growing along the East Coast of Australia. So why should she not be able to relate the names of those with whom she sailed?

Assuming Thompson and his shipmate made their escape from the wreck of the cutter and departed the Torres Strait for Brisbane, they would have had plenty of time to fine-tune their story before arriving back at Moreton Bay. The officials knew only that a man named William Thompson, had been the leader of a salvage party and that in the latter months of 1844, he was reportedly drowned far to the north.

The officials in Brisbane and Sydney did not find out about any of these events until November 1845, when Thomas Dowse began his reports and four years before Barbara was rescued. Surely at that time, the officials would have begun investigations into who was aboard the cutter and where they were from? It is also surprising that the Brisbane officials did not ask for Dowse to bring his informant forward so that they could confirm the matter.

When Dowse finally published his reports in the Brisbane Town News, William Henry Shetland

Thompson the hero, was alive and well in Ipswich. In early newspaper reports, [the Brisbane Town News, 1845/6] and then later [1850] in the new Brisbane Courier Mail, articles were written stating that all the crewmen on the cutter [except Thompson] had all been murdered by the natives. This was perhaps grandiose reporting done to dramatise the story or to cover the truth about the deaths. It is the only part of the tale, not in agreement with Barbara's version.

The 'killed by natives' version was probable offered up to take blame away from Thompson and his mate should they ever be found out and associated with the drama. Barbara Crawford Thompson was saved among the natives as per Thomas Dowse and his newspaper reports. A repeat of the second report is again tendered here.

Brisbane Town News November 1845:

'The party in this small cutter it is reported [through information received by the blacks] had landed on the coast to the northward. Whether near the wreck I cannot ascertain and they were there attacked by the savages and the whole party massacred. With the exception of the woman who, it is said, is kept almost nude amongst them and is subjected to disgusting treatment'.
End Report.

When Barbara described the events following the wreck including the drowning of William Thompson, she did not mention what had happened to the materials aboard the cutter. To any metal items and perhaps an axe or two with ropes and sail canvas, all of which were very much sought after by natives round the coast of Australia. This presents the question; did Thompson manage to set up a trade situation with the natives, giving them the wreck and all its contents, for an outrigger canoe?

The natives highly valued all metal and would have left nothing on the wreck for others to find. An axe could buy a good canoe and any piece of metal could be sharpened into a knife or spear point while timbers from the little cutter would have made good shelters or firewood for the islanders.

JAMES DAVIS

Thomas Dowse ran several articles in his newspaper [The Brisbane Town News] regarding the woman trapped with natives far to the north. His articles prompted the police magistrate at Brisbane to write a letter to the Colonial Secretary. The letter was a request asking that James Davis, a convict who had lived with the natives north of Brisbane, be allowed to go in search of Mrs. Thompson.

Thomas Dowse and his reporting had worked well on Captain Wickham, who now hoped that Davis would be able to find and rescue the missing woman. This convict [Davis] had a great reputation for his close contact with natives, especially the Kabi Kabi [Kubbi Kubbi] people. Davis had lived with the natives for about 14 years. The Kabi tribal boundary began about 50 miles north of Brisbane and ran almost as far as Rockhampton some 650 klms beyond.

James Davis was born in 1814 and was only a boy of fourteen years when he was transported to Australia in 1828. He was convicted of robbing a church poor box and was sent to Sydney. While doing his time, Davis again found trouble, probably for attempted escape and received a colonial sentence of three years over and above his original crown sentence. He was sent to the punishment settlement for second offenders at Moreton Bay. This was too much for the young Davis, [now aged 15 years] soon after he arrived at Moreton

Bay he and another prisoner escaped into the bush. After a few weeks living alone, they were eventually 'recognised' and they settled down among the Kabi tribe at Wide Bay, some 250 kilometres north of Brisbane.

Portrait of James Davis (in his later years)

The convict companion of James Davis was killed a short time later by an angry native. The man [or boy] found a dilly bag filled with human bones hanging in a tree, he obviously thought that it would be useful as a carry all and he violated this native grave by tossing out the bones. He only wished to salvage the bag for his own use but his error earned him an instant death.

Thomas Pamphlet may have schooled James Davis in the Kabi language and culture before the boy escaped into the bush. This man was doing time at the Brisbane penal settlement after having committed a second offence in Sydney. Pamphlet had been stranded with the Moreton Bay natives after a shipping accident in 1822 and on his rescue and return to Sydney committed larceny. This got him a second trip north.

Although Davis was lucky to escape his friend's fate, he managed to survive and live peacefully with the Kabi tribe for many years. James Davis resided with the Ginginburra people, [a Kabi sub group] for almost 14 years and while there, sired at least one child [a son] among them. He was adopted by a tribesman named 'Pamby Pamby' and lived with the natives near the present day town of Gin Gin, Queensland. He inherited the name 'Duramboi', the name of Pamby Pamby's dead son, whom the old native thought had returned to him in the guise of James Davis. Davis was not the only convict to escape and live with the aboriginals in Queensland. Several desperate men made daring escapes from Moreton Bay into the bush, the last absconding in 1841. Some of these men were indirectly connected to the Barbara Crawford story. These were John Sherry [Boralchou] Baker, Henry Daley, Samuel [Tursee] Derrington, David [Turrawandi] Bracewell, John [Moilow] Graham and the last escaped convict to come in from the Kabi area, was James Davis.

The convicts who were directly connected to Davis, and therefore, indirectly to Barbara Crawford, were Derrington, Bracewell and John Graham. All three had lived with different tribal groups of the Kabi people while the penal settlement at Moreton Bay was in operation. Their involvement with shipwreck victim Eliza Fraser and her strangely odd tale in 1836, became an important, indirect connection, to Barbara Crawford. The length of time that Barbara spent with the natives in the Torres Strait, was the result of official nonchalance, caused by Eliza Fraser and her new husband Captain Alexander Greene. Eliza Fraser Greene and her husband had made quite a few unsavory comments about Australia officials when they returned to England looking for compensatory handouts.

While begging poor in Liverpool and London, Eliza Frazer Greene and her husband, accused the Australian officials of not assisting Mrs. Fraser when she was returned to civilisation. This accusation was not true, the citizens in both Brisbane and Sydney had collected funds and she received quite a substantial amount in compensation. Eliza may have wanted to make sure that she was well paid for her three weeks with a native tribe and decided that she would collect as much as she could on her arrival back in England.

Listed below, is a brief run down on escaped convicts from the Moreton Bay colony, most of whom, were sought by William Thompson during his time as a police constable. These men were part of the Eliza Fraser story and therefore, a part of the Barbara Crawford Thompson story.

Samuel [Tursee] Derrington

Samuel Derrington escaped from Moreton Bay on December 22, 1827 but for some time, he could not find a tribe that would take him in. One day during 1829, he arrived at Tin Can Bay and there the people recognised him as a dead warrior named 'Tursee', here he finally found his niche among the Kabi people.

Derrington remained with the tribe until early 1837, at which time he gave himself up to the authorities at Moreton Bay. Derrington claimed rightfully, that he assisted in the rescue of shipwreck survivor Eliza Fraser. Derrington was refused a pardon and his story was not believed; though it was substantially true. Derrington had Eliza Fraser brought to Tin Can Bay from Fraser Island and would probably have taken her back to civilization but for David Bracewell.

David [Turrawandi] Bracewell

David Bracewell escaped from the Moreton Bay settlement on February 8, 1831. He traveled to Eumundi, Queensland, where a sub-group of the Kabi under Chief Huon Mundi ruled his area, which was about 150 klms from Brisbane. He was adopted and given the name Turrawandi [Wandi] and was recognised as a Motharvane [spirit returned] to the Eumundi tribe. Huon Mundi was a tough old fellow whose tribe enjoyed a rugged reputation. Bracewell while living with this group, heard about a white woman [Eliza Fraser] who had become stranded among the blacks. Her arrival aroused his interest and he asked where the spirit woman was being held. He was told that she had gone to Tin Can Bay for a corroboree.

David Bracewell made his way overland to Tin Can Bay and stole Eliza Fraser away from that people during the night of the corroborree [native festival], taking her back with him to Eumundi. It is believed that he raped Mrs. Fraser along the way, causing her to dislike him intensely. Even his promise to take her to Brisbane did not mellow her anger.

Bracewell then decided to keep her with him at Eumundi but as he already had a native wife and family, he could not claim her as his wife returned from the dead. He had to make do with telling the Kabi that she was a sister-in-law who had died and returned. Bracewell was in turn deprived of Eliza Fraser by the convict John Graham, who had also lived with natives of the Kabi group at modern day Noosa on the Sunshine Coast.

John [Moilow] Graham

John Graham escaped from Moreton Bay on July 14, 1827; he traveled to the Noosa area [Tewantin] and was recognised as the dead husband of a lubra named Mamba. She and her two sons, one named Murrowdooling and the other, Caravantee.

Mamba 'recognised' John Graham and thereafter, he enjoyed a good family life for the next six and a half years. Grahams native wife Mamba died about 1833 and he decided to return to Moreton Bay. His timing for the return should have been perfect, for he arrived just three days after his sentence had expired and he thought himself a free man. But this was not so, a new law had been passed in 1830, stating that all returning runaway convicts must serve out their sentences.

John Graham remained at Moreton Bay until August 1836, when he was called upon to go after a white woman who was stranded among the Kabi somewhere to the north. The woman was Eliza Fraser and Graham was told that if he could save her, it would probably mean a full pardon. He was able to secure the pardon by going to Eumundi where Bracewell had taken her. Graham claimed her as his dead wife Mamba, whom he said, was returning to him as a spirit. This manouvre was enough to stop Bracewell. John Graham's native 'family' were at the Eumundi camp and they backed his story that Eliza was indeed Graham's wife 'Mamba', enabling Graham to take Eliza Fraser to waiting soldiers and rescue.

Timber seekers found Bracewell six years later in 1842. They convinced him that the penal settlement was being broken up, telling him that it was a good time for a return to civilisation. Bracewell agreed and told them about another convict, living with the Kabi tribe. This man was James Davis, who was living at Gin Gin, several miles to the north.

The timber getters went after Davis in the hope that they would be able to talk him into returning to civilisation. When Bracewell tried to convince Davis that the penal colony was being dismantled, Davis accused Bracewell of betraying him to the officials. Bracewell was a particularly nasty type and when Davis refused to believe what he was being told, he [Bracewell] began singing a native war chant, trying hard to stir up a fight. James Davis though, was too smart to go into battle with another white man and he eventually accepted Bracewell's story, as being true.

Both men returned to Brisbane willingly but both had to complete their sentences. They would remain there as working prisoners until their time expired. Bracewell was killed by a falling tree at Woollston a year or so later.

James Davis, on hearing that John Graham received a pardon for saving Eliza Fraser from the natives also wanted his freedom quickly. Davis knew that he would have to do something special to earn a pardon and for the next two years, he kept an eye out for any heroic deed he could perform.

For now though, we must return to Eliza Fraser, her story is well worth briefly repeating, simply to show how it caused difficulty for Barbara Crawford.

Fraser Island 1836

When the ship 'Stirling Castle' was wrecked at Swains Reef in 1836, Captain James Fraser, his wife Eliza and almost all [one man drowned at the wreck] the crew escaped in two boats. They sailed together for several days until the two boats were separated shortly before the main group arrived at Great Sandy Island [later named Fraser Island].

Captain Fraser was speared to death about three weeks after their arrival and the rest of the men were kept and divided among different native families as they became part of the tribe. Eliza Fraser was ignored by the natives, she was not seen as a relative by any of the families who lived on the island and had to fend for her self for almost two weeks. She was thrown a few scraps of food but she had to follow along behind the women, imitating their food gathering so that she would not starve.

Lithograph of Eliza Fraser in 1836

Eliza Fraser had given birth to a baby just after the wreck of the 'Stirling Castle'. Through necessity, she had allowed it to drown as soon as it was born. She was now heavy with milk and the aboriginal women seeing this, knew that she would be able to assist a sick young mother. This woman could not nurse her own child and Eliza was given the job, she was handed the baby and the women motioned her to feed it. This was the only reason that Eliza Fraser was fed and looked after by the native women. She was not considered to be one of them and none of the native men or women wanted anything to do with her.

Eliza fed the child for the three weeks that she was allowed to remain with the Fraser Island women. They gave her small pieces of fish and snake but this diet did not go down well with the vociferous lady from Stromness in Scotland. During this period, she witnessed the death of her husband Captain Fraser.

He was recognized as a spirit relative by one of the natives but was speared to death, probably because the natives became jealous of his attention to his wife.

Eliza Fraser also witnessed the burning death of one of the crewmen by natives who had not 'recognised' the man as one of them. This was probably inflicted on him more as an experiment by the natives, rather than a purposeful killing. It is also probable that the natives did not understand why the spirit men would not take up the role they had been given in each family. They were supposed to be providers in the way of all tribal men. These spirits just moped about and did little if not nothing and yet still expected to be fed.

The natives believed that they must shed their skin somewhat like a snake when they died and as dark skin turns white when it receives a severe burn, the natives theorised that at death, they were given white skin all over. The natives that set fire to the crewman probably wanted to see what colour skin was beneath an already white skin. They knew that when native skin burns, the scars are generally white and this is why the spirit theory came into being.

Eliza Fraser, was rescued on Wednesday morning, August 17, 1836, by John Graham. She was handed over to Lieutenant Ottar by that convict at Inskip Point at 1 pm that same day. Once in Brisbane, Eliza Fraser was allowed to recuperate for some weeks before leaving for Sydney. She must have recovered very quickly after her arrival in Sydney town, for after being introduced to a Captain Alexander Greene [who must have seen something of value in Mrs. Fraser] she quickly fell in love. Captain Alexander John Greene and Eliza Ann Slack Fraser were married on February 23rd 1837 just six months after the death of her husband Captain James Fraser. The happy couple then returned to England, where they claimed that Australians had done little for her [they did not reveal that they had married]. They then attempted to solicit funds from both the lord mayor of Liverpool and then later, the people of London. They were unsuccessful with the mayor of Liverpool. He virtually threw the pair out of his city.

The couple then removed to London where exactly one year after her rescue, Eliza again tried to obtain money by fraud. She and her new husband related a very sad and somewhat overdone tale of her stay among the natives of Wide Bay. They were soon found out but not before the London public had given 500 pounds for Eliza and her new husband, thankfully, 450 pounds of this money, was held in trust for her children sired by Captain Fraser.

Eliza Fraser Greene returned to the Antipodes a few years later with her husband and children, they first lived in New Zealand and perhaps moved to Australia shortly afterward. While visiting the city of Melbourne in 1858, she is said to have died in a carriage accident. Eliza, without ever knowing it, made Barbara Crawford's chance of being rescued early, almost non-existent. The Colonial governor was left with a bad taste after the Fraser affair. He did not wish to get involved with another problem of the same ilk. Therefore Barbara was not given the benefit of a proper search and although they had no idea where the young woman was cast away, they still made little effort to find her or even validate the rumours. Even the pleading of the Brisbane Police Magistrate, newspaperman Thomas Dowse or convict James Davis could not arouse the sympathy of the officials.

A journey home

James Davis realised that it was possible to receive a remission for going after Barbara Thompson by imitating the Eliza Fraser story. He became convinced that he could rid himself of the shackles holding him by raising public sympathy for Barbara. It appears that he may have attempted to create a similar rescue scene for a stranded woman as that which John Graham had enjoyed nine years earlier. Davis hoped that a search for Barbara Crawford, emulating Graham's deed, would also gain him [Davis] a full pardon. James Davis knew everything about Thompson and his young woman. He knew that they had gone after the wreck of the whaling ship and he knew all the men in Thompson's group. Proof of this, especially of his knowing Thompson and Barbara Crawford, is supplied by the German missionary, Dr Lang, who met Davis at Pine River just before he [Davis] left on his trip in search of Barbara Crawford Thompson.

Dr Lang reported that Davis [R. Cilento and C.L.Lack, 'Wild White Men', Royal Historic Society of Queensland] told him in December 1845, that: 'he was going in search of a white woman named Thompson who was with her husband and three or four other men in a small boat [cutter rigged] that had gone missing'.

Davis had told him that the local newspaper had reported that the woman was trapped with natives far to the north. Davis stated to Dr Lang, that he had known 'both the parties' and while commiserating the case of the 'poor woman', had generously offered to 'proceed to the spot, a distance of about 250 miles. From where he would bring her back or ascertain the truth about her'. Davis then proceeded on to Wide Bay and Fraser Island where he spent about two weeks enjoying the company of his friends and relatives. The Kabi knew nothing about Barbara or William Thompson and James Davis did not bother continuing further north, nor did he attempt to raise a posse from among his own people to find out where she was. It is sure that he already knew that she was well out of reach of land parties from Brisbane, why else would he not continue the search northward.

The Colonial Secretary replied to a letter written by the Administrator in Brisbane, who had asked for funds to enable a search to be made for the missing woman. His reply, on February 12,1846 stated, 'Regarding the application for funds to search for Mrs. Thompson by the man whose name appears in the margin [John Davies]. We regret to inform you that His Excellency, states that no funds for a pecuniary reward are available'. This reply came several weeks after Davis had taken it upon himself to undertake a search. Although the Colonial Secretary misread his name, it is James Davis about whom they are writing. Thomas Dowse proves this in his newspaper reports. So Davis left Brisbane on December 11,1845 in an apparent effort to confirm the reports and to find the woman.

Sir Raphael Cilento and Clem L.Lack ['Wild White Men in Queensland'] wrote a short edition paper on the Barbara Thompson story. This they presented to the Royal Historical Society in Brisbane, stating that the 'native bush telegraph' had ferried the news of the wreck, the names of the main participants and their condition, from Cape York all the way down the coast to Brisbane.

The 'bush telegraph' though, must have jumped over or bypassed the Kabi tribe completely. This powerful people inhabited the land from Brisbane to Rockhampton, yet heard nothing about the missing whites. They told James Davis, that they had seen a small craft go north but reckoned that if it was missing, it must have been wrecked on the northern end of Fraser island. None could have survived, for the tribe had neither seen nor heard anything of them. One must remember that the natives spoke no English and were very wary of white men and their settlements. The further one proceeded northward along the coast, the worse this problem became. Had a few northern aboriginals managed to find a way around the Kabi, they would not have been able to relate reports such as those being given to Thomas Dowse and his newspaper. The Cilento/Lack paper was simplified and mostly only hearsay. It does not show proof of how the 'Bush Telegraph' could report the names and other details pertaining to the group. Especially when no one knew [except one or two convicts in Brisbane] who was in Thompson's party. One would think, that Sir Raphael Cilento and Clem C. Lack, should have realised that wild aboriginals could not have given such precise reports about unknown white people.

Sir Raphael and Mr. Lack should have remembered the search HMS 'Rattlesnake made for news about the Kennedy expedition. In 1848, only one year before Barbara was found, the 'Rattlesnake', had spent a great deal of time with the Cape natives seeking news of the ill-fated explorer. It is believed that the Yardigans or as Barbara knew them, the Yegilles killed Kennedy. News of the Kennedy party could only be gained near where he died on Cape York and this information had to be sought through the Goodengarkai people. For news to come down the coast to Brisbane in thirteen months, with all the precise details of the wreck of the cutter, would have been an oddity. News of Kennedy and his expedition had to be sought at the Cape by Owen Stanley. Not one report arrived in Brisbane from the native 'bush telegraph' to say that Kennedy had reached this or that place and when he was killed, the 'bush telegraph' remained very silent.

Confusion reigns

A few whites [convicts] spoke some of the many native dialects of Australia and its surrounds [mostly near settlements] but questioning was most often done with the use of sign language. This changed over the next several years [after 1850] due to the British concentration on learning native words and then teaching the natives Pidgin English.

The lack of any knowledge [by the Kabi tribe] regarding the cutter, its occupants or of their fate, tends to place the convict James Davis, in a very suspicious light. He was really the only man in Brisbane having had direct ties with both the Thompson group and the Kabi people. It seems that the reports on the story of Thompson and Barbara Crawford's plight could only have come from James Davis. If Davis had been inventing the story and copying the Eliza Fraser saga, he would have been surprised to know how close to the truth his reports were. Surely he could not have struck upon the exact details of Thompson's fate and the predicament in which Barbara Crawford had been left by sheer guesswork.

Especially as it was at least four years before anyone would know her real fate. Davis did know Thompson had gone north on a salvage expedition 14 months earlier and he knew that the group had not returned but he certainly had no idea what had befallen them.

Davis wanted out from under the yoke of the convict system and if he could use the woman's plight to gain a remission, he would do all he could to achieve that end. His revelations may have been lucky guesswork but then again maybe there was something else to this unfolding drama. James Davis may have even known Thompson's plan to go to America with his young lady and thinking that they may well already be in that country, he released the reports.

The way of the Press

Thomas Dowse had become somewhat fervent in his reports on the missing white woman. After James Davis returned from his search at Wide Bay in December 1845, there was little more to tell Dowse about the woman and suddenly the whole story goes deathly quiet. During the whole episode, Davis and Dowse never once mention the names of the natives or the tribal area from whence they had come to tender the report. If the references to northern natives were not fabrication, the natives were certainly not from the Kabi tribe. When Davis arrived at Fraser island, he did not seek to extend his search north of Wide Bay. The journey to his native headquarters seems to have been a sham, a friendly visit to his relations, done to enhance his chances of a remission while really just having a break from Brisbane. That Davis did not attempt to go any further north than Fraser Island, on his pretended quest to find Barbara, leads us to believe that either he already knew her fate and perhaps even her whereabouts or he was making the story up to gain remissions.

Ruling the wreck site

One particular item that may have been overlooked by Dowse and Davis was that the wreck site of the 'Clarence' was recorded in the journal of Richard Rule. His journal report for the wreck and subsequent voyage in the whaleboat was printed fully in Dowse's newspaper. Rule gave the position for the wreck site as 18.40 latitude and 150 longitude. This placed the wreck east of Bowen [Nth Queensland] at Chesterfield or Bampton reefs 880 klms off mainland Australia.

Fraser Island [the destination of James Davis while on his search for Barbara Crawford] is about 900 klms, southwest of Richard Rule's recorded position for the wreck of the whaler. This information would have been available to the officials in Brisbane and to whomsoever accompanied Thompson on the salvage operation. Perhaps the fact that both Davis and Thomas Dowse were child convicts leads to the lack of investigative spirit into where the whaler lay.

Who's who?

There are two major issues to come out of all this. Firstly, James Davis had to be the man giving Thomas Dowse his news reports on Barbara Thompson and secondly, that Davis was being fed much of this information, especially that regarding the fate of the salvage party. This had to be given by someone who knew about the salvage party and had been connected to them during the search for the whaler and perhaps beyond. It must be accepted that natives could [at that time] not have delivered such precise information.

James Davis could not have concocted such a precise piece of reporting without having spoken to Barbara Crawford or some other survivor of the group. Davis, having lived with natives for many years, could have guessed at the fate of the girl but he certainly could not have known exactly what had happened to William Thompson.

James Davis should not have known if the cutter had been wrecked, had gone to another country or arrived safely in Port Essington. Only the return of Leighhardt from Port Essington could tell them if Thompson had been there. Davis had no idea whether the group was alive or dead or if they were in Sydney or England or America. If he offered up false or misleading information, he would have been 'dragged over the coals' so to speak.

What if the salvage party suddenly turned up quite safe-and-sound or what if they were now living at Port Essington, surely he [and Thomas Dowse] would have looked quite stupid for having released such reports? Davis would have left himself open to more penal servitude had his story been found to be a hoax.

There was just no way that anyone, other than a member of Thompson's salvage party, could have known anything of their fate before Barbara Crawford was rescued, unless someone from that group made it back to Brisbane.

Someone certainly prompted Davis to begin mentioning Thompson and Barbara Crawford more than a year [fourteen months] after the couple left Brisbane and four years before Barbara was found. It is even more certain that someone wanted Davis to begin telling how Thompson and his party had lost their lives. Who could have been so closely involved with the salvage party that he or she knew the fate of all those involved?

Dowse reported;

'The crew of the cutter had been massacred by natives and Thompson had drowned'. Why did he not simply state; 'all had been killed by natives except for the woman'. James Davis was obviously being given precise [though modified] details to give to Dowse. Why was a slightly different story told regarding the fate of the crew? Could it be that the blame for their deaths was being purposefully lain at the feet of the natives?

Someone else must have arrived back in Brisbane, someone who knew exactly what had happened to Thompson when the cutter was wrecked. It could not have been the marooned man; he would have had no idea what happened to Thompson after being left behind on a desert island. Whoever the unknown 'mole' was, it appears that he/she did not want to become too 'well known' around Brisbane.

Barbara Crawford was destined to live the life of a native at Cape York for five long years, so it was not of her doing. Her time in the Torres Strait could have been shortened had James Davis been allowed to do something about it.

Davis did not receive a reward for his efforts and served out his time on Ticket-of-leave. He was still only 29 years old when he returned from living with the Kabi tribe to the colony in 1842. He was 32 years old when he made his trip back to Wide Bay in his quest to find Barbara. He continued to live and work on ticket-of-leave until his sentence officially ended about 1850.

James Davis legally married twice, both times to white women during his years in Brisbane. He eventually became the owner of a small shop on George street. His aboriginal son visited Davis regularly over the ensuing years and the two often went off hunting and fishing together.

It is said that James Davis, realised a fortune by marrying wisely but one wonders if he might have also gained some of that wealth from whale oil. When James Davis died about forty-five years later, he was financially well off and he bequeathed a large sum of money [10,000 pounds or about $30,000] to the Brisbane hospital.

THOMPSONS SWAN SONG

November 1844

Eighteen-year-old [almost 19] Barbara Crawford Thompson made very few statements to her rescuers regarding her lover and his demise. She was not asked the more obvious questions one would wish to know about those she travelled with or if she was, this information has disappeared.

Perhaps her questioner [Oswald Brierly] was lax in his questions but as he was the predominant questioner, almost everyone has accepted his tabled notations as being the most proficient information taken. The lack of questioning may have been an oversight by Brierly or if Barbara did tell all, he may have preferred hiding the truth for the sake of Barbara and the Government's reputation.

Barbara spoke only briefly about leaving her family and the 18 months she spent with Thompson in Brisbane. She offered not a single bad word for her man. She stated only that he was a wonderful man who was well respected at Moreton Bay. It appears that Barbara did not wish to relate too much about her past with Thompson. When first questioned, she apparently feigned language loss and thereby avoided the initial heavy questioning on the matter.

The rest of Barbara's statements were answers to questions centred on her life with the natives, little else was asked regarding her past or childhood. She did tell Brierly [when requested] the name of her parents and that she and her family had arrived in Australia as free settlers, per the ship 'John Barry' in 1836. She also stated that her father was a respected man who ran a respectable business in Sydney.

As the 'John Barry' came to Australia laden only with convicts in the year 1836, it was necessary to research the voyages and passenger lists for that ship in 1835 and 1837. On each of these voyages, the 'John Barry' arrived purely as a passenger vessel. The Crawford family's listing was found in the passenger register of the 'John Barry', for the year 1837.

Why was the passenger list of the 'John Barry', not researched properly by previous authors covering this subject? The terrible voyage that was endured by her family on the way to Australia, was a drama unto itself. So much more would and could have been realised if researchers had taken the time to look into the Crawford family history, rather than simply following the story as told by Brierly and his colleagues. History is just that, history and nobody should attempt to change it by hiding what has come to pass. Moral, religious and political codes have all been used to cover up historic events, cover ups that should never be allowed to happen.

The wreck of the 'America'

Barbara gave a relatively good description of the loss of the cutter 'America' to Oswald Brierly in October of 1849. Although appearing to struggle to remember precise details, she stated that; 'We arrived the day before the storm and during the very early hours of the following morning, the wind and sea grew strong'. Just before noon, a squall hit the area with such power, that the two men were unable to do anything to protect the vessel.

When the full strength of the squall [or perhaps cyclone] arrived, it caused the cutter to be pounded against the reef. This damaged the vessel so badly that there was no chance of repair. A heavy sea that laid her over on her beam dashed any hope at all when it also lifted 'America' onto the reef. Thankfully this saved the three on board because the cutter did little more than grind her timbers around atop the reef.

Barbara now makes a statement that can be a little confusing; 'We were with the ship about two weeks when the men became hungry and fell down from that'. 'They decided to swim for the shore, I stuck to the ship. After a while, the blacks began calling out and they held up their hands and called, 'Toomarh, Toomarh'

Barbara seems to be saying here, that it was about two weeks before the seas settled at which time, Thompson and his mate made their swim. This could mean that they had been wrecked for about two weeks or that it had been two weeks since they left the island on which they were camped while in the area of the whaler wreck. The latter seems the more likely, a tropical cyclone has usually dissipated long before this amount of time has passed.

It is also doubtful that Barbara actually watched the men make their swim. In fact, she does not describe Thompson's swim or drowning at all. She simply states that he was drowned while going ashore. All this is very vague and Brierly does not appear to have pressed her for stronger recollections.

After Thompson had departed, Barbara had to wait until the next day before the natives arrived on the beach opposite the cutter and began calling out to her. Once contact had been made, the natives retired to their camp and the following morning they came to take her off the wreck. She does not state that she was deeply afraid of the natives and again we are suspicious, it appears as if Barbara knew that the natives would be taking care of her for a while. In previous tales about Barbara Thompson, she is depicted as being in dire straits while still aboard 'America'. Barbara was at no time hanging by her fingertips to a wreck that was in danger of sinking. She was able to remain in relative comfort for quite a while before being rescued. For the cutter to have remained intact for any length of time shows us that the vessel atop the reef and was out of reach of the seas, affording the three people some protection until the storm had abated.

Even the most timid seaman, would have tried to reach the shore quickly if their position looked untenable. If the cutter seemed safe enough, Thompson would have had the sense to wait for the storm to abate. Then he and the other crewman could have made for the island. Barbara was not questioned on the condition of the vessel while she awaited rescue. The cutter did not have the strength of a large sailing ship and in heavy seas, it would most certainly have been smashed and washed away in the surf and Barbara, [not a swimmer] would have drowned. The area, in which William Thompson supposedly drowned, was relatively well protected from open water. The whole region is dotted with reefs and islands, only in severe storms and strong squalls does the sea get large enough to really trouble shipping in that area.

What to say

At this time, it is possible that Thompson 'came clean' [if he had not already done so] with Barbara regarding his past. He may have explained to her what would happen to him, if it were known he had taken her from her family while still a convict. It is likely that Thompson directed Barbara in what to say if rescued by a passing ship. If help came before he returned, she should tell her rescuers that he [Thompson] had drowned while swimming ashore. Thompson probably told her that if he made it, he would send a ship to look for her. Barbara, when found, was insistent on the fact that Thompson had drowned. Maybe she was protecting him but it is likely that after five years without his return, this was what she truly believed. Brierly and his compatriots did not press the issue.

Trade or not

Another scenario for this series of events could have been that Thompson, after surviving his short distance swim, managed to have talks with the very intelligent mainland aboriginal Tomagugu. This man was one of two natives fishing at Nurapai when the cutter arrived. Once the waters had calmed, Thompson may have approached and made Tomagugu understand that they needed a canoe and food, perhaps using the firewood axe as a bartering tool. Thompson may have also made it clear that he would return for the girl later. If she were cared for, the white men would return with many good things for Tomagugu and his family.

Spirit ships were becoming more frequent in the area with the opening of Port Essington and although few had stopped to trade, some natives already had axes and other goods taken from shipwrecks. In fact, it is entirely likely that the three survivors were able exist aboard the cutter for two weeks during and after the storm. It is quite possible if not probable that Thompson was able to set up bartering talks with Tomagugu and that he was able to secure a canoe on which to place some of the oil casks. It would have then been a simple matter to tell Barbara and the natives that he would return shortly with more goods and a new vessel. Tomagugu's statements tend to give the impression, that he had 'talked' with Thompson. His comments to other islanders that she 'was only a little ghost girl badly handled by the sea' and not a relative returning, tends to show that he wished to be responsible for her. In fact he was always attempting to return her to whites whenever ships anchored nearby. He was one of the first natives on the scene when her eventual rescue came and this indicates that Tomagugu knew someone would come for her. He constantly told

Barbara's that he would help her to get back to her own kind and that when he did, she should tell the whites to give him many good things. It therefore seems very possible that William Thompson bartered for, rather than stole the canoe and it is quite possible that Barbara was told of the dealings by Thompson before he left. All three may have stayed aboard the cutter while enlisting the help of Tomagugu to load the oil [if they had some] onto the canoe.

Last but not least, the word used by Tomagugu in telling Barbara they [the natives] would come for her tomorrow, 'Toomarh. There was only one way that this could be used and that was by having been taught to say it by contact with whites. There was no such word in the local dialects and Barbara could not identify its meaning even after five years on the islands.

The Escape

William Thompson and his mate watched the natives wandering about on shore. There were cooking fires burning in the distance and the occasional smell of roasting turtle meat could almost be tasted by the hungry men. Both men knew they had to escape from the wreck, at least to the mainland. If they could somehow get a canoe they would be able to make it back along the Australian coast and like the whaleboats, have some chance of getting to Brisbane.

A few days later, the seas had calmed enough to allow the men to swim the few metres to shore. They made plans to steal a native canoe or, if the natives were approachable, barter for one. Both men understood the girl could not go with them. She could not swim and was now a burden, she would slow them up and should they find a way back to Brisbane, she would become a danger to Thompson.

Thompson told Barbara that they were going ashore to try to get food. Late that night, the men slipped into the sea and headed for the shore. Silently they walked along the beach to where the larger of two outriggers was lying tethered to an anchor rock that lay on the beach. The canoe had a sail bundled inside and on a platform built between the hull and the outrigger, what looked like a very small hut. A canoe of this type would give the white men a much better chance of survival, compared to the smaller dugout canoe that lay beside it. Thompson and his mate had been making friendly gestures toward the natives while they were fishing and when the storm began to ease, the natives stood on the beach offering friendly greetings. William Thompson knew he could trade with them and he did so with the ease of a man with much experience. He made arrangements with Tomagugu to have Barbara looked after until he returned, at which time a large reward would come Tomagugu's way.

So, after telling Barbara that the natives were friendly and that they would look after her until he could get a rescue underway. Thompson and his mate, with native assistance, loaded the four oil casks aboard the big canoe and with a little direction on how to set the sail given by Tomagugu, they drove its head due south. It did not take long to understand the strangely upside down triangular sail and after a short period adjusting to the moods of the outrigger, they gained the tip of Cape York.

Relief

With the dawn came a lessening of tension. Both men visibly relaxed as they kept the vessel inside the main barrier reef but far enough offshore to avoid any further contact with natives. Calm seas and fair winds enabled the men to make good sailing time. They avoided human habitation by landing only where no native fire smoke could be seen. They had been able to lash four of the precious oil barrels to the deck of the canoe and because of this were forced to travel at a much slower rate. They had fishing line and hooks from the whaler, fruit and greens from Tomagugu and they were able to catch, cook and eat reef fish from the canoe as they progressed slowly toward Moreton Bay.

Moreton Island

After four weeks sailing, Thompson began to recognise landmarks and it was only then, that they began to thoroughly enjoy their progress. Finally, the sandy islands of Moreton Bay came into view and the two men waited until sundown before landing. They rolled the oil casks up the sandy beach among dunes and then dragged the canoe to where they buried it as best they could.

The following morning, they made contact with local natives and Thompson told them to go quietly and bring James 'Duramboi' Davis to their camp. Davis arrived the following morning and when told of the drama that had unfolded, was not at all surprised by their tale of survival. Thompson had many convict contacts with whom he could dispose of the whale oil. At least two of them had set up shops to cater for farmers and the new settlers now arriving at Brisbane. Once they had sold the oil, Thompson could live quietly at Ipswich [Limestone] until he felt safe again. He may have even stored more of the oil casks at a secret location near the wreck where he could get at them when needed. True or not, this would have certainly ensured loyalty from Davis and possibly explained that mans ability to gain his wealth over the ensuing year.

One year after he arrived back in Brisbane, Thompson had re-established himself. He had waited until the anniversary of the wreck had come and gone and Leighhardt had finally announced his return from Port Essington to Sydney [November 1845]. Thompson now felt he could allow Davis to announce the loss of the cutter, giving that convict a chance to gain a full remission. Thompson probably felt some guilt for having deserted Barbara and may have thought that by releasing the story, a search would be made for the girl. Although Leighhardt had not yet returned, shipping brought news of his imminent arrival. So at the very least, Thompson would have felt less guilt once the story had its release but he did let a great deal of time [9 months] pass before letting Davis have his say.

Nurapai Island

The natives who were fishing and gardening at Horn Island [Nurapai] when the cutter 'America' ended its days, were Tomagugu, a mainland native, his wife Sibi, [Murralahg Islander] and another Murralahg Islander named Alekki. With them were a few other families and relations from around the region.

While at Horn Island, the men fished the reef and the women and elders tended the gardens as they had done for centuries. Horn Island [Nurapai] had always been the garden island for native tribes living around the tip of CapeYork. It was not considered a residential island and was not owned by any tribal group. Horn Island was the garden and fishing centre for the region, here vegetables were nearly always in good quantity for those who tended the gardens there. Alekki was also on Nurapai with his family; he had arrived in a large outrigger canoe named 'Bidtham'. This canoe was owned in a partnership between Tomagugu and his relative, old Salali from Murralahg.

Bidtham was a typical sea going canoe of the type generally used by islanders on their turtle hunting expeditions. They were sturdy vessels, extremely well made by New Guinea natives. The canoes had cooking platforms between the hull and outrigger and a sleeping and shade hut toward the stern, this being slightly aft of and higher than the cooking platform. These platforms were also used for pulling large dugong and turtle aboard where they could be cut up for cooking. The canoes were chiefly used for fishing and turtling in the open sea between the islands and often made fishing voyages that lasted for many weeks. There were several other natives on Horn Island but only Tomagugu and Alekki arrived to assist Barbara from the cutter. They only, are mentioned by Barbara, for they were the men who conveyed her to shore and safety.

Brisbane 1845

William Thompson had taken a chance with his salvage operation and failed, it would now be his destiny to remain part of the colonies for the rest of his life. His boat was gone and he was fearful of taking Barbara back to Brisbane with him. Barbara had accepted that as she could not swim, she would have to remain on the boat until she could be rescued.

Thompson was a survivor, a man who would have been able to make his way down the Queensland coast without too much trouble. It was a simple matter keeping clear of heavy seas and natives. After all, at least three other small boats had already rowed into Brisbane from wrecked vessels that had been at a similar distance from the colony. He knew the voyage could be made because the crew of the 'Clarence' had made it. His competence in the bush and handling of Australian natives gave Thompson confidence in his ability.

The two men could easily have arrived back in Brisbane by early February 1845. This coincided with the reports on the outrigger and the four casks of whale oil discovered on Moreton Island. The reports were printed in the Brisbane Town News during that month and may have been placed there to ensure that Thompson stay 'in line' or as a cover should anyone find the evidence. Davis probably wanted payment for his assistance. He knew that if Thompson became a problem, that he [Davis] could prove William Henry Shetland Thompson was the leader of the salvage operation.

Sailing in the canoe from the Torres Strait to Brisbane should have taken a little over a month and a half or about three weeks longer than the whaleboat from the 'Clarence' had taken for the voyage from Bampton Reef. By taking the weight of the four oil barrels into consideration and allowing that Thompson had been able to secure the outrigger at the beginning of December, six or eight weeks for the journey south should have easily been possible, especially while sailing inside the Barrier Reef on calm seas.

Once back in the Brisbane area, William Thompson could control the flow of information to James Davis. This would give answer to the question of how Thomas Dowse received such accurate reports on Thompson's salvage party.

This though, does not tell us why the reports took so long to be brought to the attention of the Brisbane officials. William Thompson would have been back in Brisbane by early February 1845, yet the reports on the missing cutter did not begin until November of that year. Only the reports on the oil casks and the half-buried South Sea canoe went to print in February 1845 and these, as far as anyone in Brisbane was concerned, had nothing to do with anyone.

The question as to why James Davis did not report the wreck of the cutter in February 1845 when Thompson returned also deserves an answer. Ludwig Leichhardt had still not returned from his overland trek to Port Essington. Although his arrival back was announced by shipping coming from that port, he did not leave Port Essington until about December 17, 1845 and worse still, Brisbane was told that Leighhardt would skip Moreton Bay and progress straight to Sydney.

Therefore no one could officially say the 'America' was missing or that anyone had died as the result of a shipwreck. Several convicts knew that Thompson had told Leighhardt that he [Thompson] would announce his coming, they could witness this fact if need be. As it was only Leighhardt who could say if Thompson had made it to Port Essington, only when he arrived back in Brisbane could he be asked if Thompson had arrived at the northern port. When it was learned that Leighhardt was going to Sydney rather than Brisbane, Thompson probably gave Davis the go-ahead to report on the matter.

Announcing the loss of the cutter 'America' in the Brisbane Town News without some form of believable report is unlikely. Davis had the respect of the convicts at Moreton Bay and Dowse was no exception. It was probably only due to James Davis' renown and aboriginal connections, that Dowse decided to print the reports. Davis and Dowse would have been punished had the story proven false so it is sure that Davis was believed by Dowse when Davis reported that the native 'Bush Telegraph' had delivered him the information.

It is doubtful that the officials knew or suspected William Henry Shetland Thompson had been involved in an attempt to salvage whale oil. If they had known Thompson had gone after the oil they would have also known who was with him on that voyage. It is obvious, that they did not know because there are no official letters of permission or letters begging the rights to salvage, from Thompson or anyone else at that time.

James Davis knew exactly what Thompson and his party had been up to; he was the one who would benefit most from telling the story to Dowse. If Davis invented these reports, his story telling was almost identical to reality. Only the way in which the 'America's' crewmen died, differed from the truth and Thompson himself surely would not have told Davis that part of the story.

William Thompson did not want any connection to the deaths of the crewmen for one main reason. If it were at any time discovered that he was in charge of the salvage party, he would be charged with causing death, marooning and even murder. Blaming the deaths of the crew on the aborigines was the smart thing to do. The whole truth [or part thereof] only came out when Barbara returned to civilisation, she believed that the crewmen had died by accident and therefore, only the marooning would have been a problem for Thompson if he were still alive. Given that Barbara believed Thompson was long dead, it is understandable that she did not cover up the marooning of the old man.

The oil that later mysteriously arrived on Moreton Island in four large oil casks was obviously transferred to other smaller, more manageable containers upon arrival. Thompson could then take them to the mainland for sale. He took the trouble to leave a few gallons behind, as a foil for the officials. It is a very feeble claim by Dowse, that the aboriginals would want the oil and not the casks, containers such as the like, were highly prized by them, especially for the metal holding them together.

The timing for all these events had been wonderful for William Thompson. The colony was officially thrown open at the end of 1842 and land purchasing by officials and released convicts began about April 1844. Finally, when shiploads of settlers began arriving in early 1845, confusion reigned. While this was happening at the new settlement, no attention was paid at all to Thompson or his doings. The more dangerous officials were gone and Brisbane was soon to become a small country town. The officials had little time to follow up on any small wrecks and when Davis applied to go in search of the group, the Colonial Secretary really wanted nothing to do with the situation.

When Thompson arrived back in Brisbane, he found it easy to re-adapt to life in Ipswich. The November 1845 release of the story gave him no trouble; he was to all appearances, not associated with it at any time. A man named William Thompson had drowned at Horn Island, William Henry Shetland Thompson was in Ipswich alive and living on his newly purchased land. Henceforth, Thompson traveled through life with interesting dips and rises. He was a felon who used forgery and he cheated and lied to gain anything else he desired when he did not merit them.

Had something not interfered, Thompson would have been afforded a prominent position as a mini hero in Queensland's almost two-century history. Queensland historians and officialdom alike should be castigated for having disregarded and forgotten their first police hero. Perhaps they know the reasons why he has been left out of our history.

Caught

The overall evidence though, now surely points to William Henry Shetland Thompson as being the man who became Barbara Crawford's lover. This man [in the opinion of the author] was definitely the one that entered Barbara's Crawford's life and he certainly did not die at Cape York. He lived on and while working as a Superintendent at a Boiling down works at Ipswich in 1846, met and married a young lady named Frances Handcock.

The marriage took place on April 14,1846 and Thompson soon became a family man again. The couple raised two children, Elizabeth, born on March 17,1848 and a boy named Francis, born on July 19,1849. Fate has many strange faces and none worse than the one that would look down upon the new family of William Henry Shetland Thompson. It should be noted that Thompson took his time to start a family again. He was with Barbara for twenty months without children and it took twenty-eight months to have a first born with Francis.

Elizabeth Thomson [first born daughter of William Henry Shetland Thompson] married William Pearce of Ipswich on January 10, 1865. She died in childbirth on October 24, 1867, at age 19 years, the same age as Barbara had been when rescued, the child of Elizabeth also perished at the same time.

Francis Thomson [William Thompson's son] also had a short life. He died aged 18 years on December 4, 1867, six weeks after his sister had passed [could her passing have been too traumatic for her brother?]. This took place on or about the 23rd anniversary of the wreck of the 'America'. Elixabeth and Francis Thompson were the only legitimate children born of William Henry Shetland Thompson in Australia.

William H.S. Thompson confused a few issues when the letter P was dropped from his surname on his marriage certificate at the time he married Frances Hancock. The clerk filled out all the details in the register, leaving William with a new name, 'William Henry Shelton Thomson'. This error did not carry through and he and his children were listed correctly in all other registers under his correct name. Perhaps William thought that the mistake on his marriage certificate would better hide him if at anytime, the Barbara Crawford Thompson story came out.

Marriage certificate of William Henry Shetland Thompson. The registrar got his name wrong ....

The death of a legend

William Henry Shetland Thompson died on Friday, May 29, 1857 aged 65 years. So ended the life that had begun in the old Shire of Clackmannan, Scotland in 1792, a life that progressed to Louth in Ireland before finally ending at Ipswich Queensland.

Thompson had been dead and gone for 10 years, when both his Australian born children died in 1867. Although Thompson had a very exciting and colourful life when he was a convict police constable, his luck with raising a family proved to be much less fortunate.

William Henry Shetland Thompson was interred under that name at Ipswich cemetery. All other relevant registered details for his marriage, childbirth, properties etc also carried this name and he, at no time after 1841, was listed under his real name, Henry Shetland.

After the death of William Thompson, Frances Handcock Thomson did not wait long to re-marry. She did so only a few months later in Ipswich. This leads one to suspect that Thompson was ill in the last months of his life. She must have been very young when she married Thompson, her next child [a girl] was born just 16 months after Thompson died and she went on bearing children until 1866, giving birth six more times over a period of 12 years bearing eight children, five boys and three girls. In total, she gave birth to 10 children in the twenty-year period. Frances died on May 19, 1892, two years before her second husband also passed away.

84

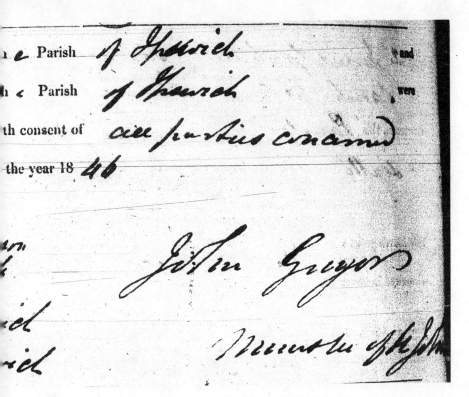

.... *but it still proved to be William Henry Shetland Thompsom.*

W. H.S.Thompson, wore many different hats while he lived. He was at times an unsung hero and at otherssimply a cad. It is strange that he has not been recognised for his deeds, especially as these occurred in avery small colony while it was in its formative years. Could it be that those who could give recognition to aman of some fame, knew of an act committed by this same man that caused them to forego giving him suchrecognition?

William Thompson may have eventually been found out but the officials concerned were no longer in aposition to deal with the problem. To raise the issue would have left the government with a compensation claim against it at a time when it could not afford such claims. After all, the girl had finally been rescuedand Thompson was married and settled at Ipswich. It was far better to leave him unrecognised for any of his past deeds [good or bad] and to convince Barbara's parents that her reputation was more important than money. It can here be noted that William Henry Shetland Thompson died just seven years after Barbara returned to Sydney aboard the HMS 'Rattlesnake'. If by some chance, William Henry Shetland Thompson could be found not guilty of being the man in Barbara Crawford's life, the Author happily apologises to his memory. It would also be nice to think that history would then also apologise for having left this unsung convict police hero out of Queensland's rugged past.

A FLOWER GROWS WILD

Barbara's story

The island, near which the 'America' was wrecked, was known to the natives as Nurapai and to whites, as Horn Island. The cutter had gone in and anchored alongside a reef, now known as Madge reef, a [derivation of the Kaurareg word 'Madjii' meaning reef]. The reef was a favourite fishing area for the Kaurarega and it is situated just a little to the east of Murralahg [Prince of Wales Island] running for some distance, toward Nurapai.

Nurapai Island was used by the Kaurarega and some of the mainland tribes from the tip of Cape York, as a garden island for their sweet potato and yams. The women and the elderly regularly did the gardening, while the men and boys went fishing and turtling.

On the afternoon on which the cutter 'America' anchored near the reef at Horn Island, the whites noticed natives fishing along the reef at about half a mile distant. The white men were perhaps a little nervous of the natives but William Thompson had vast experience in dealing with aborigines and after some hand waving and friendly gestures, they decided to stay put until morning. This proved to be a mistake, for during the night a squall struck the area and by morning the boat was in trouble, the seas began pounding her against the reef, until she became so damaged as to be unusable.

The natives were also troubled by the stormy seas and were not seen near the water for some days. During that time, the three survivors were without food and supposedly grew weaker as time went by. With no hope of saving the vessel, all that could be done was to sit tight while the squall ran its course.

On the day following William Thompson's departure from the wreck, the local aborigines hailed Barbara. Waves breaking on the reef made it difficult to hear them but she could make out the word 'Toomarh'. They motioned her to stay where she was and the next morning; came to take her off the wreck.

Barbara had suspected the worst when William returned with [to her eyes] a flimsy looking native canoe. In her young mind it was sure that she would be drowned trying to stay aboard with the oil casks rocking and rolling about. Thompson set about convincing her to stay with the cutter until the natives came to get her. She was not at all happy with this but William told her that she would be safe with these friendly natives until he could return with a boat to rescue her. If it so happened that he did not return, she should tell anyone who might rescue her that he and the mate had drowned, while swimming ashore.

Barbara was not too convinced but she realised that by not being able to swim, she would be at risk aboard the canoe and would certainly slow the men down. She begged William to hurry back in case the natives decide to cook and eat her instead of waiting for his return with gifts. She made the following statement in her own words while being questioned by Oswald Brierly, soon after her rescue:

'We were anchored near where the whaler was wrecked [had Barbara made a small error and meaning to say, where the cutter was wrecked? Or was this a cut off from an earlier statement?]. 'We ran in and anchored as might be tonight and the next morning, as of this time at present, [Barbara was talking to Brierly just before lunch] we were smashed on the rocks'. 'We were wrecked in the middle of the day. The natives were on the reef turtling. The squall came upon all of us [natives and whites]. We were with the ship about two weeks when the men became hungry and fell down from that'. 'They decided to swim for the shore, I stuck to the ship. After a while, the blacks began calling out and they held up their hands and called, 'Toomarh, Toomarh'.

Barbara wenrived at and for some unknown reason, she now felt that she was not going to be eaten. The older man was an elder of the Kuarareg people of Murralahg Island who had recently lost his favourite daughter. The young native girl had been taken by the sea and now the little group of natives were telling the elder, who was obviously an important person, [Chief Peaquee] that the sea had given her back as a ghost child.

Peaquee peered at Barbara with the ominous look of a judge. He took some time studying her both back and front, until he too agreed, that this was indeed his daughter 'Gioma'. At that moment, his wife and the mother of Gioma, [Gameena] arrived and she proved to be much faster in accepting the situation, she placed a comforting arm around the young Scottish girl and cooed softly to her.

86

The Kaurarega knew that Barbara was still very young, just barely into her teens and they treated her as such. She was sent to live with her adoptive aunt [Urdzana, wife of Saapor] who was allocated the job of bringing Gioma back to life. Barbara later stated [to Brierly] that she was allowed to keep her own clothing until she adapted to the Kaurareg way of life and she discarded the material as it wore out. This may have been so but it is much more likely that Barbara's clothing was divided up at the time she was originally deprived of them. The natives were extremely envious of the material that 'ghosts' could provide and they would not have wanted a returning relative, to actually wear the strange garb among them.

Urdzana began the teaching process that was required to bring Gioma into the world of the living. She slowly taught her the language that would enable her to live safely among the Kaurarega. Barbara was given the job of assisting with the minding of small children in the main village and as they learned the language, Barbara too, became fluent.

Learning

As time went by, she was introduced to the womanly requirements for females of the Torres Strait islands. She was allowed to remain in the village, rather than be out working until she could converse normally. She also needed to understand the way of life of the Kaurareg people and for many months, minding the children, was to be her daily routine.

Barbara's skin began to turn reddish bronze and then later, dark brown. She suffered badly from sunburn and blistering and the women brought native remedies to help heal the more troublesome areas. The little children though, were great fun for Barbara; soon tricks and teasing became part of their daily games. They taunted Barbara, telling her, that now the sun was browning her up nicely and she was getting her colour back, she looked about ready to become a meal for the men.

Teasing like this always caused her to shiver and the children laughed hysterically thinking they had made a great joke. Barbara, although frightened by this talk, knew that they were taunting her in the same way they teased each other. The whole tribe was making an incredible effort to teach her their lifestyle and Barbara came to understand that she was in no real danger. Slowly, she learned their language and their ways, along with her role in their tribal life. Her age was the key that helped her to accept and learn much faster than an older woman could have done.

She was taught the names of fish that were good to eat and those that were not. She learned how to catch good eating fish and dig for turtle eggs, how to find edible plant life and what she could grow in a food garden. Finally, she was taught how to cook native style. Many of the young girls visited her and as her knowledge of the language progressed, their talks grew longer. Much giggling and laughter was enjoyed by the girls, as they whispered together over what wonderful traits certain warriors had over others.

The nudity of the natives did not cause embarrassment for Barbara and after the first few weeks among them, she developed less awareness of her own body. She soon took to dressing the same as the native women and quickly came to understand that native girls began their sexual activities from about age eleven and that unmarried pregnancy was very common.

Barbara did not understand the native method of solving the problem of pregnancy outside of marriage. Young girls were permitted the privilege of sexual freedom but should they become pregnant the child, once born, would quickly be done away with.

Burial alive, [Marramatta] or the swift blow of a native club ended a new but unwanted life. Boy children of unmarried parents were sometimes saved alive but girls were always disposed of. A child could not be supported if the father was not ready to marry the expectant girl and this placed an unwanted burden on the girl's family, disposal of the newborn was the quickest solution. Abortion was unknown among them so they had to wait until the child came, before it was put down.

Native women and girls were not only interested in teaching Barbara, they also wished to learn. One question often asked of Barbara in the early days on Murralahg was 'How do white women have their children? Is it the same painful experience for them as it is for us'? The younger girls who came to visit her, must have been convinced that these 'Marki' [ghosts] were able to have children on the other side.

Going Native

Barbara realized that she had been saved among the Kaurarega not only through barter but also because Peaquee and his wife had accepted her as the ghost of their dead daughter and she knew she had to play the part with vigour. Barbara also learned of her betrothal to a warrior named Boroto. He had been betrothed to the real 'Gioma' since her early childhood. Barbara had seen this powerful looking warrior watching her from time to time and now she understood what was to become of her.

When finally she began working with girls her own age, Barbara's life became one of gardening, fishing and minding the young children of the tribe. Still, her time was not boring, much girlish talk and fun went on when friends came to visit with her. Barbara learned the customs and laws that governed the tribe, of their loves, hates and above all their fears.

Many times girls of the village would appear with gifts of bead necklaces or bird feathers for their ghost-girl. Barbara's favourite item was a beautiful mother-of-pearl shell cut into a half moon shape that she could wear on her breast. Islanders and mainlanders alike prized the amulets and young warriors gave them to girls that they fancied.

Barbara was also taken by canoe to a place where the real Gioma had been lost to the sea, at a small islet known as Giomalahg [Black Rock Island]. She felt sad for the death of the young girl whose place she had taken in the eyes and hearts of the parents and the tribe.

Tomagugu also came regularly to visit with Barbara. He constantly told her that he knew she did not belong with the Kaurarega and that he would try to help her to get back to her own people as soon as it was possible.

This in itself points strongly to the possibility of bartering between Tomagugu and Thompson. Tomagugu, of all the natives in the region, did understand the true nature of the white visitors and he alone knew that she did not belong. It was also a reminder to Barbara that she was not a native and her real mother and father were far away in Sydney town.

King of the islands

The area in which the cutter was wrecked had been a great stroke of luck for Barbara. Although the islands of the Torres Strait were peopled by fierce headhunting cannibals, they were controlled by the Badu Island tribe who were in turn led by a wild white man.

Inter-tribal fighting was rife and many of the islanders practised headhunting. This was done, not only against the mainland tribes of Australia and New Guinea but also each other. It may seem strange to say that Barbara was lucky but in fact, she was. The existence of the fierce white man 'Wee-nie' [Wini], caused the Kaurarega and other natives tribes in the Torres Strait, to show respect for these returning 'spirits'.

Gioma

After her first 12 months on Murralahg Island, Barbara had in truth, become 'Gioma'. She learned how to make and wear her Dadjee [full-length kunai grass skirt] and how to find Kuki Oebada, [seagull eggs], among the rocky outcrops on the islands. She learned to call Chief Peaquee 'Baba' [father] and Gameena, 'Amma', [mother]. One day at the beginning of her second year on the island, a message came from far off Badu Island. One of the chief headmen of that place had called for the spirit girl to be brought to see him.

Barbara was told that this man was also a spirit and that he wanted to meet with her. Perhaps he had marriage in mind. Barbara was excited at the prospect of meeting a white man who shared her predicament but she shuddered at the thought of going to such a dangerous place. The island had such a fierce and fearful reputation that she would not let herself be drawn away from the safety of Murralahg.

Although she felt curious about the white man and wanted to see what he was like. Barbara told her adoptive father that she did not wish to leave Murralahg to be with the Badu people. She was happy to stay with her father and mother. Peaquee replied that she had been betrothed to the warrior chief Boroto, well before she went to the land of the spirits and now was the time for her to go and live with her Ulai [husband].

Barbara had mentally prepared herself for this eventuality, she had been betrothed to Boroto and there was nothing, she could do about it. The girls had teased her many times about the warrior who watched her from afar whenever he was not away hunting. Gioma had come to enjoy him looking at her and at times, she even cast a nervously flirtish eye his way.

Boroto had not yet brought marriage gifts to Peaquee, nor had he finalised his bride price. It seemed that he was waiting for this new Gioma to show that she was ready for him. When Boroto found out that the white man on Badu was asking for Barbara, he was prompted to end the waiting and he paid the bride price post haste.

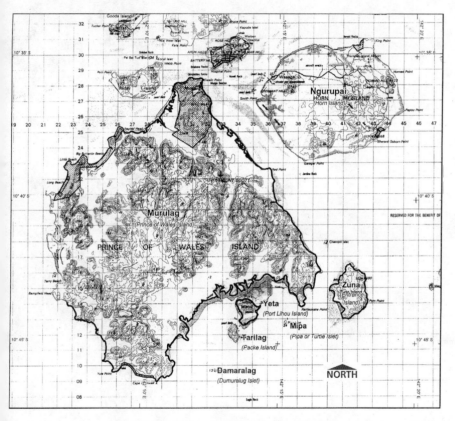

Map of Prince of Wales and other islands around Cape York

The spirit ship [steamer] that needed no sails

The Lookout

Barbara had found herself a favourite position high up on a small hillock where the boys sometimes went turtle spotting. She loved to watch the occasional tall ship go sailing by and she wondered what they would do if they knew that a white girl was trapped on this island with no way of escape. Ships were becoming more frequent in the area and Barbara knew that it would not be long before they would find her. Sometimes, while at her lookout, Barbara would watch the dugout and outrigger canoes, as they hunted for the succulent Sulur [green turtle] or fished for the sweet tasting Kopuru [whiting]. She was excitedly surprised one day, when one of the girls, came running to tell her of a Marki canoe that moved without sails. Barbara hurried to see this unusual sight but realized while watching it, that it was a ship driven by steam, just like the little harbor tugboats. The ship still had masts for sails in a good breeze but the single funnel was coughing out coal smoke and her sails were reefed as she moved across the horizon.

The steamer was on its way to Port Essington and it moved very slowly, giving Barbara a good deal of time to feel her white connections. She sat with face downcast and a tear wound its way down her sun-browned cheek. She thought of her mother and father in far off Sydney and wondered if they could feel that she was still alive, or had they given her up for dead?

Such a deep and sad loneliness overcame her, that she could not stop her tears for many hours, she hung forward, slumped over one of the small boulders, while sobs racked her body. She felt pain for the loss of her family and agony gripped her heart as she remembered William and now the terrible frustration of being trapped, so far from her home.

Boroto

Although it was still Barbara Crawford who sat high on the hill watching the tall ship, it was Gioma the native girl, who made her way back down to the village before the darkness came. Gioma needed to belong she needed comforting arms to hold her on that far off island. Now that her civilised life had gone, she had to adapt or die. The light from the village Mue [fire] flickered as the evening brought forth the darker shades of night. Barbara felt the hair rise on the back of her neck, as she made her way down the hillside, it was strange how the shadows seemed to come to life as darkness descended.

Barbara feared headhunters, so much so, that her thoughts surprised her. She had taken to saying angry words against them in her mind. She also noticed that her mental words had become an uneven mix of Scottish and Kaurareg.

Her walk back to the village became a quickening trot as her fears increased and the fear seemed to be following, moving just as quickly as she and right behind her. She was too terrified to look back and the trot turned into a fearful gasping sprint that drove her straight into the camp at full speed, sending her diving into the little hut where Urdzana was preparing turtle soup.

The laughter of the older native woman, continued on into the night and much teasing was done before Gioma finally drifted off to sleep. Urdzana's words echoed in her mind, telling her that if she were so scared of the dark and those who would have her head, she certainly needed a good strong warrior like Boroto to protect her.

The Protector

Urdzana was right; Gioma did need a warrior to keep her protected, more so now that she was of the marriage age. She could no longer stay with her relatives after her betrothed had paid his bride price, she must now move to the hut of her husband. There was also the problem with the Badu people. Their attentions would only increase if she did not take Boroto as her husband.

A few days later Gioma, with much shyness, joined Boroto at his hut, carrying her Quizdilli [bag for carrying] and her sleeping mat. Although she could see that he was pleased she had finally come to him, he picked up his fishing spear and headed for the sea. Gioma was now married and her new husband had gone for the food that would give them sustenance. Both had duties to perform and in the way of the Kaurarega people, they did as they had been taught.

Gioma waited until the women were heading off on their daily search for yams. She followed them quietly to begin her new life as wife of a warrior. Teasing and giggling were directed at her more than ever and many ribald comments came her way before this day was over. She had learned many things while living with Urdzana, her duties to the household and to husband, these being the most important of all her lessons.

For Barbara Crawford, the black skin of the Torres Strait natives no longer scared her nor did she feel that they were different to her. She had been adopted into the Murralahg tribe at the tender age of fourteen years. She did not have the moral code of an older Victorian era white woman because she had not yet been taught to dislike all the differences in human beings. Barbara knew that her co-habitation with Boroto was not something that would be accepted by white' society but she was alone outside of that world and she needed a protector to support and feed her.

Barbara shivered as she entered the hut that Boroto had built while awaiting his bride. She placed her sleeping mat alongside the small fire that cracked quietly in the Tarti, [hole] dug to keep its coals warming the earth near their mats, for during the winter months, human adaptation to the tropical climate soon allowed winter chills at night. Boroto sat cross-legged, binding a shell that had been ground down to a point, onto a Kaibu, [spear] while keeping his demeanour calm and acting totally disinterested in the atmosphere within the wedding hut.

As the fire dwindled, Gioma settled onto her mat and turned her back to the embers, enjoying their warmth as she stretched out while pulling her dadgee skirt up around her shoulders for added warmth. Only the sound of the little waves ebbing and flowing upon the island shoreline could be heard and soon Gioma felt the closeness of Boroto as he lay down beside her. She kept her back shyly, nervously, to him, as she lay on her side with both arms folded across her chest.

Gioma began to shake as her nerves and the strangeness of the situation soon overtook her, she did not know the way of the native men and she did not know what to expect nor what she should do. She feared Boroto for his savagery and for his power. She knew what William had expected but this was different, she kept her back to Boroto but could not ignore his hands, he ran them silkily and with sinuousness up and down her side. Snakelike they traveled along her body, her skin seemed on fire and her muscles began to quiver. Fearful and yet excitedly nervous, she could smell the pungent acidity of his maleness but suddenly as if by magic, that disappeared and Barbara began to feel that most primitive of all urges over-riding her innermost thoughts. She suddenly turned fearlessly, wantonly and hungrily, to receive him…

Headhunters and Cannibals

Gioma came to know and fear enemy tribes from surrounding areas, including mainland Australia. She was told how these wild tribes loved a fight. She had also heard how fierce tribal groups on other islands would send their young warriors to take heads at night. They lay hidden among the trees, waiting for those who went alone or unarmed. Barbara eventually witnessed the result of one of these raids.

An old man and a teenage girl who were well known to her had been gathering shellfish along the shoreline when they were taken by surprise. A raiding party of five or six warriors quickly caught and dispatched the two Kaurarega, leaving them lying near the water's edge. Blood, from their headless bodies stained the wet sand, giving the little wavelets a pinkish tinge. When the bodies were discovered, Barbara and some of the other girls ran down to see what had happened. It was only by scars and other body marks that Barbara recognised who they were.

Barbara ran back to the village, her young mind shocked at the savagery of the killings. She cowered inside the hut, wishing for the comforting arms of Urdzana. The way these people accepted such a horrible death frightened the white girl. They did not have a compassion for life, the headhunters did not care if a person was a toddler or an old man, a head was a head and that was the way of it.

Even Boroto was at times a stranger to her. He did not understand the ways of white love and he did not show her any real affection, his sexual attentions were brief and seemed more a relief for him rather than enjoyment for both. He did understand her fear though and he gave her sympathy whenever he saw that fear in her eyes, for she had already been dead and knew what awaited them in the spirit world.

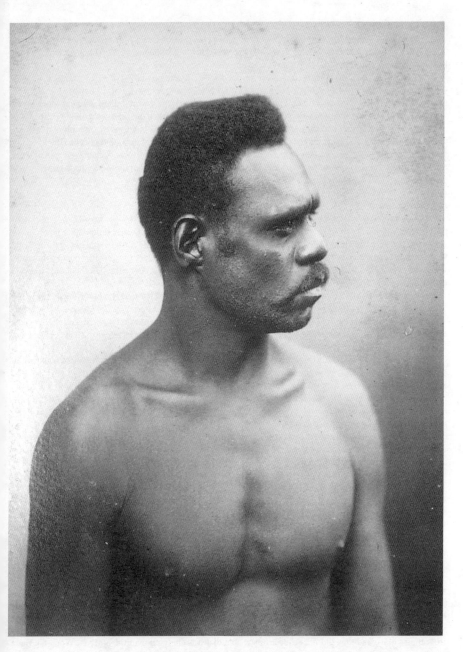

Boroto was concerned when Barbara went aboard the spirit ship

A wild wild world

Sometimes, giant fires were lit on the mainland shores as a challenge for the Murralahg Islanders to fight. A challenge was always accepted and a fire was quickly set blazing by the young Kuararega [pl.: Kow-ra-rega, singular: Kow-ra-reg] tribesmen in answer to the challenge.

Gioma watched the young men with whom she fished, ate and regularly talked and laughed, as they went off to capture heads from an opposing tribal group. She sat and watched when the men returned with their gory prizes. She cringed as they wrapped the heads in leaves and covered them with coals until they were well cooked. She shivered as they un-wrapped the heads and plucked out the eyes, holding them up for the women to see and she listened in horror, as they shouted. 'Look, this is how we deal with our enemies this is our food.' She hid beneath her mat as the men cut off the lips [Ira Guda] and cheeks [Baga] of the slain and she shuddered at their taunts while they devoured their horrendous meal. These events though not occurring often, were common and Barbara, like most of the women, was afraid to see these horrific acts, yet none would or could interfere.

Enter the Queen

Gioma soon became well known in the Cape York region. She was taken to the mainland often, where she met with Baki, the unofficial queen of the local Goodengarkai tribe. Queen Baki was a much-loved woman of the tribe that controlled the very tip and several miles south on the western side of Cape York. She was not an official queen but she had an excitable nature that made her a very outspoken woman a thousand years ahead of her time. Baki easily befriended anyone who visited her and soon had them enjoying her brashness.

The man in Baki's life was her husband Dowathoo. He supported her totally and obviously loved her dearly. He always stood behind her, taking care of the work she would normally do, thus allowing her to socialise and create a name for herself in the area. Queen Baki feared no one and maintained her notoriety, even when whites officially came to Cape York. She was just too outgoing to let a few spirits keep her from having fun.

Barbara was also taken to visit many of the smaller islands where fishing was the main occupation. As time went by, she became well known to all the friendly tribes in the area. In her second year with the Kuararega, she was taken by canoe to Warraber [Sue] Island. Warraber lay about one full day's sail to the northeast and was about the same distance from the island of Badu, which was more to the northwest. Gioma felt no fear at being mentally [though not physically] closer to that dangerous place, she was with her people and Boroto was there to protect her.

The Kaurarega had arrived at Warraber to catch turtle and dig for yams. So for the present, they would be away from Murralahg at least for several days. As allies of the Badu islanders, the Kaurarega were totally at ease when they arrived and the women set to work building temporary huts and making fires, while the men went after fish and turtle.

Men of Badu

Many other island peoples were also at Warraber and a woman from Badu began showing Gioma a lot of attention. The woman wanted Gioma to come to Badu with her, to live among that people, telling Gioma that she would want for nothing and have great respect among them. Gioma was a spirit girl and she belonged at Badu with their spirit chief.

Gioma told her that she would come at some time but for now, she preferred to stay with her own people. This was not what the woman wanted to hear and she became angry. She and her husband left Warraber and paddled away toward Badu.

Two days later, a large fleet of war canoes was seen coming out from the direction of Badu. Gioma counted 16 of them and all were filled with finely dressed fierce looking warriors. Boroto had gone off with the other men and was busy fishing. He had left Gioma [Barbara], in the company of Eerawie, a young girl from their village and they did not suspect the trouble that was charging over the horizon. When the Badu canoes arrived, Gioma and Eerawie decided they would hide themselves. They watched the finely dressed young fighting men as they landed. Barbara could not count them all, there were so many of them. The two girls watched silently from their hiding place, telling one another they would have to be taken by force to the evil island of Badu. Each war canoe had its leading warrior who directed the action on his particular canoe, without this man, the canoe would be like a rudderless ship.

Both girls peered down in fear at the sandy section of beach where the canoes had been run in. They stared in awe as a young warrior of grand stature and elaborate dress, stepped ashore. He stood with one of the Murralahg warriors [whom Barbara recognised] and this man told the Baduan that Gioma had been seen earlier working at this very spot.

This young Badu warrior, named Dora, had arrived with his helper who was a Kaurareg named 'Adi', who seemed very keen to assist in finding the spirit girl Gioma. Adi was very much afraid of the men from Badu. They would have his head in an instant and be eating his eyes before nightfall if he did not help them to locate the ghost girl.

It was Wini [Wee-nie], the spirit wild white man of Badu who had sent the warriors to fetch Barbara to Badu. More than 200 of them all dressed in their finest plumage, just to fetch one young white girl. Although the Kaurarega were few in number their reputation as fighting men, must have impressed Weenie. Why else, except perhaps for showing off, would he send so many warriors to escort her back to his lair.

Gioma and Eerawie had hidden themselves well and the warriors were unable to find them. Barbara heard Adi tell Dora that, 'he knew she was nearby and that she must be hiding herself'. Dora expressed his anger at this and spoke loudly when stating that 'he would come again for her soon and that next time, she had better be ready to go with him'. Although the Badu men could have slaughtered the Murralahg people, it is probable that Weènie had told them to leave her in peace if she did not want to come.

The Baduans had failed to bring back the spirit girl but made up for the loss by returning with a few trophies of another kind. They found an old man and a young woman [probably the same couple that Barbara described to Brierly] who belonged to a family with whom the Baduans had an ongoing fued. Both were quickly killed and their heads became gory prizes for the young men of Badu.

Once Barbara was no longer referred to as an unmarried [Nurakai] woman, she had now become an Ipikai [married woman] and the king of Badu no longer showed interest in her once her marital status had been relayed to Badu.

Barbara though, was destined to meet Wee-nie, for some time later he attended a Corroborree [Kanrabi] at Murralahg Island. It should be noted here, that Barbara never went, nor was ever taken to Badu, Wee-nie met with her only once, at Murralahg.

The pain of it all

Life for Barbara was not easy in the islands, one day she suffered a bad injury to her knee, while collecting seagull eggs among the rocks. The injury was severe and terribly swollen for weeks. The healers came and put their potions and lotions on the knee but the damage was bad. Although she was still able to walk, she would limp a little for the rest of her life.

Gioma suffered with the cold during the winters. After her first two years at Murralahg she would wake many times during the cold nights and find herself too close to the fire. One night, with the fire crackling warmly, an ember jumped from the fire onto her sleeping mat, burning her right side severely while she was asleep. The women came to rub cooling grease upon the burns and for many days they treated her. Finally, her wounds healed, leaving Barbara with permanent scars down her side. Her eyes also began to suffer and she developed a bad case of Opthalmia. Her right eye began to lose its sight, while her left was always inflamed. Although her health seemed to waver, she always maintained her inner strength and carried on with her life.

Wee-nie [Wini] of Badu

Late in Barbara's second year on the island, a big Kanrabi [Corroboree] was to occur on Murralahg Island. Gloriously dressed islanders and mainlanders from all around the Strait came in peace and friendship, while showing their traditional dance and multi coloured dress. It was also a time of flirtatiousness and in many cases inter-island marriage. Barbara was told that she would now meet the spirit warrior from Badu. The men from that island would cause her no trouble at Kanrabi time although she could expect some showing off because they were always among the finest dressers.

Excitement within the tribe grew as the festival arrived. Gioma could not wait to see her fellow 'spirit' and hoped that she could speak to him in English. When she first saw the white warrior of Badu, Barbara thought that he was just a middle-aged man who, like her, had become tribal while living among the natives. Barbara could only speak the Murralahg dialect with him, as he could not speak English and she could not speak Badulahgi.

She asked him 'where did you come from' and he told her that he had been shipwrecked and that his name was Gienow [Gino?]. He also told her that English ships, came to his home port for fruit but none of the ships of his country [Portugal, Brazil, Chile or Argentina?] went to England. His name in the language of the Badu, was Weenie [Wini]. Two brothers who had lost their father had taken him in as a returning spirit. The brothers were particularly happy with their new father, for he had acquired the ability to repair broken canoes in the spirit world.

When Barbara first saw the man, she held no fear of him and said that he was polite to her. Wee-nie wore seaman's trousers decorated with shark's teeth and the well-known tall headdress of Badu but he was otherwise dressed the same as the Badu people who accompanied him. He asked her if she wanted to go back to the white world and Barbara told him that she had her mother and father alive in Sydney and that she wished to see them again.

Barbara found him to be 'quite pleasant' to talk with and she gently refused when he asked if she would like to return with him to Badu. Barbara was now married to Boroto and had her adoptive parents and friends on Murralahg.

In almost all other histories written in regard to the meeting between Barbara and Ween-ie, the writers have stated that Barbara was taken to Badu and that she was unwanted by the headman of Badu. The truth is that the actual reports were not researched and the truth of their meeting has been overlooked.

Historians have since believed that Wee-nie summoned her to Badu where the meeting between the two whites took place. This was totally incorrect, Barbara never went to Badu for she feared that place and felt that if she went there, she would not be able to return. Barbara found herself drawn to the shipping channel where she could watch the tall ships and steam driven vessels, as they became more frequent through the strait. This was something she could not do at Badu, which lay many miles to the north.

The legend of Wee-nie

Much has been said about this wild white man of the islands. In the 160 years that have passed since old Weenie met with Barbara Crawford he has been given a dark heritage, one that he may have not deserved. His eventual death while in his seventies came at the hands of Thursday Island policemen. He was killed in 1864 when the police and at least one of the Jardine family, used a hidden sniper [Frank Jardine?] to shoot him from a boat lying offshore.

The incredible desire for revenge shown by the British can be seen in the [unsubstantiated and probably erroneous] reports given, on what happened next. The Jardine's reported that the Badu people took the body of Wee-nie out to sea and after hacking it up, fed it to the sharks. True to the British need to mete out punishment, officialdom pronounced that this was how Ween-ie was disposed of.

Wee-nie though, was a revered chief on Badu and he had a large family. His sons [by three different wives] would have created mayhem if his body had been desecrated in such a manner. Wee-nie would have been buried with the full traditional honours allotted for a chief of Badu, probably at a place protected from the wrath of missionaries and officialdom. It must also be remembered that the whites were too scared to get too near the Baduans and shot Wee-nie from the deck of a boat ready to run for cover. It is hard to imagine the shooter staying around long enough to watch the natives cut Wee-nie up and feed him to sharks!

The attack on Wee-nie, [allegedly led by the Jardines, from Somerset house at Cape York] shows that he was very much disliked by the whites in the region. He did not want anything to do with white people or missionaries and would not allow them near his people.

The Jardine's were hated and feared by blacks on the peninsula, what they could not cheat for, they killed for and only the friendly Goodengkai [of Queen Baki] held their peace. Such was the way that Frank Jardine ran Somerset that he was later given a year leave of absence and told to stay away until things cooled down.

Wee-nie apparently told Barbara that he had killed his four surviving white companions who were shipwrecked with him, before arriving at Badu. This may have been true but it may have also been a commentary regarding the schooner 'Thomas Lord' which vessel arrived at Badu in June 1846. The captain sent a boat ashore and was shocked to see a band of natives led by white man, attack and kill four of the boat crew. All four were beheaded as if in warning to the others to stay away. As this happened only a few months before Barbara and Wee-nie met on Murralahg, Wee-nie may have been trying to tell Barbara of this incident.

. Some say that he was a ferocious killer and that he had ordered the natives of Badu to kill all spirits and missionaries that arrived on the island because they would cause problems for the Badu people. He is said to have joined in on headhunting raids and eventually killed some of the leaders on Badu so that he could achieve the rank of overall chief. This was mostly untrue of the old white warrior. He gained his rank among the people through his age. He was almost an elder when he arrived at Badu and his two adoptive sons were already married and held some esteem on that island. When police shot him dead in 1864, he would have been about 70 years old and was the great chief of his tribe. Wee-nie [Wini] may have been a killer and a headhunter but others say he was a middle-aged gentleman who adored his lifestyle, living happily with his three wives and children.

It is probable that Wee-nie knew what was in store for the natives once the white missionaries gained a foothold. He did not wish the whites to interfere in his paradise nor destroy their culture. Maybe that is why he always refused to meet with mission people, it is well known that he opposed the Badu people accepting them, or their teachings.

The Jardines though, appear to have been hungry for wealth be it mineral or from the sea and would stop at nothing to gain and maintain that wealth. Frank Jardine probably was the one to have killed Wee-nie, there was not enough room for two such men in the Torres Strait.

And so ended the life of this shipwrecked sailor who adopted and came to love the wild lifestyle of the Torres Strait islands. Hopefully historic truth will prevail and the horror stories offered up by those who would change history could be revealed as being just that, stories.

Jardine in fear

So fearful of the natives were the Jardine's that their residence [Somerset house] was set up like a fortress. Loopholes for rifles and swivel guns protected every point and a number of naval marines were sent to help protect the homestead. Natives had no trouble killing about five marines and boasted that the end would soon come for Frank Jardine. The marines were replaced with native police and this caused more trouble.

One of the native troopers [not a Goodengarkai] took a Yardaigan [Barbara called them the 'Yegillies'] native woman into the bush and murdered her, he then cut out and ate her liver. Retaliation was swift and some of the friendly Goodengarkai natives were attacked and killed by the woman's tribe. Jardine then arranged a terrible slaughter of the Yardaigan natives and the British, annoyed at Frank Jardine, pulled their support from the region. Somerset house quickly lapsed into a state of ill repute frequented by disreputable characters that used the area for profiteering. Eventually, Frank Jardine had to be given extended leave from the area because of his horrific acts against the natives of the Torres Strait.

. Henry M Chester replaced Frank Jardine and maintained the area until Jardine returned twelve months later. Frank Jardine died in March 1919 and was buried by natives who, though in awe of Jardine, apparently disliked him so much they buried him standing up.

A bride for Weenie

As for Wee-nie, there is the question of whether he wanted to have Barbara as part of his harem. In truth, it is more likely that Wee-nie did not want Barbara at all. He may have asked her to come with him out of concern for her predicament or just because he might have liked the thought of a white woman as one of his wives. Wee-nie though, already had three wives and he certainly did not need her and he probably already knew that she would not wish to go to Badu. Barbara was also traditionally married to Boroto by the time Wee-nie became really interested in her plight. This was more likely the true reason that she did not accompany Weenie back to Badu.

Many years later one of the men of Badu was asked if he could remember the meeting of the two ghosts. The old man [who had been a boy at the time] stated that Wee-nie had not wanted the white girl, complaining that, 'She talk too much that one, all time talk talk talk'. This of course would have been Wee-nie's way of saving face at Barbara's refusal. He could let his people think that she was a nagging female and this was why he did not want Barbara at Badu with him. Her refusal of his offer is the more believable version of their meeting.

THE HEART OF THE WILDFLOWER

Gioma sat atop the rocky hillside silently watching the sun's golden orb as it hung low on the western horizon. She tilted her head to the left to let the cool evening breeze play softly over her burn scar. If only things were easier on the island. Her knee was always sore and her vision had become blurred in her right eye, while her left eye was red and sore. The burns she had suffered when her sleeping mat caught fire had caused her much pain and although the larger burns inflicted on her body had healed, the scars often ached where the nerves had been seared.

Her nose was also suffering and she could never seem to keep the sun from burning it up. No matter how much native remedy she rubbed in, the skin was always split and sore. Still, the aching in her young body was overcome at this time of day. She sat in peace and watched the sun slowly sinking below the horizon and for a few moments, the pain had all but disappeared. It was replaced sadly and as usual, by the terribly immense feeling of loneliness that always came with the setting sun. Far out on the horizon, a tall ship ran away from her toward the strait with all its sails set, the waning sun coloured the giant sails gold and orange and the ship glowed as it bathed in the wondrous sunset. The ship was homeward bound and Barbara watched the vessel in all its glory.

The sheer magnitude of her vast empty world, flooded Barbara with the need to be with her real mother, to hear baby Jane's tinkling laughter when her father tickled her sides. How many evenings had Barbara sat on that lonely hilltop? How many tears had glistened gold on her cheeks at this her favorite, yet saddest time to be alone? How often had she travelled by canoe around the islands, fishing and digging for yams, how many times had she grown sweet potato for her food? She looked to the east at the garden island of Nurapai where she had last seen William and tears welled swiftly into her eyes…

The Enemy

To Barbara it was strange how much the mainland native culture of Australia, differed from that of New Guinea. The New Guineans had brought agriculture to the islands and to the few Australian natives with whom they made contact yet most Australian natives were hunters not growers.

Barbara loved her little garden on Nurapai and knew if she ever had to leave the islands, her garden would be one of the many things that she would miss. Yes she had grown to love the way of the natives, yet still she yearned for her family.

But Barbara, in her enforced role as Gioma, had also come to love many of her native friends and her adopted family. She enjoyed the Kaman [warmth] of the early morning sun and the smell of the Ari [rain] at monsoon time. These were small things but they had become so much a part of her being and she knew that whenever she had to leave, she would be heartsore and torn.

Barbara had been quick to learn the difference between a Bobata [grandfather] and an old man [Keturketai] and how to 'sagul na gi' [make fun] with the women. Her life in the wild was, for the most part, peaceful and many of the native women liked Barbara very much but she also had her enemies.

Battle for dominance

Yu-ree [Yuri] was a tall mainland woman who had been the wife of a Kaurareg warrior. This man had recently died leaving Yu-ree frustrated and searching for a lover. Yu-ree began giving Boroto that special vital look that women of all races and creeds seem to give when bewitching menfolk. As custom would have it, Yur-ee began hiding herself outside Boroto's hut, calling softly to him late at night. Gioma resented this but held her peace, for in the world of the Kaurarega, this practice was followed by any woman who had lost a husband and it was up to the man being seduced, to respond or not.

Boroto did not resist Yu-ree's attentions for long and he began to visit with her regularly. Gioma did not have the native temperament to accept this and felt that she was no longer one with Boroto. She had lost that belonging feeling and did not care for him the way she had before.

Once while sitting around the village fire talking with some of the women [Barbara to Brierly, October 1849], Yu-ree told Barbara to fetch a water bowl for her. This was an insult directed at Barbara, an insult that

tried to show who was the most dominant of the two women. Barbara, being angered at the affair between Yuree and Boroto, told her to get it herself. Yu-ree got up to fetch the bowl and then flung it with malice at Barbara's head. Barbara evaded it and then threw the bowl back at Yu-ree. This now created a dangerous situation for the young white girl; Yu-ree went after a club, with which to sedate Gioma once and for all. Had she got hold of it, she would certainly have dispatched the spirit girl with ease.

Barbara though, had a secret weapon, something that Yu-ree knew nothing of, she had her fists. She knew she would have to take the fight up to her much larger opponent and she sprang after Yu-ree before she could reach the club. Fighting with ones fists was not a recognised method of one-on-one fighting among the Torres Strait natives and this was entirely new to them.

Barbara grabbed Yu-ree and spun her around, beating the native woman unceasingly on the face and head while hanging onto Yu-ree's hair. She slammed her knuckles into the mainlanders unprotected nose time after time, just as she had seen the sailor men fight outside the hotel in Sydney. She refused to stop hitting Yu-ree, trying to avoid the severe injury or death that would befall her if the larger girl got free and reached the club. Yu-ree did not understand how to defend herself against this new way of fighting. She could not stand up under the onslaught by the much smaller girl. Yu-ree screamed for Gioma to desist but Barbara hung on to her by the hair and kept hitting. She stopped only when the much taller woman fell to her knees.

Once released, Yu-ree half crawled, half stumbled away from Barbara and staggered back to her position at the fire. Both women stood panting in its glow while blood trickled down from Yu-ree's nose and one of her eyes showed definite signs of swelling to a close. The other women sat open-mouthed at the sight of this little spirit woman and her strange method of fighting. Yu-ree lowered her eyes and licked her swollen lips then sat down. Barbara was never challenged by Yu-ree again, she accepted that the spirit girl was the main wife of Boroto and that she [Yu-ree] would always be secondary.

Boroto though, had now completely lost his place in Gioma's affections. Barbara realized that she could never accept a lifestyle so different from that to which she had been raised. She had tried many times to tell the natives girls about her god. She also told them of the loving ways between married men and women of her world but they did not believe her and just laughed at such an idea, perhaps one day they would believe but not now. Barbara's description of her fight with Yur-ee may have been concocted in a show of bravado for her questioners but the anger within her obviously destroyed her will to stay with Boroto. It is also possible that she saw herself losing Boroto and without a protector, she would be at the mercy of any that would covet a 'marki'.

Trials and Torments

Many of the customs of the Kaurarega people were mentally tormenting to Barbara. She witnessed terrible events that caused her grief and much sadness. She had seen the young women of the islands have their babies disposed of in a way that horrified her. This to our world, was the ultimate in savagery, to them it was survival, could it have been that much different to having an abortion?

As we treat unwanted animals, so they treated babies that were unwanted. Fatherless children were just more mouths to feed in a very tough world. Perhaps an example within our own ranks could be shown by the actions of Eliza Fraser. She gave birth in a longboat just after leaving the wreck of her ship. The survivors were in a very bad position and there was nothing else to do once the baby was born but to let it float away. They were miles from help in a storm tossed sea and a newborn child in those circumstances would not have had much chance of survival anyway. This attitude, to those of the present day, does not appear right but in earlier times, many similar events were played out among all races, life was tough and death was seen as just part of everyday living.

Babes in the Woods

Barbara seems not to have chosen to discuss whether she had children at Murralahg. When Dr Thomson [Surgeon on the 'Rattlesnake'] examined her, his diary should have revealed her health condition at the time she was found.

The Author was able to secure part Dr Thomson's diary for 1847 through 1851 but was dismayed to find that the diary covered the first voyage of the HMS 'Rattlesnake' for 1847/8 and then missed 1849-50, continuing on in late 1850. This left out the examination of Barbara by the doctor and also the report on the death of Captain Owen Stanley.

Dr Thomson's examination of Barbara would have shown two very important things. First, it would have confirmed her age and second, that she had borne children. It is sure that Doctor Thomson did record his work for the voyage of 1849. Why then, is that section of his diary unavailable? The diary showing the entire voyage on which he served aboard the 'Rattlesnake', is missing only that period [October 16,1849 to February 1850] during which Barbara was aboard the ship.

Barbara Crawford's age at the time she was taken from her home would have obviously been an embarrassment for the Colonial Governor. She had been stolen away by a convict at age 12 years and then abandoned in the islands while still aged 13, first by Thompson and then later, by the officials in Sydney and Brisbane.

At age 14 years, she was married off to Boroto and probably had her first child at age 15. Her second child may have been born shortly after Barbara turned 16 and she was almost 18 years old when the 'Rattlesnake' first arrived at Cape York. When Barbara Crawford Thompson was finally returned to her parents in Sydney, she was a young woman of 19 years and 3 months.

The cause of her five years of suffering, had been a colonial prisoner, one who was still serving a crown sentence at the time Barbara was deserted by him at Nurapai island. If this were to become public knowledge, the British government would have been very critical of the Colonial Governor in charge at that time. It is therefore understandable that the officials did not make a more in-depth investigation of the story once Barbara Crawford returned to her home.

The trauma suffered by Barbara Crawford during the years 1842 through 1850, was something for which the Crawford family and especially Barbara, should have been well compensated. Charles Crawford had also suffered and spent a year of his life in prison for what was probably a trumped-up charge. This could have and was probably easily arranged by Thompson and carried out by his cohorts in Sydney, keeping Barbara's father off Thompson's trail.

Brierly's Kaurarega Census

Oswald Brierly faithfully recorded the parentage of all natives he came into contact with at Cape York and the other islands in the regions he visited. Although at first puzzled by the numerous mothers, fathers, sisters and brothers that each native appeared to have, he went on dutifully recording their names and the names of their children. It was only when he came to understand that Uncles and Aunts became small fathers and mothers and that cousins became small brothers and sisters, that he could correctly arrange each family tree.

Some of Brierly's notes about the Kaureg people are quite interesting and he is very professional in his notations regarding the sire and dam of each person he meets. Of the available information recorded by Brierly, only two children are registered without having their parental names submitted.

These are Ootzoo [female about 3 or 4 years old] and Numa [male about 2 or 3 years old]. Barbara told Brierly that Numa was Tomagugu's son but this is incorrect if Brierly's parental listings are to be believed. In his records, he lists the child Numa, yet does not show its parentage, this left Numa without recorded lineage. Tomagugu and his wife Sibi [he a mainland aboriginal and she a Kaurarega woman] are registered as having only one child and it is not Numa, it is still only a babe in arms.

Numa was with Barbara or with Boroto wherever they went and the boy arrived on the scene almost at the same time as Barbara when she met with her rescuers. Although Barbara may have only been a minder for this child, it is more likely that there is a closer connection

Barbara also had plenty to say about the naming of the girl child Ootzoo. Babies were usually taken to the oldest chief elder and he would, after great thought, name each child as they were brought to see him. The female child Ootzoo [muddy water] was named by chief elder Qui Qui in recognition of her light muddy coloured skin. Both Ootzoo and Numa, are thought [by the Author] to have had more than a passing relationship with Barbara Crawford and this will be further discussed in question time at the end of this work.

Suffice to say, that Barbara Crawford does nor really discuss any of the many other children with whom she had contact at Murralahg, Ootzoo and Numa seem to have been her pride and joy. It is interesting to note that Brierly lists the parentage of all children with whom he is aquainted yet only two, Ootzoo and Numa are left with parents un-named

The mainland blacks do not appear to have had the same traditions as island natives where children were concerned. All four grandparents of mainland natives, assisted in looking after their grandchildren. At Murralahg Island, the mother of the husband was taboo for the young wife and contact between them was rare. A child was usually left with the parents of the wife or a minder, when the couple went away fishing or hunting.

The years spent among the Kaurarega on Murralahg were an education for Barbara Crawford Thompson. She learned the ways of a savage people who understood no religion and believed only in spirits and ghosts. In the five years she spent with the natives, Barbara formed a bond that developed in the sands of time and she adored many of her friends dearly.

She knew why these people killed so savagely and she understood their loves, hates and fears. She realised that the natives thought that whites were ghosts of departed loved ones or of enemies who were returning to earth. She also understood that the natives feared the white men's guns and the terrible wounds these weapons caused.

By early 1847, Barbara Crawford Thompson had become a full member of the Kuarareg tribe. She came to appreciate the tribal way of life and learned to trust even her not so handsome knight in black shining armour, 'Tomagugu'. When HMS 'Rattlesnake' arrived on its first voyage to Cape York in October 1848, Queen Baki [a good friend to Barbara] was among those who greeted the men of that ship with surprising friendliness. She received many gifts from the white men. This was especially so, because she was instrumental in gaining intelligence on the death of the explorer Kennedy near the Cape. Baki was an intelligent woman and her husband, 'Dowathoo', adored and doted on her. He not only fished and hunted for her, but he also cooked and looked after the children as well. He was an enigma and was certainly born at least 150 years ahead of time. Barbara also made several girlfriends, the Kaurarega women Auda, Eerawie and Wamati and the mainland girl Kolletta were just a few. Barbara did not appear to trust Wamati although she was the daughter of old Salali and Aburda who assisted Barbara in her escape to the British warship HMS 'Rattlesnake'. The old native couple also had two grown sons, Wagal and Nooma. All were friendly toward Barbara during her time on the island. Soanna and her daughter Amooee were both women of Murralahg and were also firm friends with Barbara.

The Snake

Gioma [Barbara] lived, worked and played with her husband, her family and her friends, until one day during her fourth year [1848] on the island, she heard that two spirit war canoes, one large and one small, had anchored off the mainland coast. Barbara wanted to see the ships but had come down with fever [perhaps Malaria] and was not capable of the journey.

There were two vessels anchored at Evans Bay at that time, HMS 'Rattlesnake' and her tender, the 'Bramble'. Their mission was to secure news of the fateful Kennedy expedition. They were also ordered to set up trade with the natives and learn [some of] the language of the area.

Barbara stated that while ill, she taught Wamati, Eerawie and a few of the other girls to say 'White Mary on Island' in Pidgin English so that when the natives went to trade with the white sailors Barbara might be brought to the sailors attention. This might have been the case but Barbara knew that Tomagugu would bring the whites to rescue her if she so wanted. Tomagugu though, apparently did not approach the sailors at that time. Barbara may have been ill but she may also have believed that her life now belonged to Boroto and to Murralahg and its people.

Barbara states that an attack of the fever was the reason she did not attempt an escape but the ship was there for the better part of October 1848, giving her plenty of time to recover. Tomagugu came at that time and informed her of the arrival of the ship. He asked if she would like him to take her to the vessel but she refused.

Many of the native women were too shy to go near the spirits but Queen Baki, ever outspoken and fearless, ran the proceedings with great aplomb. She enjoyed talking big, quickly leaning enough Pidgin English to be understood and because of that, she enjoyed an even more prestigious position.

Some 17 miles away, Barbara, now 17 years old, would remain with her tribe for another year; she was still the wife of Boroto and probably had not yet had trouble with his girlfriend Yur-ee. If she did have a child or children to look after, this combined with shame or a third pregnancy, could have been the reason for her hesitation. Another reason could be that she was satisfied with Boroto and her life among the natives, she was becoming tribalised and it would take a big lifestyle trauma to shake her out of it.

Barbara Crawford Thompson had no malice or ill feeling toward any of the natives at Murralahg. The natives had saved her, fed and nursed her in her pain and illness and they had kept her alive and safe for almost five years. She had nothing bad to say of any person of her tribe and had only lightly complained of the jealousy that some of the women had toward her.

She had only one real complaint and that was of her man Boroto, having an affair with the young widow Yu-ree. This incident appeared to be the only traumatic thing that really annoyed her during her five long years with the islanders.

THE RETURN OF THE SNAKE

On October 16, 1849, the British warship HMS 'Rattlesnake' lay at anchor for the second time in two years near the Australian mainland at Paguda [Evans Bay] at the tip of Cape York. The ship had been in the area since the first day of October and already contact had been made with friends they had met and made at the same time the previous year. The natives were from the same mainland tribe [Goodangarkai] that included Tomagugu and Queen Baki and others were as usual, coming from the surrounding friendly islands.

The brig consort 'Bramble' and the cutter 'Asp', which belonged to the 'Rattlesnake', were anchored nearby with the schooner 'Sir John Byng'. This latter vessel arrived on the scene on October 14, under Captain Levien. The 'Sir John Byng' had come to deliver fresh supplies to the 'Rattlesnake' before going on to Manilla so there were now four vessels at anchor in Evans Bay. Four of the men from the 'Rattlesnake', Thomas Huxley, John MacGillivray, Oswald Brierly and Captain Owen Stanley, were soon to become very prominent in Barbara Crawford's future.

The 'Bramble' under the command of Lieutenant Yule RN, had already made visits to the area in 1845, with HMS 'Fly' and in 1848, with the 'Rattlesnake'. 'Bramble' was probably one of the vessels Barbara had watched as these survey vessels went about their work charting the reefs and islands.

HMS 'Rattlesnake' trading with the Kaurarega

For the first few days of October 1849, the winds were too averse for the island natives from Murralahg to come and trade, so the officers were able to draw and paint mainland items of interest. When the winds finally settled, the natives of Murralahg began preparations for the voyage to Evans Bay. Barbara was told she would go over in the canoe known as 'Bidtham', which was owned jointly by old Salali and Tomagugu.

It is interesting to note here that Barbara stated that Tomagugu had partnered Salali and his son Alekki, because he [Tomagugu] had lost his big islander canoe [perhaps stolen or traded by someone who was in need of a good canoe] a few years previously. Most of these large canoes were bought from the natives of New Guinea and the cost was such that partnerships were common.

Barbara's report

Barbara stated that on October 14th 1849, 'We set out at about 8 o'clock in the morning and went across [from Murralahg] to the small island of 'Wamilahg', where Tomagugu and his family were living. We did not reach this place until late in the day where we met with Tomagugu and his father Tchaicow. They told us to go on to the larger island of 'Wamalahg', which is situated a little to the south. We did so and soon arrived to set up our camp. The two other canoes arrived carrying Tomagugu and his wife Sibi ['she was of our island and had married Tomagugu and gone to live with him at Wamilahg' Barbara to Brierly].

Barbara went on

'Soon our fires were going and our sleeping mats had been laid out and we all ate cooked turtle. Boroto and a few of the men had tried the tobacco [traded by the mainland natives] from the ship and all got quite sick. Boroto lay ill in the sand all night. I did not sleep well that night, I also did not eat, I had not eaten anything for two days for thinking of the ship and how I should get off' [the island].

'About two in the morning, I heard Meakool calling everyone to the canoes as he had been delivered of a bad dream about the Yegillies [probably the Yardaigans, a warlike Cape York tribe] attacking during the night. All of the women and children dashed for the canoes and spent the next two hours off shore, then at dawn; the men called them back in. A few of the old people and some of the men [had] stayed ashore. I went with Wamati [Aburda's daughter] and Auda her sister, around the island to look at the ship and to collect firewood for when the men would come back. As we were looking at the ship, Wamati suddenly asked if I would stay with the ship people. I told her 'Oh no, I am too black. They would not have me now, I only want to get medicine for my knee and my nose.'

Wamati began to annoy her at this point. She was trying to feel Barbara out, to see if she was going to escape with the white men. Barbara realised this and she kept doing and saying all she could to cover her excitement. When Wamati asked her to go and cook Turtle and Koti [yams] for Wamati's husband, Barbara told her angrily 'Cook it yourself. I have no husband or child to cook for'. Did this statement mean that Barbara was still a Naroka, [maiden] as she had been almost five years earlier, when the Badu people had come to take her back to their island?

It appears that Brierly in his wish to maintain Barbara's reputation tendered these words [see question time] to make it seem that Barbara had no native husband. Many writers since that time have defended this as being so.

But perhaps it simply meant that Barbara had mentally given up on her native 'husband' and family and now wanted only to go back to civilisation. She may have subconsciously felt that Boroto now belonged to Yu-ree and that she [Barbara] no longer wanted him because of the affair. It is without doubt that Barbara and Boroto were a couple and it is time that this part of her history is accepted as fact.

Boroto had gone off with the other men fishing and Numa [the boy child] was with him. The girl [Ootzoo] was probably with her maternal grandparents on Murralahg. When the men, including Boroto, returned later that day, the women cooked the turtle they had caught but many of the canoes had returned empty and the meal did not go far.

It is interesting to note that while relating this information to Brierly, Barbara mentions that several of the men became ill from the over-indulgence of tobacco. Her only real concern was shown for Boroto, she worried over how he lay sick in the sand all night. Perhaps she knew that all too soon, she would see him [and any children they may have had] no more. The following day, October 15th 1849, Barbara sat hoping that the men would take her to the mainland where the marines were washing clothes and trading. The men again went fishing and much to Barbara's annoyance, they put off their visit until the following day. This was possibly because the winds were still not fair enough for the canoes to arrive safely at the position where the spirit ship was anchored. Some of the small island communities had earlier been to the ship trading and they came to the camp where Barbara was staying. Sibi [Tomagugu's wife] gave her a pipe from the ship and other natives crowded around Barbara asking her to get this or that for them when she went to visit with the spirits. Tomagugu told the natives to leave Barbara alone. Then he took her aside, telling her that as he and Alekki had saved her life she therefore belonged to them and anything she could get from the white men should be given over to them only.

Barbara had travelled to Wamalahg from Tomagugu's home island with Sibi and Tomagugu in a canoe belonging to old Den [who was a mainland native]. The following morning [16th of October] all of the islander canoes had left Barbara behind. They were gone and already halfway across to Evans Bay where the white men were washing their clothes. It is now obvious that Tomagugu had arranged for a small mainland canoe to take Barbara across to where the ship lay.

Boroto did not want Barbara to visit the ship and he bade all the canoes from Murralahg leave her behind but Tomagugu had a surprise in store. Although he feared Boroto's revenge should he blatantly help her to escape, he arranged for a mainland family to be last to leave and that Barbara would have to force herself aboard the canoe rather than be assisted in any way. Barbara had been purposefully left behind by her own people and she ran [Barbara was in such a hurry that she left her Dadgee skirt behind and was almost completely naked] when she saw the last canoe leaving. Although she still could not swim, she jumped into the water grabbing the side of the little mainland canoe. The occupants of this canoe would not pull her aboard until the canoe reached deep water, thereby absolving themselves of intentionally taking Barbara to the white men. It should be understood that Boroto did not wish for Barbara to visit the ship at all for fear of losing her, he knew that she was likely to return to her own kind. Every native in the region half believed this and worried that Boroto would take revenge against those who transported her to the white men.

The Kaurarega also had prestige in the region by having a spirit living with them. To lose her would be very bad for their reputation. On the other hand, they knew Barbara could get much-needed axes and other tools from the ship. Boroto did not want his wife to go to the ship for all the obvious reasons. It was therefore vital for those who assisted Barbara to appear to have done so unwittingly. Only this excuse would save someone who did assist her, from being beheaded. This then was how Barbara eventually made it to the mainland aboard a mainland canoe. The big canoes, [including 'Bidtham'] were already either gone fishing or had left her behind, fearful of Boroto's vengeance should they assist Barbara. The mainlanders could claim they had known of Boroto's order not to take Barbara to the ship.

Looking Black

When they arrived at Evans Bay on the morning of October 16, 1849, Barbara and Koletta, [a female Cape York native] stepped ashore and walked along the beach toward four white men who were wandering along deep in conversation. A few mainland blacks were walking with the white officers and while the spirits chatted together, the whole group idled slowly along the beach toward the two girls. The nervous excitement that Barbara must have felt as the whites approached her can only be imagined.

When they came together, the white men walked around Barbara without giving her a second look and Tomagugu [who had suddenly arrived] began trying to tell the whites that he had brought them a white woman. Barbara, whose heart was beating like a steam hammer, turned to Tomagugu and said; 'Komi, arra-gi arra-gi, atzir nathya krongipa' ['Friend, talk not, talk not, I know how to speak']. Barbara then spoke to the white men in English saying, 'Why do you leave me, I am a white woman'. The marine officers were at first taken aback by her revelation but after a few amazement filled moments, they crowded around to inquire where she was from. She told them that she was a Scots girl, at which, they yelled for the coxswain whose name was Scott and told him that one of his countrywomen was among the blacks.

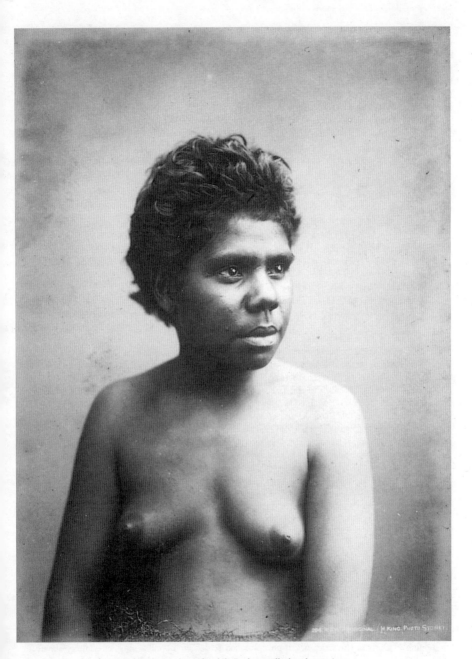

Koletta listened quietly while Barbara talked to the marines

At this moment, Boroto, Numa and Alekki arrived on the scene. Boroto was trying to contain his anger at Barbara for going to see the whites. He kept trying to edge her away from the area but Barbara would have none of it. Coxswain Scott ran to the young woman and took over the proceedings, giving her a shirt with which to cover herself, Tomagugu promptly gave this to the boy Numa. Scott then took her hand to lead her into the bushes where he and Sergeant Mew of the marines washed her and then combed her hair whilst dressing her in two shirts. [Brierly] 'A white shirt she wore as a man would wear a shirt and a blue one she wore somewhat as like a petticoat'.

Barbara could understand Scott better than she could others in the crew but it was not until a short time later when she was with the better spoken officers, that her speech and understanding showed rapid improvement. Captain Owen Stanley, Commander of the 'Rattlesnake', was below in his cabin when Barbara was found. Oswald Walter Brierly, [Linguist, Artist and scientist] Thomas Huxley [scientist and assistant surgeon] and John MacGillivray [botanist and artist] were ashore at Evans Bay and when informed of the situation, hurried to see the white girl.

Paradise lost

Captain Stanley had taken his ship 'Rattlesnake' to anchor, near the western tip of Cape York. He had done exactly the same thing in the same place the year before. His men carried on trade with the natives while learning as much as they could of the two major languages that were spoken in the area.

Brierly, Brady, Dr Thomson and Lieutenant Simpson were shooting gulls along the beach on the clear, calm morning of October 16, 1849. The ship's washing detail were busy washing clothes for the men of the 'Rattlesnake' and it was to these men that Barbara presented herself.

The officers were only a short distance away and were surprised when one of the sailors came running to tell them that a young white woman had been found among the natives. They, [the officers] then set off at a run and were soon at the washing place. There they noticed a rather unkempt and bedraggled looking young woman, [Barbara had just been immersed in seawater and would hardly have looked a perfect 10] sitting on a bank wrapped in two oversized men's shirts. But finally, after five years of adventurous life in an alien environment, Barbara Crawford Thompson had been found and was now finally back with her kind, just as Tomagugu had said she would be. The white men asked Barbara if she was going to stay with the natives or did she wish to come aboard the ship. This was one of several times that the officers asked Barbara this question. It seemed to them that she had turned almost totally native in her manner and speech. Barbara though, told them she wanted to go on board the 'Rattlesnake' and back to civilisation. She continued conversations with the natives and answered questions thrown at her by the whites, for a girl still 18 years old this must have been a very traumatic, yet excitement filled moment in time.

As they were departing the beach, Barbara noticed Boroto growing distressed at her departure. She told him that some of her women friends from the spirit world were on board and she wanted to speak to them. She also told him that there were many items she needed and these would be much easier to get if she went to the ship. She asked the officers to give Tomagugu, Alekki and Boroto axes and some tobacco before she departed, as these men had been the most instrumental in her survival while on the island. Boroto though, would not be put off and he paddled out to the ship and waited on deck for his Gioma to return with him to the island.

Barbara Crawford Thompson was soon taken aboard where she went below deck to meet Captain Owen Stanley in his cabin. Stanley could not believe his eyes when he saw the girl and he observed that although healthy enough, she had obviously been subjected to the elements. Barbara's skin had turned almost black, she was slightly lame with knee damage and she suffered from Opthalmia [inflammation of the conjunctiva of the eyes]. She had also suffered some large burns, which she told Captain Stanley, happened when her sleeping mat caught fire one cold night.

After a period of adjustment and reverting to civilised dress, Barbara made herself ready for what should have been intense questioning on how she came to be in such a predicament. The examination and questioning of Barbara Crawford began once she had settled comfortably into her quarters aboard the ship.

Thomas Huxley, Oswald Brierly and John MacGillivray trading with the Goodengarkai tribe at Cape York

Oswald Brierly became chief questioner and recorder while Huxley and MacGillivray both had time asking their own questions of the girl. Barbara briefly related how she came to be at Cape York and that she had spent 20 months married to a man named William Thompson before arriving at that place.

One of the very first questions Brierly asked of Barbara, was what had happened to her wedding ring. Barbara stated that she had worn it on a string around her neck while on Murralahg. She said that the girls had seen her crying whenever she looked at it and one night while she was asleep they removed the ring and tossed it into the fire.

This part of Barbara's story may be true but it is unlikely Barbara received a gold wedding band from William Thompson. He was a convict and as such, had very little of value, gold would probably have been replaced by copper or wood. The couple had not been officially married and Barbara may have been a little caught out when Brierly asked her about her wedding ring and so she told him a story that somewhat emulated Eliza Fraser's wedding ring story. Barbara had told Brierly that she had married Thompson in Brisbane. It is therefore probable, that she concocted the ring story to save face. This does not make Barbara Crawford a liar, it confirms that she was deeply ashamed of what had happened to her since she left her family home in Sydney.

HMS 'Rattlesnake' at sea

At home with the 'Snake'

Apart from her medical problems, Barbara was reasonably healthy but according to the men of the 'Rattlesnake', she did struggle to answer some of the questions asked of her. Barbara at times thumped her forehead with the palm of her hand as if trying to remember her English.

Barbara still maintained her Scottish accent while speaking English but her battle with translation was at times amusing to the officers. Her understanding of the many different accents among the sailors also troubled her in the early stages. It is true that Barbara's might also have found this a good way of not answering questions she found too embarrassing or when she needed to cover for William Thompson.

Boroto caused some concern for the sailors. He would not go away and steadfastly refused to leave the ship unless Barbara went with him. It was only after several bribes were given that he finally departed. It became obvious to the officers that Barbara was very much a part of the local native society. They noticed too, that she had children around her while ashore and that Boroto was without doubt emotionally connected to her.

They again asked her if she would rather stay with the people of Murralahg to which she replied that she was a Christian and wanted to return to her family. Barbara knew that the extended family of any children she may have had to Boroto would take good care of the children, she also knew that mixed race children would not be accepted into Victorian society.

Captain Stanley had made a cabin available for his two sisters when the ship had originally sailed from London; they accompanied him as far as Madiera on the voyage out. Due to his very heavy work commitments, Captain Stanley had not yet had time to clear out the cabin for its intended use as his workroom, so with a little spit and polish, it again became a ladies cabin.

Thomas Huxley as a young man

Making ready to leave

Barbara Crawford was saddened now that she was leaving the Kaurarega people. She had become part of their way of life, it was probably only when Boroto strayed, that she made the decision to depart the island if and when the ships again anchored nearby. Once made, that decision was not going to be changed by anyone, she had earlier given herself to that life and when she could not accept the way of the natives, she knew that she must return to civilisation.

Boroto kept making a pest of himself and he often called out to his Ipi [wife] begging her to come back to Murralahg with him. When she refused, he resorted to threats of violence. Boroto paddled his canoe to Barbara's cabin porthole with his brother Gunagi. They called to Gioma asking her to come home. Barbara replied that she wanted to go with the ship to visit some of her old spirit friends and she would return when she had seen them. This was too much for Boroto, he told her that if she came anywhere near the village, he would take her head off and tear out her eyes. This threat only tended to strengthen Barbara's resolve and she no longer went ashore.

Thomas Huxley and his wife in later years

Gioma's 'mother' arrived in her canoe and she cried bitterly, telling Barbara that Boroto was going to cut the head off her 'mother' if she did not return. She wore the mother of pearl necklet that Barbara had left on the beach with her 'dadgee' and Gameena offered them to her if she would come home. She begged Gioma to come and look after her 'Gurri Koop' [garden] on Nurapai but Barbara refused her plea.

It is not mentioned if any of the children were brought to the ship and this leads one to believe that this information might have also been deleted. The family would have brought all of Barbara's friends to try and convince her to return including any children connected to her.

Sydney Bound

The 'Rattlesnake' remained at the Cape for nine weeks before leaving the area and sailing to the coast of New Guinea. During that period, Barbara made herself a dress and other items of clothing while teaching Brierly and the other scientists much of the Nya-oomee language. Finally the 'Rattlesnake' weighed anchor and set sail, Barbara watched her native friends from the deck as the ship slowly left them far behind. With tear filled eyes, she went below to her cabin, avoiding the wondering stares of the sailors.

While en-route to Sydney [January 1850], Captain Owen Stanley suffered a stroke, which severely affected his abilities. Little did they realise the serious condition of the captain. He remained ill in his cabin for the rest of the voyage.

The 'Rattlesnake' 'spoke' a vessel bound for Brisbane while they were between Brisbane and Sydney. They gave news of Barbara Crawford's rescue to the other vessel, which was relayed to the local newspaper when it arrived in Brisbane. The rescue of Barbara Crawford Thompson probably created a lot of 'told you so' comments in the former penal colony and would have deeply worried at least one of the locals of that town. The Brisbane Courier ran the story of her rescue almost before she arrived at Sydney in early February 1850. When Barbara Crawford arrived back in Sydney she was kept aboard until her family were notified of her arrival. She then gave her thanks to the officers and crew for bringing her home before quietly going ashore where her parents were waiting to take her home.

Four weeks later, as HMS 'Rattlesnake' lay quietly at anchor in Sydney harbour, Captain Owen Stanley RN, passed away at 8am on Wednesday, March 13, 1850. Captain Owen Stanley, after whom the New Guinea mountain range received its name, died just 30 minutes after his cabin boy found him in the throes of another stroke at 7.30am. Captain Stanley's brother had died just a few months earlier, also passing on a 13th; it was in fact August 13, 1849. His Reverend father also passed away during this period, dying on September 6,1849 just six weeks before Barbara was rescued. Three members of the Stanley family had died within six months of each other, his father, brother and Captain Stanley himself.

Owen Stanley's wife had the unenviable sadness, of burying her brother-in-law in Tasmania after having been notified of the death of her father-in-law in England, before then traveling to Sydney, where she mourned the loss of and buried her husband.

WILDFLOWER IN THE MIST

The chill winter air lay silent and almost still, occasionally little wafts swirled about in the growing fogbank that was drifting shroud-like across the colonial township of Sydney. What breeze existed had not the strength to raise a ships flag but it was sufficient to drive the fog slowly and relentlessly across Sydney harbour.

A three-mast ship was towing out in the late afternoon, her hawser dripping saltily as the swell rose and fell beneath it. The large three-mast ship followed dutifully behind a small steam driven paddle tugboat that was dwarfed by the great tall ship.

The paddle steamer chugged forward with its long thin funnel standing out of the orange and grey mist like a pen from its inkwell. Only the swash, swash, swash of the paddlewheels and the clunk and hiss of its little steam engine could be heard as it towed the much larger vessel slowly toward the waiting arms of the ocean.

The evening light was fast fading, as the two vessels arrived at their separation point a few miles offshore. The towline was released as an offshore breeze, seemingly on cue, took hold of the sails. The crew of the paddle steamer gave three hearty cheers to see the big ship on her way and watched as the larger vessel moved slowly off under her own power.

The little steamer now had to hurry to make it back through the heads before darkness and the fog set in. She was soon swallowed up in the mist as she chugged much faster now, back toward her port. The helmsman on the tall ship watched them go, as his shipmates lit the big oil lamps fore and aft.

The great sails were already twisting round to meet the breeze that toyed playfully with them. Then, as if on command, the zephyrs strengthened, apparently having decided which way they would blow. They began to fill the big rusty brown canvas sails of the Englishman and her sailors scurried from yardarm to yardarm, dropping the last of her canvas into place.

At first, the fog seemed to be moving faster than the ship, and it wrapped itself like some monster of the deep, round every part of the vessel. The helmsman watched these changes and marvelled as always, at how the fog held sway, while the ship like a knight's mighty charger, drove its unicorn-like beak into the heart of its foggy foe.

The helmsman's attention was drawn back to the deck as a young woman made her way toward the mainmast. She stood for a moment as if trying to gain her sea legs. Turning slightly, she leant against the big bole of the mast. Then facing toward the bow of the ship, she wrapped her right arm round the mast as far as it could go. She hugged it tightly and placed her ear against its cold strength, listening to the 'flump, flump' of the sails and the creaking of the yardarms as they twisted and turned. She like her mother before her was listening to the ship as it spoke down the length of the big mast.

The fog rolled onward, over and around them as Barbara stood quietly beside the mast. The ship bowed to the swell, rolling eternally in from the vast Pacific. Her mind swept aside a thousand turmoil filled years to when as a child of six, another ship had carried her away from her native Scotland. It had brought her to a distant wild land that had fought to weaken her resolve but in the end she had won, she had survived all that could be thrown at her, and she had won. She shivered and pulled the shawl close about her, feeling proud of her very being.

The fog and mist seemed to have grown heavier as the ship turned its head to the southeast. A tear ran warmly down her cheek on that cold July evening and a strong feeling of sadness overtook her. She had lost so many of those she had known and loved, life had dealt her such a strange hand.

The helmsman's mate rang the ship's bell, 'clang clang, clang, clang ' and the Wuna Marki fog deepened. It curled around the masts and wafted around and over the sails. Its icy tendrils continued their ghostly dance and as darkness took hold, the yellow light from the big oil lamps added to the already eerie atmosphere.

The helmsman could now barely see the woman at the mast. Still she stood there holding the great bole as one might hug a friend. She turned her face skyward to where the topsails had all but disappeared from view.

The young woman finally turned and hurried toward the double doors that led below, she needed to be with her husband now, to feel his comforting arms. She needed to forget the savage events she had witnessed and those who had used her. Perhaps some day the truth would be known but for now, she just wanted to forget. The helmsman's mate again struck the bell and the fog grew deeper and darker around them. Soon, only the muffled echoes of the bell could be heard, mournfully clanging as the ship slipped silently away into the grey mists of time.

'Gna piki utsimen'
[Her dreaming has ended]
[Kaurarega]

Drawing of a Cape York native woman wearing her 'Mue Dadgee' shirt (sketched by Thomas Huxley)

EPILOGUE

The life of Barbara Crawford Thompson was one of incredible trauma and adventure. Little is known of her later life and until now, it was not known if she had ever officially married. Some authors have made statements of possibility but have not provided documents proving their suspicions. Now that much of her personal history has been found, it is safe to say that she lived an extremely dramatic life and has now an interesting part of Australian history. No matter where or when she finally died, Barbara Crawford has provided us with a story that will never cease to amaze.

In the officially recorded colonial history of Australia, very few young girls were witness to such horrors or suffered such undignified treatment while still too young to fully understand what was happening around them. She was a victim of fate and its strange quirks. So much happened to her within the space of just 15 years, that had she not been so young, she would surely have died.

The return to her parents, must have been a most emotional homecoming, especially after bearing up to such a terrible sequence of events. After Barbara had arrived back with her family, she regained her health quickly and on July 14, 1851, she was a witness at the marriage of her sister Jane Crawford, to Mr. Henry Whittall at St Andrew's church, in Sydney. Like Barbara, Jane was unable to sign the marriage certificate due to her own illiteracy.

Four months later, in November 1851, just 21 months after her return to Sydney, Barbara married a man named James Adams. Her sister Jane witnessed the marriage and signed her name with a cross. The certificate at first glance appears to have been signed by the bride and it is possible that Barbara may have learned to sign her name by this time. The writing on Barbara's wedding certificate though, does appear to have been wholly written in one hand, by [except for the James Adams signature] perhaps the minister or registrar and so it is doubtful that Barbara herself signed it. It is probable that James Adams was also much older than Barbara Crawford, who may still have been looking for a father figure. It also appears Barbara waited until she turned 21, to marry without the need for consent from her father, Charles Crawford.

Barbara's sister, Jane Crawford Whittall, died aged 36 years on October 30, 1868. She had two sons, Henry, born on May 13,1860, and Richard, who was also born in the month of May seven years later. Henry lived until he was 15 years old, dying on October 13, 1875. Richard lived for only 13 months and died on June 10, 1868. Jane may well have had other children out of wedlock but I have recorded here only the two sons by her marriage. It seems likely that the birth of her last child may have been troublesome for both mother and child, Jane died only four months after Richard's death.

Barbara Crawford Thompson Adams' life after marriage is for the most part unknown but Author Adelaide Lubbock [noted for her biography on Captain Owen Stanley] stated that a fund had been raised for Barbara on her return to Sydney. Lubbock relates that Barbara Crawford wasted this money, spending it all [perhaps her years among the natives had taught her to share] on her family.

Adelaide Lubbock also stated that Barbara married and went to England where she entered the carnival circuit as 'The Wild White Woman'. If this is true, there must be some evidence of that fact hidden in a library file somewhere in England. This also may have been a mistaken reference to the Eliza Fraser story, that lady did get involved in fairground work in England during the 1840's.That many sections of Barbara Crawford's dramatic tale were hidden from the public eye, can only be shown on the evidence [or rather the lack of it] supplied by those involved in her rescue. Captain Owen Stanley had hired Oswald Brierly as ships artist. Yet he does not appear to have done a single portrait of Barbara Crawford. Breirly knew that she was part of Australian colonial history, yet he asked only a very few questions regarding the important points in her story. In the opinion of the Author, the men aboard the 'Rattlesnake' decided to keep her story simple for the sake of her reputation.

Adelaide Lubbock, in her biography on Owen Stanley, was quite correct in stating that Barbara married, although she did not know to whom. Many have rejected this information as guesswork on the part of Ms Lubbock but the proof has finally been found and is shown here for the first time ever. Barbara Crawford is said to have died in Sydney at age 84 years in 1912. The year of her death may be correct but her true age would have been 81 or at most 82 years.

No. 699 _Henry Whittall_ of th.. Parish _Brighton_

Jane Crawford of th.. Parish _Brighton_

married in this _Church_ by _Banns_ with consent of _Father of Jane Craw~_

this _fourteenth_ day of _July_ in the year 185/ _fifty one_)

By me _William Cooper_

This Marriage was
solemnized between us
{ _Henry Whittall_
{ _Jane Crawford_ her mark
{ _Benjamin Richards_

In the Presence of
{ _Barbara Crawford_ her mark

Marriage Certificate of Jane Crawford and Henry Whittall

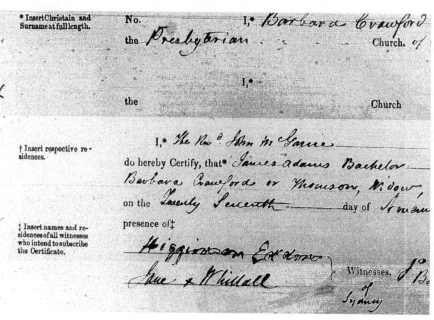

Marriage certificate of James Adams and......

An accurate summary of the life of Barbara Crawford is not something that can be easily recorded. Her tale is filled with many ' ifs and buts', especially in regard to William Thompson. This book however, has introduced startling new evidence never before seen by the public. Previously, very little has been made of the ordeals suffered by this young woman and it is because of the unfairness of it all, that this work was undertaken.

The new evidence recorded herein has been presented for the first time since these events have taken place. The tragic voyage of the 'John Barry' for some unknown reason seems to have escaped notoriety. Barbara's true age, her family, her first 'marriage' to William Henry Shetland Thompson and the details surrounding his past have all been overlooked until now. The possibility of Barbara having had children by the Kaurareg native Boroto, her marriage to James Adams and much of her family's history are also items that seem to have previously escaped detection.

It is probable that Australian officials and the family of Barbara Crawford wanted the whole affair kept quiet, not only for Barbara's sake but also because of embarrassment to the government and perhaps other compensatory reasons.

The problem with changing or distorting history is that it takes away the truth and allows for falsehood to take its place. Historic truth is our human heritage and without it, no country can hope to exist comfortably and truthfully as a nation. No matter what problem may arise regarding this young lady's reputation past or present, she is part of history and as such, the truth behind her story must be revealed. I believe that I have correctly shown William Thompson's identity and how he made his connection with Barbara Crawford. It is open for those who do not adhere to these theories, to prove otherwise.

There are a few items of interest that are still missing from Barbara's story, the fate of Charles Crawford Snr and the rest of his family have yet to be found. Barbara's passing and the latter half of her life after her marriage is also of interest to historians and this information still eludes us. Charles Crawford may have died in Sydney about 1860 but this has yet to be substantiated.

..... *Barbara Crawford or Thompson Marriage certificate*

It is believed that Barbara outlived her husband James Adams and married again before dying in Sydney, possibly as already recorded, in 1912. Too many others have recorded that year for her death, so I shall not at this time, dispute the point. The Author was able to discover that a woman named Barbara Donahue paid for the exhumation and reburial of a woman named Jane Crawford when the old Sydney cemetery was being closed down about 1902. If this was the doing of Barbara Crawford Adams, I am unable at present, to verify the fact.

Barbara Crawford must be shown a place in Australian history that will compensate for her sufferings. She is well worthy of honour for the shame she was forced to bear, not only during her lifetime but also in the histories that have since been written about her. Barbara should be recognised on a public scale that will no longer allow her to be ridiculed with phrases like 'Boroto's Gin' and the 'White Lubra of Murralahg'. She was only a girl of 12 years in March 1843, when she was taken away by a prisoner of the Crown. This man took advantage of her and then abandoned her to a fate no young girl should have suffered.

It is almost certain that Barbara Crawford's dramatic ordeal, was watered down by all involved in her rescue, with the later inclusion of the Australian officials. When her ordeal was reported, the Governor would have been content to hush the matter up. The entire story would not be told and people were left to imagine what really happened to her while she lived among the natives. The man who spirited her away from her family has been totally ignored. Was this only because he was reported as having drowned and was therefore, 'out of sight, out of mind'? It appears [to the Author] that from the moment Lieutenant Gorman took over as commandant in Brisbane, serious corruption appeared. Gorman ran the colony on a remission reward system that was sorely abused by the convict police. Limestone [Ipswich] developed a reputation after the Gorman years and many suspicious events unfolded in that little town. For Thompson, this would have been his happiest period in the colonies. Be that as it may, should someone ever prove that William Henry Shetland Thompson was not involved in the Barbara Crawford story, the ordeal that this girl was forced to endure should still afford her, a place of esteem in Australian history.

Yes, it is true that Barbara Crawford had become almost totally native and it was probably only because of Boroto's philandering that she decided to return to her family. Shame could well have kept her among the Kaurarega forever but her youth probably gave her the strength to overcome and thankfully she returned to her fold.

This though, does not detract from the terrible cultural changes she was forced to endure before she could acclimatise herself to a very different lifestyle. Barbara Crawford also suffered puritanical ridicule from those of the Victorian era, including many historians. They and others that followed took the view, with very little research, that she was a mature married young woman when cast away. It was therefore their belief that this woman should have committed suicide, rather than have allowed a savage to touch her. They who caused Barbara Crawford this ridicule cannot be forgiven for their derogatory statements about one so young and about whom, they did not know the truth.

Barbara was only 13 or 14 when stranded in 1844, her will to live proved greater than the moral code concocted by a prudish Victorian aristocracy. To her, the whole ordeal may have appeared to be just life and at her age, easily put in a back room. The truth is that Barbara Crawford Thompson became part of Australian history and it is sure that in her old age, she would have realised how large a part of our history she really was.

Today, the 'holier than thou' attitude still exists and still condemns her and anyone that a self-righteous society can destroy. Perhaps as a reward for her suffering, little Black Rock Island [Giomalahg] just off Prince of Wales island could be given the name, 'Barbara Crawford Island' for it was the death of a black child at this place, that enabled Barbara to survive.

FIN

WILDFLOWER QUESTIONS

Wildflower Questions have been set down so that readers can adjudicate on questionable sections within the Barbara Crawford story. The Author has recovered vital evidence in her case and has presented several previously unknown facts that are accompanied by documentary evidence in support.

Barbara Crawford's true age on leaving home, her family life and year of arrival in Australia. The disastrous voyage out to Australia. The proof of her marriage to James Adams and other data regarding her story has never before been shown publicly. This newly discovered information is presented here for the first time in the 160 years since these events took place.

The identity of William Thompson, though still hard to prove, appears to have finally given in to investigative reasoning. One must hark back to the way in which this story was presented by her rescuers and subsequent historians to realise the very large array of differences, compared to what is now certified truth.

No matter what, the fact remains that there are several puzzling situations in her history as told by previous writers and we shall deal with those in this question time.
Author

Why did Charles Crawford fail to report his daughter as being missing?

It is highly likely that William Thompson became a good friend of the Crawford family on his visits to Sydney. He was [like the Crawfords] a Scot and if he met with the family in January of 1841 as suspected, he had plenty of time to gain their trust. To all appearances, the only way Thompson could have taken Barbara away from her home would have been either as a wife or domestic servant. This reasoning is arrived at because of the fact that the Crawfords did not report an eloping Barbara, as being missing.

Because Charles Crawford made no complaint to the authorities, an elopement can probably be disregarded. That Charles should allow his daughter to run with a man at her age, even for those times, does not sit well. It is more likely that Charles was deceived into believing that Thompson needed a domestic servant in Brisbane and that was how she was spirited away.

It would have been just a little harder for Thompson to make sure that Charles did not know exactly where he would take Barbara and that Charles Crawford would keep his silence on the matter. Thompson may have had some hold over Charles or perhaps his standing in the police force worried Charles Crawford. This may have been why Charles did not report the matter; perhaps he believed that Thompson could cause him difficulty if he went to the authorities. In fact, Thompson may have known that Charles was or even arranged for him to be involved in a few underhand dealings, later using these to silence Charles. In reality, the fact that Charles Crawford did not try to do anything before Thompson contacted him in May of 1843, two months after they had disappeared, points to Thompson controlling the matter. The Crawford's therefore probably believed that Barbara was working as a domestic servant, until the letter arrived.

Who Was William Thompson?

William Thompson was believed to have drowned at Cape York and because this was universally accepted to be true, his history has apparently never been thoroughly investigated. Personally, I am convinced of the identity of this man and it will be a challenge for other historians to prove otherwise.

No other William Thompson was 'well favored and much liked' by Lieutenant Gorman and Captain Wickham. No other William Thompson had the experience with local natives or had the reputation to cause Ludwig Leichhardt to offer him a position with the Leichhardt expedition to Port Essington in 1844/5.

As Oswald Brierly and Thomas Huxley noted, 'Thompson would have become a person of note in Brisbane had he remained at that place but the temptation had taken him'. I believe that somewhere in Queensland Archives, there is proof that the true Barbara Crawford story has been covered up and that Thompson was well known to the officials at the colony. To admit this would have placed Australian governing officials in a precarious position, leaving them very open to Victorian ridicule, compensation payments and heavy condemnation.

Was William Henry Shetland Thompson really the Man in Barbara's Life?

It is strange that the officials in Brisbane did not investigate the Barbara Crawford Thompson story in depth at the time she was rescued. There were so few men with the name William Thompson in or around Brisbane, yet it appears [on the surface] that his identity was not investigated. The officials in both Brisbane and Sydney knew the comings and goings of all those that visited the Moreton Bay colony up until about 1851. Perhaps they preferred to believe that Thompson had come from places unknown and did not try to find who he was or from whence he had emanated.

Brisbane was still under heavy security while these events were taking place. The populations of both Brisbane and Limestone [Ipswich] combined, in 1843, could hardly have topped a thousand men and women, including military guards etc. It should have been simple to find out where Thompson had his origins and who he was. In fact, if he, as Barbara pointed out, was 'well known and much favoured'; he would have had some registration with the officials on one file or another.

Housing for settlers was not readily available in Moreton Bay and migrants or freed convicts had to be well prepared for a rough lifestyle. They were required to build their own cabins and house themselves without hindrance to the officials or to the dismantling [1844/45] of the penal colony. William Thompson's residence at Limestone [Ipswich], considering he spent 18 months and more at that town, would have also been known to the officials in Brisbane.

The Author has been able to find only three men with the name William Thompson that resided in Brisbane during the period 1840-1845 and only two have a claim in this instance. We have already discussed both in previous chapters and my reasons for accepting W.H.S.Thompson as being Barbara's man are shown.

William Henry Shetland Thompson lived at his shack near Ipswich until his death in 1857. His death occurred, just seven years after Barbara returned to her family. Thompson lived as most others do, with mistakes and errors of judgement disrupting what could have been a successful life.

How Did Thompson purchase a Cutter if he were still a convict?

William Henry Shetland Thompson certainly would have saved a little money over the years he spent as a convict. His work as a convict police constable was paid work and although the money was certainly not a large amount, nor was the buying price for a small cutter. He was considered a free man in 1841and from that time, earned his keep in one fashion or another. It was not until at least July 1844, that he purchased the boat, giving him three years in which to have put aside a few extra pounds.

That money would have come from work done for the penal colony on Durkins boat and doing timber assessments for the government. It should be realised that when convicts were issued with pardons or even tickets-of-leave, they were automatically given the right to purchase materials in connection with the livelihood they chose.

Thompson also managed to buy a small allotment at Ipswich and that, along with the money paid for the cutter, would have left him very low on cash. It is possible that John Durkin had nothing to do with the salvage attempt, he may well have decided to sell his boat and retire back to England, giving his friend a reasonable price.

What was the true position of the wreck of the 'Clarence'?

Richard Rule gave the name of the reef on which the wreck took place as Brampton [or Bampton] Reef or shoal, he gave its position as approximately Lat. 18,40 and Longitude as 150, which should have placed it at or near the Chesterfield and Bampton Island shoals. This information is stored, in letterform, at the State Library of Queensland.

The position given by Richard Rule for the wreck site seems clear but there is a small case for Bramble Reef, which lies about 50 kilometers off Cardwell, North Queensland. It seems odd that most of this story takes place at the tip of Cape York which lies another 900 or so kilometers north of Cardwell.

Whereas the reefs known as Chesterfield and Bampton lie far out into the Pacific some 800 east of Bowen, which is fully 1200 kilometers south of the Cape. Whoever was navigating the 'America' was surely a grand seaman, some of the world's trickiest sailing through uncharted reefs, was done to complete a 2000-kilometer dash to Cape York.

Bramble Reef lies just 400 kilometers south of Cardwell and might well have been the wreck site. It is unlikely that Richard Rule gave the correct position for the wreck, had he done so, this information would have prompted salvage ships to head off after the cargo of whale oil. Maps of the new coastal route through the reefs were readily available at the time 'America' was in the area.

The question is, why then, would the whaler 'Clarence' be fiddling about among the islands of the Great Barrier Reef? The position given by Richard Rule is where a whaler could be expected to be while heading back from a hunt or while chasing whales heading south. So why would a whaling ship be near the mainland among dangerous reefs? Could it be that the crew had a hankering for native women or wanted to trade for Tortoise Shell while on their way home to Sydney. Trading with the natives was becoming popular, anything could be got for a machete or a nail made of iron. Several ships that were on their way home had been reported as trading with the natives for Tortoise Shell prior to 1844.

Would the salvage party have taken the risk of sailing so far [800 klms] out into the Pacific Ocean into a reef-studded environment, without knowing if the wreck was still there? All this tends to have one believe that Rule may have given the incorrect position for the wreck. One that would keep at bay those who might covet her cargo.

Richard Rule knew how to navigate and he knew exactly where the wreck sat. Perhaps the fact that the five survivors from the 'Clarence' were only given stores for four days when they rowed into Brisbane, might have given rise to a few 'sour grapes' toward their employers and the government.

It is likely that the men then looked for someone with a boat, one that would take a risk on salvaging the whale oil. If Richard Rule did not join the Thompson party, then a navigator had to be found and charts were needed for the wreck area. Overall, two sites for the wreck must be considered, Bampton reef, 800 Kilometers east of Bowen and out into the Pacific and Bramble reef some 900 Kilometers south of Cape York and very near the Australian coast.

Did Thompson manage to salvage any oil at the wreck site while in the cutter 'America'?

This is something that probably did happen and would explain the drowning incident where two of the crew was lost while getting firewood. Was it really firewood or oil barrels they were carting? If it were the latter then Thompson may have managed to salvage four or more barrels of oil and bring them with him to Nurapai Island. There is still much confusion and perhaps the truth will never be known but then again, how did the four oil barrels and a South Sea Islander canoe arrive mysteriously at Moreton Island in February 1845?

Did Thompson really drown at Nurapai Island?

It is known that William Henry Shetland Thompson never drowned, he lived out the remainder of his life at Ipswich. Thompson was [Barbara to Brierly] 'an excellent swimmer' and was unlikely to make the mistake of swimming ashore in seas that were too rough, the cutter was atop Madji Reef and in no real danger so why not wait until the seas abated. According to Thompson's qualifications as a bushman [given by Barbara] he was much too experienced to make such a stupid mistake. William Henry Shetland Thompson had made several dangerous swims across flooded rivers and streams in the past. His most recent bout with rough water, took the lives of two of his crew when the cutter's little dingy was swamped in surf. William Thompson quite strongly and capably swam to safety while the two crewmen drowned.

How long was the Cutter at Nurapai Island before Thompson made his swim?

Contrary to our belief, there is a doubt as to how long the three survivors remained on the cutter after it was wrecked. Barbara stated that they were 'with the boat two weeks, when the men grew weak from hunger and decided to swim to Nurapai island'. Barbara quite possibly meant that two weeks had gone by since they left the search area of the wrecked whaler. In which case, the survivors may have only been aboard the wreck for three or four days before the men made their fateful swim. This of course, would throw a small [but only small] spanner in the works if it were correct. The men would have left the wreck on the third or fourth day after the worst of the storm and certainly when the sea was calm enough to make a short swim.

Although this shortens the time spent on the actual wreck of the cutter, it does not prove that William Thompson drowned. It just gives him less time to assess the situation especially if he needed to barter with an unknown tribe of natives. But the man who could ride up to a squadron of 300 spear-packing natives and convince them that all was okay, would surely be able to sign language with a couple of native fishermen. The Torres Strait natives were already in fear of the white man on Badu island and had seen ships and other white men, so if William Henry Shetland Thompson is our man, then he obviously did survive. He is registered as having married in 1846 and raised two children at Ipswich, Queensland. If he is not our man, then someone known as William Thompson did die at Cape York. This man would have been, 'a much favoured and well liked resident of Brisbane', whom everyone, yet no one, knew!

How did Thompson purchase land at Ipswich in 1844, while on a salvage trip?

Thompson made his purchase of land in April of 1844 before leaving Brisbane and paid the total amount [as per the contract] one month after the purchase. He was still in Brisbane when final acceptance of the sale was issued by the Government on August 4, 1844. Thompson was not in Brisbane on November 15, 1844, when the deeds were issued but he was back living at Ipswich, before February 1845. It would have been a simple matter to have someone collect or have the post office hold his deeds until he returned to his home at Limestone.

Would a canoe voyage from Cape York to Brisbane have been difficult?

All sea voyages in small craft are difficult, it should be remembered that Thompson and his crewman had some experience in shoal waters, mainly because they had spent almost three months sailing around in reef waters apparently looking for the wreck of the whaler. Thompson also knew that two crews from two different whalers had already made the voyage to Brisbane quite comfortably in whaleboats. A sea-going canoe would easily have done the same trip in relative safety by staying inside the reef and hugging the coast. It most certainly would not have managed the voyage south without at least one person in command.

What was Barbara Crawford's character?

As one follows her statements and actions during her dramatic teenage years, it is plain to see that she had little fear of life or its pitfalls. Barbara was probably a precocious child who found it easy to commune with adults. She had been outgoing enough at twelve to befriend William Thompson and therefore it is possible, that she may have even taken it into her head to run away with him. The problem arising from this is the same, why did her parents not go to the police, when she first went missing?

It is probable that Barbara was an attention seeker who, because she was one of eight children, needed to be noticed. She may have found the father figure she perhaps needed, in William Thompson. He could give her the solitary attention that she might have craved. This scenario perhaps eventuated whilst near the hotel next door to her home. She is much more likely though to have been an innocent victim of a self-assured William Thompson who found a safe way to lure Barbara to Brisbane with her parent's permission.

Did Barbara try to protect Thompson from officialdom?

It is not only possible but it seems highly probable. William Thompson would have given Barbara simple schooling in what she should say to anyone who might rescue her. She knew that she could not leave the wreck of the cutter because she could not swim. She also knew that she would be a hinderance on board an overloaded canoe.

This made it easy for Thompson to be rid of an encumbrance that would bring him nothing but trouble on his return to Brisbane. He told Barbara that if he did not return for her, it was because the sea had taken him. She should therefore tell whoever rescued her, that he had drowned at Nurapai and she should always stick to that story. It is amazing that nobody noticed that exactly the same information regarding

Thompson's death and the loss of the cutter had been released to the public almost four years before the only survivor and therefore only witness could report the events. Barbara Crawford, being the only living survivor of the whole drama, was still at Prince of Wales Island when the story first came out.

From her records, Barbara always spoke highly of William Thompson. Her thoughts of him were probably hero worship taken on when he first came into contact with the Crawford family. She, like many other young females, exhibited enormous loyalty to the man who was first to be sexually involved with her. It can only be expected that she would not let the officials know all of the details surrounding her abandonment. This perhaps, could be one of the answers to our next question.

Why has Barbara received little publicity during the 160 years, since these events took place?

Barbara Crawford's five-year ordeal at Cape York has been one of the great little known histories of early Australia. Even the three weeks spent by Eliza Fraser among mainland natives, overwhelms the Barbara Crawford story. Perhaps the reason is that so little was known and therefore, too little could be written down, to compile a good story. Another factor is that Barbara did co-habit with a black man and this was a forbidden item in Australia, even forty years prior to the 21st century.

Also, Barbara was an intelligent girl and probably did not tell all that she knew about William Thompson or her time with him. She loved him dearly and probably had no idea of his real fate. She did not tell the truth about her age when questioned and everyone who has written about her since she was rescued, has treated her as a fully mature woman and not as the child she really was.

This has given writers and historians the fuel to treat her memory with disdain, some even calling her derogatory names and relating to her with racist overtones. In comparison, Eliza Fraser was vociferous and many statements were made in relation to her time with natives. A film was made of Eliza's story, which denoted her as being more of a comedic tart than what she really was.

In regard to the possible cover-up of the whole affair by officials and Barbara herself. This may have been arranged intentionally. At first by the three scientists aboard the HMS 'Rattlesnake' and then, when Barbara was brought home, the governor down played the whole affair. Barbara and her parents may have also preferred her story to be kept quiet.

Did Barbara officially marry William Thompson in Brisbane?

No, not officially, even if Charles and/or Jane Crawford had given their permission. There is no record of a marriage, nor is one registered anywhere in New South Wales marriage records. [Queensland as a state, did not exist at that time]. Only a faked marriage or one in the style of 'Gretna Green', could be the answer but this did not constitute legal marriage in Australia.

What happened to Barbara's 'wedding ring'?

Barbara claimed that Thompson had married her and when asked by Brierly, what happened to her wedding ring, she replied that she kept it hanging from a string round her neck. At night she would look at it and cry. She stated that the native women did not like this show of sadness for her past life as a ghost and they took the ring and threw it into the fire.

This explanation was probably put forward to stem the embarrassment of not being married to Thompson. Natives do love ornamental objects and a golden ring [it may also have been made of wood or even copper] would have had many uses in the islander society. It is more likely, that if Thompson did give her a ring, she gave it away or it was stolen. The explanation for the loss of her wedding ring hints at the similar occurrence in the Eliza Fraser story. That woman hid her wedding ring on a belt made from native twine. The Eliza Fraser story was well known in Brisbane when Barbara began living at that place and Barbara may have 'borrowed' a little.

Was Barbara only twelve when she 'eloped' with Thompson?

Barbara Crawford was born between July 13, 1830 and July 12, 1831, this would give the registered age of 6 years attributed to her when the ship 'John Barry' arrived at Spring Cove in July 1837. The shipping record lists all of the Crawford children in order of age, beginning with Alexander and ending with Andrew, there was a space of approximately two years between each birth. All are listed as being born in Dundee and not in Aberdeen from which place their parents originated. These records are deemed to be accurate because there was no benefit to the Crawford family by them giving the wrong age for the children. Food rations and tickets were given as per the age of the children and any falsification of age would have only been to the detriment of the family.

Barbara's birth date [as proffered by the Author] would have fallen at some time in November of 1830, perhaps between the 20th and the 25th of that month. The reasoning is that Barbara probably waited until she had turned twenty-one years old in November 1851, before marrying her beau, James Adams. It is unlikely that Charles and Jane would have wanted to lose their daughter for a second time, especially as Barbara had only returned home 22 months before her marriage to Adams.

Charles Crawford was aged 30 and Jane Crawford 29, when they arrived in Australia in July 1837, their oldest child [Alexander] 14 years and the second youngest [Andrew] was aged 2 years. The baby of the family is not named in records but was 6 weeks old when the family disembarked in Sydney. The accuracy of the ship's passenger list in showing the age for each of the family is undoubted. This is proven by cross checking the list with the age given on death certificates, for those of the Crawford family we have found.

Jane Crawford [the mother] was 29 when she arrived in Australia and this age tallies correctly with her death in 1853 when she was she was 45 years old. Her youngest daughter [Jane] was 4 years old when the 'John Barry' arrived in Sydney in 1837. She married Henry Whittall in July 1851 and required her fathers consent. This shows that she was under twenty-one at the time. She was in fact nineteen years old. Her death certificate stating she was 36 in 1868, is the final proof that the ship's passenger list was correct. There are many statements referring to Barbara's young age made by Brierly and his companions while aboard HMS 'Rattlesnake'. As the age given for each member of the family are proven correct in all records available, it would be presumptuous to believe that only Barbara was shown with an incorrect age. Had Barbara been 16 years old when she eloped [as she claimed] she would have been a twin to Mary and this fact is never mentioned. Shipping officials would have also noticed the difference in age between a six-year-old and a child of ten. There was absolutely no reason for Barbara to be wrongly listed. Food supplies and ticket expenses were not affected until after age twelve. To give the reader some idea of Barbara Crawford's age at the important times during her life, one should note that she was six years old when the 'John Barry' arrived in Sydney in July 1837.

Therefore, if Barbara had been born in November 1830 she would have been 12 years and 4 months old when she went to Brisbane with Thompson in March 1843. She was 13, almost 14 years old when she was deposited with the Kaurarega in early November 1844 and 18 years old, when rescued in October 1849. She was 19 when she arrived back in Sydney in February 1850. Barbara Crawford [or Thompson] was 21 years old when she married James Adams on 25 November 1851. She, unlike Jane, [2 years her junior] did not need her fathers consent and probably waited until perhaps the day after she had turned 21 for that reason.

Barbara Crawford Thompson Adams was probably 81 or 82 years old at the alleged time of her death in 1912, that year as the year for her demise has yet to be proven.

Was Thompson 'well known and much favoured' by Captain Wickham

Captain Wickham did not arrive in Brisbane until early 1843; he had just over 17 months to become aquainted with Thompson, who would have spent much of his time at Ipswich, 50 miles up river. It is more likely that Thompson's record spoke for him and the officials probably went by this, rather than having other than the occasional meeting with him. It is probable that Barbara did not see any of the people she spoke about. Leichhardt, Wickham, Gorman and Simpson would not have been on Thompson's list of people that Barbara should meet.

The statement by Barbara, that Thompson was 'much favoured and well liked in the Moreton Bay colony' absolutely reassures us of William Thompson's identity. There was no other 'well known' William Thompson living in or around Brisbane at the same time as William Henry Shetland Thompson.

It was only he, who had the bushcraft to merit an invitation from Ludwig Leichhardt. Had he not been with Barbara and already made arrangements to go on the salvage operation, he surely would have taken up Leichhardts invitation. Barbara Crawford showed much admiration for her William Thompson. Her memory of how he was invited to go with Leichhardt's expedition was still strong after five years apart from her man. This part of her story re-assures us that Barbara Crawford was a very intelligent young lady, who knew the importance of the events of her time.

Did Ludwig Leighhardt really invite Thompson to join his overland expedition to Port Essington?

When asked about William Thompson, Barbara quite happily described to Brierly this mans importance, she told how Leichhardt approached Thompson to act as guide for the expedition, based on Thompson's knowledge of the area and native tribes in Southeast Queensland. Her statement is somewhat borne out by a letter to the Colonial Secretary [sent by Leichhardt four years later] requesting that the convict Thomas Hand, be allowed to accompany the 1848 fateful expedition to Western Australia, from Brisbane. Thompson had refused Leichhardt in 1844 and therefore, no official request was made at that time. Brierly and Huxley were also convinced of this fact, so there is no reason to doubt Barbara on this point.

How did William Henry Shetland Thompson meet his fate?

William Henry Shetland Thompson married Frances Handcock in 1846, he sired two children by her and both his offspring died eight weeks apart, in 1867. The girl Elizabeth [19] died in childbirth and her brother Francis, died two months later at age 18 years. Thompson worked at R.J Smith's boiling down works at Ipswich and he was still gainfully employed there as a superintendent in 1850. William Henry Shetland Thompson died of natural causes, aged 65 years in 1857. He was buried at the Ipswich cemetery. Not one of his Australian line survived, both of his children by Frances Handcock died, without having children.

Was it possible that another William Thompson took Barbara from her family?

No, there was really no other possible contender for this role, the only other Thompson at Moreton Bay, was the Englishman, William Henry Thomson, who was sent to Moreton Bay about 1833 when almost through his original sentence. He was a Roman Catholic who was sentenced to seven years in 1827. He committed a minor crime in Sydney for which he received 18 months on top of his original 7year sentence. He was sent to serve the rest of his time as a second offender at the Brisbane penal colony. After examining the convict muster for the ship 'Marquis of Hastings' and convict records for the Moreton Bay colony, I am convinced that he could not have been connected to Barbara Crawford.

This mans release from servitude was due in 1836, one year before Barbara Crawford arrived in Sydney as a six-year-old. What became of him after his release is not known. He had no claim to notoriety at the penal colony and apparently served out his time and disappeared. He did not end his days in either Brisbane or Ipswich.

William Henry Shetland Thompson is the only man of that name who had any firm connection with the Moreton Bay officials and it is undoubted [by the Author] that it was he, Shetland Thompson, who was Barbara Crawford's lover. Of course there were many other men named William Thompson in the British Empire but none with the connections in Brisbane or with the fame and bushcraft required for Leighhardt to have made his invitation.

Why did Barbara not have children to Thompson while living with him for 20 months?

This is a question not easily answered. Barbara did spend at least twenty months with Thompson and could easily have fallen pregnant during that time. It is possible that Thompson realised that while Barbara was so young, problems could arise during a pregnancy that would bring the couple under notice. Thompson therefore probably took the precautions necessary and available at the time, to reduce the possibility that she might indeed fall pregnant. He was in no position to support a child when they first arrived in Brisbane and a pregnancy would certainly call unwanted attention to them.

Did Barbara traditionally marry the warrior Boroto?

Without solid evidence, only the word of those who first made contact with Barbara can be heeded. Oswald Brierly does not broach the subject properly, nor does Thomas Huxley but John MacGillivray stated categorically that Boroto was the husband of Barbara Crawford and that it was Barbara who told him so.

It is noticeable that Barbara never talks about nor visits with Boroto's mother [Yowah] while living among the natives. This was forbidden to wives of the Kuarareg men of Murralahg. Wives were allowed some discourse with their fathers in law but not with their Mothers in law. Barbara only meets Eengar [Ingar] Boroto's father, on very few occasions and never mentions Yowah except to say that she was Boroto's mother.

Besides this, John MacGillivray [Naturalist and Artist] stated that this was why Boroto was being possessive of her. Once she had joined the 'Rattlesnake' at Evans Bay, Boroto became increasingly nervous. MacGillivray had been concerned about the way Boroto was behaving and after asking Barbara, she told him the reason as to why Boroto was so upset.

Victorian morals forbade the revelation of a liaison between a savage headhunter and a white woman and it is likely that it is this that caused the three scientists to report that Barbara had a little trouble remembering her English. They had to find some way for Barbara not being able to answer the more embarrassing questions. MacGillivray's testimony, that Barbara was traditionally married to Boroto, is evidence enough for most.

When Barbara made the statement to her native girl friend, that she 'had no husband or child to cook for'. Almost all that have read or studied Brierly's reports, seized upon this to demonstrate that she was never married to a savage. Barbara was a young girl who was well entrenched in the native lifestyle and the statement she made, possibly referred to the fact that her husband Boroto, was off with her son doing what boys do when they fish and hunt. She was stating the obvious to the girl, 'He is your husband, you cook for him, I don't have a husband to cook for, he is away. I have only myself to look after'.

Those who state that Barbara had no native 'husband' put MacGillivray's statements in contempt and place a slur on that scientist's character. The whole episode now becomes extremely contentious. John MacGillivray was a very learned man and his questioning of Barbara Crawford has proved to be just as accurate as that done by Huxley and Brierly.

Brierly probably attempted to use her statement [Authors opinion] to mislead people and cover up the truth, perhaps only for Barbara's sake. However gallant this may have appeared, the historic facts should not have been so completely covered to protect her reputation.

If all this does not satisfy, another possibility is that Barbara was just being sarcastic when she admonished Wamati. This came about because of Boroto's affair with Yu-ree. Barbara was noticeably angered whenever the affair was mentioned and she may have been telling Wamati that she no longer felt that Boroto was her husband.

Barbara Crawford is owed much for the assistance she gave the scientists aboard the British warship and to the missionaries who learned much from her reports about the natives of Cape York.

Thereafter, the missionaries spent much time preying on the natives in an effort to convert them. If these missions were still operating perhaps a prayer of thanks for Barbara Crawford would be in order as little else has been done in her memory.

Did Barbara have children to Boroto?

It never ceases to amaze how some writers fail miserably when it comes to having even a little understanding of human nature. Almost all writers on this subject discard the possibility of Barbara having associated herself with a male native.

This young lady arrived on Murralahg while still only 13 years old. Once she had mastered the language and lifestyle of the natives, she would have also heeded the call of the wild. This was the same for almost all other whites who spent living time among native tribes. Why writers wish to have Barbara appear to have lived her life on Murralahg as some type of spiritual nun, is beyond common sense and all reason.

Some writers have stated that Barbara was a 'Marki' [ghost] and that natives would not have sexual relationships with ghosts. This reasoning does not hold water. Wee-nie was also a Marki and yet he had three wives and all bore him children. It must be remembered that Barbara was only thirteen when she was cast away in the Torres Strait. She had already been in a liaison with William Thompson while still in her puberty. It would have soon become obvious to her, that she needed husband protection from one of the men of the islands. Her native 'parents' would have been happy to receive the much larger bride price that a 'Marki' would bring.

Barbara made various comments in her descriptions of life among the natives, many of these hint at her sexual freedom and the probability of having mothered children. She talks of how old QuiQui was the grandfather of the tribe and that all mothers took their children to him for naming. Oswald Brierly, who recorded all that Barbara told him just after her rescue, writes that she told him of an old native named QuiQui who gave names to newborn children. She felt that the old man was a bit of a wag because [Barbara to Brierly]---- 'when the first child came [a girl] he named it Ootzoo' ['Muddy Water']------. Her statement had begun and trailed off just as it is written here and I believe it showed that Barbara had already told Brierly [in an aside] that she had given birth to at least two children on the island.

She said nothing regarding the parentage of this 'first child' and her statement to Brierly on this subject, had abruptly ended. The muddy water reference was definitely aimed at the skin color of the child and Barbara told Brierly that this is the reason that she called QuiQui a 'bit of a wag'. Her statement, 'When the first child came', whilst not stating whose first child it was, tends to give credence to my opinion, that she did have children at Murralahg.

Brierly faithfully recorded all parents and their children, yet he does not list Ootzoo's parentage. He and also records a small boy named Numa who went with Barbara and a few others in the canoe that took her to the little island of Wamilahg. This was a couple of days before her meeting with the white men from the 'Rattlesnake'. Although Numa is also on the scene when Barbara is in talks with the officers and men, Brierly still does not give the parentage of the boy. Boroto brought Numa to Evans Bay and could have been the father but Tomagugu was also there and Barbara records the mainland native as being the father.

The boy Numa disappears from her care when Barbara waits to take the final voyage from Wamilahg to the Evans Bay. Boroto had already left Barbara and gone fishing and it is possible that the boy Numa was with him at that time. Numa is not mentioned again until he arrives with Boroto while Barbara is meeting with the white men. It is possible that the boy Numa also belonged to Boroto and Barbara. Her warrior husband kept the boy with him so that Barbara would not run away, only bringing him back when Boroto knew that Barbara was already with the white men.

Barbara told Oswald Brierly that the child belonged to Tomagugu. A possible proof of this comes when Tomagugu takes the first shirt offered to Barbara as a covering by the marine washing party, giving the shirt to Numa. If the child did belong to Tomagugu and Sibi, why was the child living on Murralahg and not on Wammilahg [several miles distance] where Tomagugu and his wife now lived and why was the child with Boroto and not Tomagugu?

It was also bad for Tomagugu to take a shirt from Barbara without first being offered the gift unless he were giving it to her own child. Boy children did stay with the women until they were about six or seven years of age so it is very possible that Boroto kept three year old Numa with him to keep Barbara from running away.

Boy children were highly thought of among natives and Boroto would have believed it impossible that Barbara would ever want to give him up. Records may exist in missionary files or from Somerset house showing the parentage of Numa and Ootzoo and although it is unlikely that Barbara Crawford [or Barbara Thompson] would be mentioned as mother, Boroto may be listed as their sire.

As for Tomagugu, he was a mainland native like his father Tchaikow. His mainland mother [Paruna] was already dead when these events occurred. Tchaikow [father of Tomagugu] was related to the Kaurarega through his mother, an old woman named Sasumuy, who was a full blood Kaurarega and who was still alive when Barbara went back to the white world.

Numa [Authors belief] was not the child of Tomagugu and Sibi and this was known by Brierly. He displays this in his journals by not giving the names of the parents of Numa or the girl Ootzoo. It was totally unlike Brierly to not list the children's parentage, all other children that became known to him or those whom Barbara mentioned, had their parentage meticulously recorded, even the mothers and fathers of well known adults were registered. In fact all native names appearing in this work are names sent down to us by Brierly and John MacGillivray. When reading Brierly's journal, it can easily be seen how meticulous he was.

It is the Authors opinion, that Barbara had two [and probably only two] children by Boroto. Both children would have spent a good deal of time with their grandparents [Barbara's adoptive mother and father] according to and as per native tradition. Had Barbara remained at Murralahg, she would have seen less of Numa, as he grew older. The boy and girl would have been under the care of Gameena while Barbara worked and in the evenings, the family would have come together at the village.

So Barbara probably had a female first born. Ootzoo was born one year before the boy Numa and during the first 18months of Barbara's stay with the islanders. Barbara's statement that 'when the first child came', leans toward her having had two children. Therefore, the year of birth for the children would have been Ootzoo in late 1846 and Numa in late 1847. Barbara may have had a third pregnancy and this might have been why she did not try to join the 'Rattlesnake' when it arrived at the Cape in October 1848. If Numa was not the child of Barbara and Boroto, then her second child may have been stillborn in 1848, when she was unable to go to the ship. Her statement that she had fever at this time does not ring true; she was more than probably well entrenched in the native lifestyle and happy with her lot at that time. Once Boroto started his affair with Yuree, Barbara made the decision to return to her own kind.

Was Barbara a prisoner of the Kaurarega?

This is an extremely interesting point, Barbara mentioned to Oswald Brierly, that she was brought to the small island of Wammilahg from Murralahg while attempting to gain her freedom. Barbara sailed to Wammilahg aboard the big outrigger named 'Bidtham' and mentioned that this sea-going canoe was partially owned by Tomagugu, who had bought it in partnership with Alekki and old Salali. This was apparently because of having lost his first canoe. This conjures up the thought that William Thompson did manage to get Tomagugu's original canoe by barter or by theft. Barbara was allowed to leave Murralahg Island to visit the spirit ship when the Kaurarega decided they could use her to get a better supply of iron tools and biscuits from the 'Rattlesnake'. Barbara was taken to Wammilahg Island, from where she could see HMS 'Rattlesnake'. Here, she was apparently watched, to see what her reaction would be.

Finally, Barbara was very angry with Boroto over the Yuree affair and Boroto, knowing this, may have begun to suspect that she was ready to leave him. When Boroto arrived back at Wamilahg shortly after the mainlanders left with Barbara, he found or was informed that she had escaped and he quickly set out on her trail, arriving at the Cape a short time after she did.

Barbara had already begun talking to the white men when Boroto arrived and he thereafter refused to be parted from her. Overall, Barbara had only to escape from Boroto and not from the rest of the tribal peoples around Cape York. She did this with the help of Tomagugu and the mainland blacks who knew they would be rewarded for bringing Barbara back to her own.

Did Barbara lose her mother tongue?

Not likely, she may not have remembered some words but she herself stated that when first she contacted the white men Tomagugu was trying to tell them that he had saved her from the sea. Barbara told Tomagugu to hold his tongue for she could tell them herself.

Barbara states that she kept up her knowledge of the English language by singing songs she had learned as a child. This may have helped but almost from the first hour on board ship, she is away and rattling in English. She does occasionally stop to think of a word but she definitely 'Talk too much that one, alla time talk talk talk'.

An interesting remark Brierly made about Barbara, occurred when he questioned her a few days after the rescue, he states; 'Mrs Thompson told me how they [the natives] use part of an iron bark tree to repair canoes. She said that she knew these trees, from having lived in the bush near Brisbane. She then she proceeded to name quite a few different types of tree'.

This does not come into line with his previous statements, 'that she struggled to remember her language'. It also shows that whoever William Thompson was, he did have a good knowledge of Australian flora. Such an incredible amount of knowledge, from a girl that they referred to as 'intelligent but quite illiterate', leads one to believe that Barbara's reputation was definitely being protected by Oswald Brierly and Thomas Huxley. She may not have been able to read and write and she probably did struggle with a few words but she would never have forgotten her language in the space of only five years. It is only when we come to the question of whom and from where came the mysterious William Thompson, that Barbara finds language difficulty.

Footnote: Brierly also noted that Barbara spoke her English without the loss of her broad Scottish accent and that she understood seaman Scott better than the other crew members.

Was Weenie [Wini] of Badu Island the wild man he was made out to be?

Ion Idriess in his semi-fictional works on the subject was probably very right about the character Weenie [Wini]. Perhaps he was just as violent as Idriess made him out to be, why else would he end up with police sniper bullets in him, at age seventy?

Sarcasm aside, Barbara stated that Wee-nie had told her that he had killed his four companions before he was wrecked on the island of Badu [Mulgrave Island]. This shows Wee-nie in a rather savage light but it may have only been pretentious bluff by a middle-aged man, trying to impress a young white girl and promote his savage reputation among the Kaurarega. It may also have been semi-truth in that Wee-nie was in fact relating the deaths of four white crewmen from the ship 'Thomas Lord' which vessel at one time visited Badu.

The overall truth about Wee-nie is that two native brothers accepted him as their father and he became well liked by them because of his new ways of repairing their canoes. Their real father had probably been an elder of the tribe and in accepting Wee-nie; they would have placed him [Wee-nie] in a powerful position. As he grew older among them, his position was enhanced because of the native tradition of respect for their elders. Barbara also stated that Wee-nie was a very polite man who treated her respectfully.

Has proof been found that Barbara Crawford married [or remarried] after her return to civilisation?

Barbara Crawford [or Thompson] married James Adams in November 1851, just 20 months after she returned to Sydney. It is possible that he was a sea captain or a sailor and may have taken Barbara back to England. Aside from funeral notices in the Sydney Herald in August 1853, giving the date for the funeral of her mother Jane, on the 26th of that month, there is no mention of Barbara or her family after that time.

In fact, her father Charles also disappears along with Alexander, Charles Jnr, Mary, Ann, Andrew and the youngest child. Charles Crawford and his family may have returned to their native Scotland after the terrible trauma they had suffered. Of Barbara's family, only Jane Crawford [mother] and Jane Crawford Whittall [sister] have known graves in Sydney. There is a vague record of a Charles Crawford dying in Sydney in 1860 but the reference does not prove it is our Charles Crawford. There is also a reference to a Charles and Jane Crawford, having been removed from the old Sydney cemetery for re-burial when that cemetery closed. The person who had them re-interred, was a Barbara Donahue but I was unable to gain further information on this exhumation. If the rest of the Crawford family did remain in Australia, I have not taken too much effort to find them; someone else can do the digging. As far as I am concerned, they can remain in peace.

Barbara's native relations

To understand the relationships that the natives of Northern Australia and the Torres Strait islands had with their families, it should be noted that natives did not consider cousins in the way of the whites. A cousin to them was a small brother and an uncle or aunt was a small father or small mother. Barbara stated on many occasions that this man was her brother and this woman was her mother and this was, for a short time, confusing to Brierly.

What was the fate of the Kaurarega people of Murralahg Island?

Most of the true Kaurareg of Murralahg Island were massacred after they were blamed for the deaths of about 16 Chinese and 2 whites [probably Mr and Mrs Gascoine of Melbourne] while the group was fishing for Trepang in the area. Apparently natives killed all of the men but the woman managed to escape onto Murralahg Island, where she was later found in a terribly dehydrated condition by her rescuers. She died before she could be returned to civilisation and it is said that a group of whites led by the Jardine's from Somerset House slaughtered the Kaurarega.

Only a few Kaurarega remained scattered across the Torres Strait islands through inter-marriage after the slaughter. The language of the Kaurarega was spoken by many of the islanders, including the Baduans and some of the mainland peoples. A little of the language is still spoken by some families, even today.

A land rights claim was submitted in 2001 by islanders proclaiming themselves as original Kaurareg people from Murralahg [Prince of Wales] Island. It is probable that they are indeed relatives of the Murralahg Island people who did not return to the island after the killings. It was not until after the second world war that some islanders began re-settling near the area. An equal claim was lain by these people for parts of Nurapai Island, which was really only a garden island and fishing area for all peoples in the area of Cape York.

Since the terrible massacre, Prince of Wales Island has been held in awe by the regional natives, many feel that there are ghosts haunting that place although this rumour may have been spread to stop them from returning. It is said that none will return to live there and this is of course, a sad superstition that is denying them the rights to land that is historically theirs. Perhaps education could induce them to return to Murralahg where they could open a tourist attraction to the memory of the Kaurarega and to their spirit woman Barbara 'Gioma' Crawford Thompson.

Why did Barbara give up her life among the natives?

Barbara Crawford Thompson spent five of her 'growing up' years among the natives of Murralahg Island. She was very well entrenched in the native lifestyle and probably would have remained with them had it not been for a few problems that arose. Barbara had begun to feud with Yu-ree over Boroto. Her jealousy over the affair combined with the danger that Yu-ree now posed to Barbara's life, brought about a change in Barbara's feelings toward her native husband.

Fate then brought about a possible escape from her troubles and as she no longer felt the same about Boroto, she decided to depart from her lifestyle as soon as a chance presented itself. Boroto enjoyed the attentions of two women and was probably strutting about like a Peacock but when Barbara went aboard the 'Rattlesnake' his true feelings came to the fore.

Barbara left not only Boroto but perhaps her own two small children as well. This thought may not sit well with most mothers but the truth of the times was, that mix race children would not be accepted in Victorian society while the mother of such children would come under ridicule from all quarters.

Barbara made the decision to leave her children knowing that they would be well looked after by their extended family. While on the island, she had much less to do with the little ones than she would have done in civilised society. Even so, she must have been torn apart many times during the nine weeks the ship remained at Evans Bay.

Did Barbara begin a career as a fairground exhibit?

Barbara Crawford like Eliza Fraser may have been induced to make money from her drama. Eliza Fraser achieved this by fraud and by playing the part of a 'Wild White Woman' at fairgrounds in England. If Barbara did try to earn money on the show circuit, it would have been a sad and ignominious end to such a dramatic part of her life. Adelaide Lubbock [Owen Stanley's biographer] made these comments about Barbara but she may have confused the Eliza Fraser story with that of Barbara Crawford.

Did Australian officials hide the truth about Barbara Crawford?
The Author believes that such was the case.

As more people become interested in our colonial past, it is hoped that somewhere in a dark dusty corner of some musty Australian or English filing office the truth will be found. Perhaps it will show that William Thompson's history has been totally expunged and that Barbara's Crawford's story has too little documentation.

It is interesting to note from the Kennet report on the Torres Strait natives in 1869, that the officials were interested in what had happened to the native warrior Boroto. Why did they have any interest in this man at all if he were an insignificant warrior? To all extents and purposes, they denied that Boroto had any real personal connection with Barbara Crawford Thompson

Countless tales of Australia's colonial history remain hidden far from home, perhaps much of this history could be found in Captain Wickham's diaries or the diary of Surgeon John Thomson of HMS 'Rattlesnake'. These works are obviously held somewhere in France or England and would prove very interesting reading.

On a final note, Barbara Crawford has been an inspiration to the Author, her bravery, her will to live and her strength of character, especially while facing acute embarrassment during her rescue, can only be commended. The purpose of this work on her life and times has been to widen the very narrow minded approach to the history of Barbara Crawford Thompson Adams.

She has been very badly treated by history and historians alike. Barbara Crawford, as an important part of our Australian colonial history, has not received the credit she deserves. Her story is a vital part of our heritage and as such, must be given its true standing.
Author.

The family and friends of Barbara Crawford Thompson were:

Charles Crawford: Her father
Jane Crawford: Her mother
Alexander Crawford: Her oldest brother
Charles Crawford Junior: Her second brother
Mary Crawford: Her oldest sister
Ann Crawford: Her second sister
Jane Crawford: Her youngest sister
Andrew Crawford: Her younger brother
Baby Crawford: The youngest sibling [name and sex unknown]
William Henry Shetland Thompson: Her defacto husband
John Durkin: convict constable and boat owner.
Richard Rule: Possible navigator of the cutter 'America'.
James Davis: Escapee and ticket-of-leave convict at Brisbane town.
Thomas Dowse: Ticket-of-leave convict, newspaperman and finally real estate agent.
Tomagugu: native of Cape York and Wammilahg island
Alekki: native of Murralahg [Prince of Wales island]
Chief Peaquee: native elder of Murralahg father of 'Gioma'
Gameena: wife of Peaquee, mother of 'Gioma' [Barbara]
Urdzana: native aunt of Gioma [Murralahg]
Saapor: husband of Urdzana
Urdzana: [wife of Saapor] Aunt to Gioma
Wagal: Son of Salali and Aburda friend of Barbara
Nooma: Son of Salali and Aburda friend of Barbara
Wamati; Daughter of Salali and Aburda, friend of Barbara
Auda: Daughter of Salali and Aburda, friend of Barbara.
Urdzanna: [wife of Boroto's brother Gunagi] sister-in-law to Gioma
Soanna: Mother of Amooee

Amooee: daughter of Soanna, friend of Barbara

Weenee: [Wini] white warrior of Badu

Queen Baki; Friend and woman of the Goodangarkai tribe of mainland aboriginals

Kugi: [young flying fox] son of Saapor [Flying Fox] small brother [cousin] of Gioma

Kuki: [Monsoon] native woman of Murralahg

Ras: [Thunderhead clouds] daughter of Kuki

Boroto: warrior of Murralahg, hus.band of 'Gioma' [Barbara]

Gunagi: warrior and brother of Boroto, husband of Urdzanna [Murralahgi natives]

Eerawee: native girl and friend of Gioma [Barbara]

Sibi: wife of Tommagugu and friend of Gioma Barbara].

Qui Qui: elder of Murralahg and name giver to children

Ingar: [Eengar] father of Boroto, native of Murralahg.

Yu-ree: [Yuri] girlfriend of Boroto and opponent of Barbara

Ootzoo: girl child of Murralahg light skin [Muddy Water]

Numa: Boy child of Murralahg [Gioma's son?]

Numah; Native warrior of Murralahg

Yowar: [wife of Ingar], mother of Boroto

Aap: male native of Murralahg

Meakool: native and probable witch doctor of the Cape, dreamer whose dreams usually came true

Kolletta: a mainland native girl of Cape York

The Goodangarkai [Garkai] mainland natives; of Cape York

Sergeant Mew: [marines] of HMS 'Rattlesnake'

Marine Lord: [marines] HMS 'Rattlesnake'

Coxswain Scott: of 'Rattlesnake'

Surgeon Dr Thomson: of 'Rattlesnake'

Officers: Inskip, Yule and Smith: of HMS 'Rattlesnake'

Surgeon Schloss: of 'Bramble'

Captain Owen Stanley: master of HMS 'Rattlesnake'

Officers and crewmen aboard the HMS 'Rattlesnake'

Captain Levien: of the 'Byng'

Thomas Huxley: assistant surgeon HMS 'Rattlesnake'

John MacGillivray: Naturist HMS 'Rattlesnake'

James Adams: husband of Barbara November 1851

Henry Whittall: Brother-in-law of Barbara Crawford Thompson Adams

Higginson Eddison: Witness at both weddings for the Crawford sisters [Barbara and Jane].

Of course there were many natives that were named who lived on Murralahg with Barbara while she played her role as Gioma. Brierly only relates a few connections to Barbara and naming all of these people would be contrary to native culture. These people are now at rest.

MEMORIAL DICTIONARY TO THE KAURAREGA AND THEIR NGYA-OOMEE LANGUAGE

The mini-dictionary listed below was written by Oswald Brierly and John MacGillivray and translated by Barbara Crawford Thompson. It has been arranged here from scattered notes left to us by Oswald Brierly by the Author, Raymond J Warren. It is recorded here with salutations to the Kaurarega peoples of the Torres Strait.

A

Aba-ipa [fem; shiver/shale] Abane [ours] Abepa/Abeepa [for; when held or kept for a male i.e. for him]. Adabu [salt-water] Adoamma [true brother/ brother from same mother] Aibol [summer] Aidu [food] Aibolo [summer] Aikeka [fem form of the word for i.e. ngai aikeka=for me (spoken by Barbara)]. Aiyeiwu [come here] Ajir [shame] Albi [we/us] Albi Nipa [for us] Alpa [let, as in us] Allai [husband] Alpa [let] Amma [mother] Anna [me/mine]. Apu [mother when talking of] Ari [rain] Ari [both/we/] Ari-gi [both/too many] Ari Nipa [for us all]. Atzir [speak/talk] Barbara's statement to Tomagugu, 'Komi, ari-gi ari-gi, atzir nathya Krongipa' Translated to Brierly as 'Friend, talk not, I can understand them. [It probably should have translated as 'Friend, both talking not [or] both not talking, I can tell them myself'].

B

Baba [father] Badu [Badu island] Baguma [lightning] Baow [waves] Barudder [Mud] Beidum [shark] Beibassam [eyebrow] Bisi [Sago] Bobata [grandfather] Bom [Pandanus fruit] Bubbu [stream] Buyeri [flame]

C

Chena [that] Chena wir [give that].

D

Dadje [long grass skirt] Dagie [Jupiter] Dana Nuki [spring water or tears] Dana [eye] Dapar [cloud] Doama [yellow ochre] Doopa [fever] Du-yama [thunder] Dza [affix; of]

E

Ekai [milk]

F

Fimi [what?]

G

Gamu [cold] Ganu [smell] Gariga [Sun] Gariga-Titure [morning star] Garkai [black fellow] Garkaji [Australian mainland native tribes] Garu [cane] Garwulgeepa [wash] Gata [shoal water] Gi [Gh-ee Negative of anything/nothing / none/no i.e. Nga ajir gi, she (has) shame none/not] Gioma-lahg [Black rock Island] Gni [yours] Gni-ipi [your wife]. Gooden-Garkai [mainland natives of northern Cape York Australia. This may have been a pidgin name meaning good blackfellows] Guba [wind] Gurri-koop [garden] Gowarra [swamp] Gizu [sharp]

I

Ibara [Crocodile] Ideepa [untie] Ikai [breasts] Inguje [urine] In-ee [male genitalia] Inilee [male] Inur [night] Ipi [wife] ipika [wife] Ipikajille [wives] Ipikai [married woman Ipikai-kage [young wife] Ira [father/mother in law] Ira-guda [lips]

J

Je [sky] Jille [plural; to be added on to a word]

K

Kaba [to dance] Kada [to stand] Kadi-tanure [stand up] Kage [child] Kai-eda [old woman] Kaibu [spear?] Kaikuru [testicles] Kainidung [new moon] Kalaka Mura [have arrived?]. Kaman [Heart] Kami [friend fem to male] Kanrabi [corroboree/festival/sing sing] Kanu-meepa [tie/bind] Kaow-quiku [young man] Kapi [light] Kapi-kissuri [moonlight] Karomat [brown snake] Kassur [creek]
Kata-murra [banana] Kaura [ear or small island] Kaurareg [native of Murralahg Island] Kaurarega [tribal group of Murralahg Island] Kawki/Keimagi [friend male to fem with affection] Kayer [crayfish] Keki [seagull] Ke-Ipekai [old wife] Keriri [Hammond Island] Kerket [anger] Kerne [young lad] Keturketai [old man] Ki [possessive; mine i.e Muleepa-Ki = my spear] Kissuri [moon] Kobar [cough] Komi [friend fem to male] Kopuru [Whiting]. Kowturri [blue crab] Kuki [seagull] Kuki [wet season/ monsoon] Kuku [knee]

Kunur [ash] Kutai [Yam] Kra-ameepa [tie or bind] Krongipa [myself?]

L

Ladeepa [tear/rend] Lahg [possessive: ours] Lahga [land] Lalki [lie]

M

Mada [female genitalia] Madjii [reef, this is probably where the name Madge reef at Nurapai originated] Mageda [body hair] Mal [deep water], Mapu [weight] Marabi [Bamboo] Mari [shell] Marki [Ghost or anything white]. Markili [ghosts] Marramatta [smother] Matu-meepa [strike/hit/wound with spear] Meepa [take it away] Mida [which] Mita [taste] Moarura [Wednesday Island] Monia [maiden/ virgin] Mue [fire] Mue dadje [fire skirt] Muggi kage [baby/infant] Muleepa [spear] Mull-pal [full moon] Mura [coming] Myaichipp [cry]

N

Nabing [this/these] Nadu [she] Nagi/Ngatu/Ngidu/Ngi [I as in me, sagul nagi= I laugh] Nagir [Mt Earnest Island] Nanu-ee [his] Naroka [maiden/unmarried woman] Nathya [tell/relate?] Nattam [namesake] Nep [grandchild] Nel [name] Norekai [young woman] Nurepai [Horn island] Ngya-oomee [language of the Kaurarega, possibly translated; 'their talk'] Nur [noise] Nukineepa [thirst] Nureepa [twist] Nga [fem; she/ me] Nuki [drinking water]. Netua-kage [son] Ngiou [thou or thee] Ngadu [who] Ngitana [you] Ngi [we] Ngi-kel [you two] Nga [who] Nganu [whose] Ngow [male] Nunu-ee [his] Ngana Kapu [my heart]. Nudu [he]

O

Oomee [possibly speak/talk] Ootzoo [muddy water] Oripara [rainbow] Owai [husband]

P

Paduga [Evans Bay] Pageepa [Spear/sting] Parma [red ochre] Paru [forehead] Piki [dream] Piroan [black snake] Pitti [nose] Palame [theirs].

Q

Quiku [head] Quizdilli [carry bag]

R

Ramu [cold] Raon [bush turkey] Ras [thunderhead clouds] Rebata [Aunt] Rugabu [sweet potato]

S

Sagul [laughter/fun/sing] Samu-dana [eyelash] Suguba-Waneepa [smoke] Sulur [green turtle] Susu [breasts; New Guinea probably Motuan]

T

Tanure [up] Tanureepa [sit] Tareepa [seen] Tarteepa [swim/ turn over] Tarti [hole] Tati [father; when spoken about] Tawpei [short] Titure [star] Topi [turtle shell] Tooki-ap [sister] Tsika [foam] Tugga [mangroves] Tumit [dirt] Tuo [smoke] Turkekai-Kage [young boy]

U

Ubi [greedy] Udlu [dog] Udlu-umai [my dog] Umai [my/mine] Umeeza [stab] Uraba [coconut] Urma [dew] Urza [loggerhead turtle] Ute [sleep] Utsem [fire] Utsemin [put out fire]

W

Waiben [Thursday Island] Wakaow [woman's belt] Warraber [Sue island] Waru [Turtle] Warup [drum] Wawpi [fish] Welmeepa [wake up] Wuna [fog] Wur [sea].

Y

Yawa [goodbye] Yirada [shade]

Z

Zapu [anything tiny]

The letter G is always presented as in the word Get. Ch is always as in Church. Oo as in cool, Ai as in eye.
Vowels were represented as in English, [with two or three different sounds].

Canoe Parts

Platform [Tamu] Netting [Sari] Outrigger poles [Togo] Outrigger float [Sarima] Bow [Bua or Buai] Stern
[Menir] Gunwhale [Bada]. Paddle [Karaba] Mast [Raba] Sail Poles [Suru] Backstays [Buzu] Sail [Rab-
Waku or Waku] Rope [Uro] Anchor [Yadi] Float Pegs [Sarim Pati].

Pronouns

Pronouns; I [Ngatu] Thou or Thee [Ngiou] She [Nadu] He [Nudu] She, We [Ngi] Us [Albei] Both
[Ari] You two [Ngikel] You [Ngitana] They both [Pale] They all [Tana] Me [Ana] For me [Ngai
Aikeka [fem]] For Him [Nu abepa [male].

Examples of Pronouns

Examples: *'Nu abeipa chena wir' [Give that for him] Ana Gamu Abeipa [My body is shivering] Ak-kaikeka*
Mu-le [Tell me/we] Albi Nipa [For us] Ari Nipa [For us many] Pale Nipa or Tane Nipa [for them]. Ngadu
or Nga [who] Nganu [whose] Fimi [what] Mida [which] Nabing [this or these] Chena [that] Aba or Alpa
[let us] Ngow =mle; Udzu = fem; [mine] Yinn [yours] Nunue [his] Nanue [hers] Abane [ours] Palame
[theirs]

Nouns plural

All nouns ending in ra, have the plural re as in Kaura-re-ga, all nouns ending with kai, receive the addition
of Jille to the end of the word, as in Ipi-kai-jille [wives]. To create a plural for a noun or an adjective not
ending in 'ra', add 'le' to the end of the word.

The recorded words and sentences listed above, are a sprinkling of the Kaurarega language written down by John MacGillivray while he was at Cape York in 1849-50. The language of the Kaurarega may now be almost gone but perhaps these few words will bring pleasure to those who still know a little Nya-oomee. Barbara Crawford Thompson taught these words to the officers of the 'Rattlesnake'.

The fate of those involved with Barbara Crawford Thompson: 1843 to 1851.

William Thompson: Believed drowned at Horn Island, December 1844.

William Henry Shetland Thompson: If in fact this man was Barbara Crawford's lover, he survived and remarried in 1846. He fathered two children at Ipswich, the first a girl [Elizabeth] in 1847 and the second a son [Francis] in 1848. William Henry Shetland Thompson died at Ipswich on May, 29,1857, he was aged 65 years.

Jane Crawford: [mother] died, August 26,1853, in Sydney.

Charles Crawford: possibly went to sea or returned to Scotland.

Alexander Crawford: [Brother] possibly went to sea.

Charles Crawford Jnr: [brother] possibly went to sea.

Ann Crawford: [sister] possibly married in Sydney.

Mary Crawford: [sister] possibly married in Sydney.

Andrew Crawford: [brother] unknown

Jane Crawford: [sister] married Henry Whittall in July 1851, in Sydney. She had at least three children

Barbara was a witness to the marriage as Jane was to Barbara's marriage some four months or so later.

Jane Crawford died 1868, aged 36 years in Sydney.

Youngest child of Crawford family [fate unknown]

Wee-nie: Died about 1864, he was shot dead by police from Thursday Island and left at least three adult mix race sons. It is believed that one of the Jardine's of Somerset house, Cape York was involved in the shooting.

Boroto: Died about 1866 or 1867, his death came before the terrible massacre of his people by whites.

This could also be a pointer to the age of Barbara's warrior husband, he became part of her life about one year into her stay at Murralahg or about 1845 when he was perhaps in his late twenties to mid thirties. The information regarding his death comes from the Kennet report on the area shortlyafter the massacre of the Chinese crew and white captain of the fishing boat 'Sperwer', near Murralahg Island.

Queen Baki: of the Goodengarkai tribe of Cape York aboriginals, lived on for many years and was still alive in 1869. [Kennet report]

Captain Owen Stanley: Died March 1850, shortly after bringing his ship back to Sydney.

Brierly, MacGillivray and Huxley: all have biographies and their fates are well recorded.

James Davis; He lived on until 1889, he died aged 75 years and willed the sum of $20,000 to the Royal Brisbane Hospital, perhaps the best thing he had ever done in his life.

Captain J. C. Wickham: Police Magistrate of Brisbane, remained at that post until about 1859, when Queensland, separated from New South Wales and became a state in its own right. He had difficulty with the government and decided to retire to France where he remained with his diaries, until his death.

John Durkin: does not appear to be listed anywhere in Queensland records after his 1841 a pplication to trade between Sydney and Brisbane. His vessel was probably the 'America' which was lost at Cape York with William Thompson and Barbara Crawford aboard. If this was indeed his vessel, Durkin may have drowned.

Kaurarega tribe: Slaughtered at Murralahg.

Footnote: *Today Sunday, October 21st 2007 at 4-30pm Queensland time. Barbara Crawford may have taken pity on my incredible need to have the unknown details of her story recognised. I believe that she has touched me on the shoulder in the form of two of her 'angels'. Glenys Hatch of Perth, Western Australia and Sherrin Blum of Shepparton Victoria are direct descendants of Mary Crawford, Barbara Crawford's older sister. This is one momentous event that I truly hoped would one day happen because for 160+ years, the Crawford family have remained hidden from public view. The fact that this has happened reinforces my belief that I have been on the correct trail all along. Oddly, the two ladies only found out about Barbara's story on the Internet two weeks before finding my book in the West Australian library in Perth. It was because of my curiosity in regard to the unanswered questions in Barbara's story, that I began digging for the truth. It was because of their own family tree curiosity, that Glenys and later, Sherrin found me wallowing about in colonial history. I can only say that I have been honoured and extremely flattered that the descendants of the Crawford family were placed in a position by fate, to contact me above all others who have written about Barbara. Admittedly, the ladies are no bonanza of new information [except in regard to Mary and Ann] but they are Barbara's family and are now extremely important in Australian history.*

Thank god for our modern communication systems and for families now trying to unearth their predecessors. I am surer than ever before that my book is extremely close to Barbara's reality and that I have been rewarded above all other Authors on this subject by contact with a family that has 'gone bush' for so very many years. *(See Chronology Addendum).*

CHRONOLOGY OF EVENTS:

Year 1806, Charles Crawford baptised.

Year 1808 JaneCrawford Morison baptised.

Year 1828, Ship Sophia arrives Sydney.

Year 1831, Henry Shetland sent to Moreton Bay

Year 1837, c May 20th. Birth of baby Crawford.

Year 1837, July, Crawford family arrive Spring Cove Sydney.

Year 1837, September 28th, death of Margaret Crawford born aboard 'John Barry' aged 14 weeks.

Year 1838, Lieutenant Gorman commands Moreton Bay Penal Colony

Year 1841/42, Crawford's meet William Thompson between July 1841 and September 1842.

Year 1842/43, Mary and Ann Crawford leave Sydney for Albany W.A. with the Hassell family.

Year 1843, Barbara Crawford disappears from her home, March 1842.

Year 1843,December. Mary Crawford marries Roderick Martin Cowden in Albany W.A.

Year 1844, September. Ludwig Leighhardt departs Brisbane for Port Essington.

Year 1844, November. Cutter 'America' wrecked Horn Island, Thompson reported drowned.

Year 1845, Barbara among Headhunters at Prince of Wales Island.

Year 1846, William Henry Shetland Thompson married at Ipswich.

Year 1848, HMS 'Rattlesnake' visits Cape York seeking information on explorer Kennedy.

Year 1849, Ann Crawford marries John Wellstead in Albany W.A.

Year 1849 Barbara Crawford Thompson rescued by men of HMS 'Rattlesnake' at Cape York

Year 1850, Death of Captain Owen Stanley, Barbara Crawford returned to her parents.

Year 1851, Marriage of Barbara Crawford's sister Jane Crawford, to Henry Whittall.

Year 1851, Marriage of Barbara Crawford Thompson and James Adams in Sydney.

Year 1853, Death in Sydney of Barbara's mother Jane Crawford.

Year 1857, Death of William Henry Shetland Thompson, aged 65 years.

Year 1859, Queensland gains statehood.

Year 1860, Death of Charles Crawford in Sydney aged 54 years.

Year 1864, Death of Wee-nie of Badu at Thursday Island.

Year 1866/67, Death of Boroto of Murralahg

Year 1868, Death in Sydney, of Jane Crawford Whittall [sister to Barbara]

Year 1889, Death of James Davis.

Year 1903, Mary Crawford Cowden dies in Albany from burns aged approximately 76 years.

Year 1907, Ann Crawford Wellstead dies in Albany W.A. aged 79 years.

Year 1912, Barbara Crawford Thompson Adams dies aged 81/82 years [unverified].

*Chronology Addendum

Year 2007, October 21st. Direct descendants of Barbara's older sister Mary Crawford made contact with the Author. This is the first known contact had by any Author with direct descendants of the Crawford family since 1850. It also appears that both Mary and Ann left Sydney [perhaps October or November 1842] for Albany in Western Australia. They commenced work as servants to the Hassell family at sometime before Charles Crawford went to prison. Both girls went on to have large families [Ann had thirteen children] in Western Australia and both appear to have altered their age by a couple of years to marry. Mary gave her age as 18 years in December 1843 when she married Roderick Martin Cowden whilst her father was three months into his prison term. Mary was in fact 16 or perhaps just seventeen years old at the time. When Mary married she was three months pregnant with the first child of seven that she birthed. The child's name was Matilda, Mary may have put her age up because of her condition or for her marriage. Ann married John Wellstead when she was twenty or twenty-one at Albany [Al-bany not All-bany] Western Australia in December 1849, giving her a birth year of 1828. Ann did not require consent to marry, she had reached 21 in August of 1849. Age discrepancies can be problematic but the ship's manifest taken when the family arrived in Sydney and while the children were still young has proven correct so far. Especially for those whom we have found certification of death or marriage Mary and Ann have been correctly aged through church records and it is only Barbara who remains and enigma in this area. In fact of the nine persons in the Crawford family, all have proven to be age correct with the manifest.Only one remains unproven at this stage and [you guessed it] that person is Barbara Crawford.

Jane [the mother's] death and Jane Crawford [the younger's] age at marriage and death are both 'spot on' with the manifest. The death certificate of Charles Crawford Snr gives his age as 60 in 1860 but this does not tally with the ship's manifest, which gave his age as 30 in 1837. We find that Charles senior was baptised in 1806 and this does tally with the manifest of the 'John Barry', especially if his birthday was after July of that year. At the time of researching for this book, I was not sure that the Charles Crawford buried in 1860, was the 'Tinman' of Kent Street. His descendants and the burial transcript assure me that it was indeed Charles [the tinman] Crawford. More research will be needed to remove all doubt regarding his age and perhaps by examining his police file, we can gain the final proof. Suffice to say that the Barbara Crawford Thompson story remains unaffected by this new information, only Charles Crawford's age is changed from 30 to possibly 36 years when he arrived in Sydney. A final notation on Jane Crawford Whittal [wife of Henry] is that she probably died in childbirth with a little girl that she named Matilda. That baby passed away a short time after Jane, Mary's firstborn was also named Matilda.

Whatever else happened concerning the family or to Barbara herself during the 160 years since these events took place, is really of no consequence to her being cast away on Prince of Wales Island. Yes it would be nice to know exactly what did happen to our heroine in the years 1851 through 1912. For now though, that part of her story remains a mystery. Barbara Crawford Thompson Adams must be recognised for her strength and the courage she displayed from an early age. She may have 'eloped' with Thompson, she may have co-habited with and had children or a child to a native headhunter but she did not place herself in that position by choice. She was certainly not old enough [when she left her home] to be classed as being responsible for her own actions.

Oh the excitement of it all!
As for the excitement of being contacted by direct descendants, one cannot express the enjoyment of such a meeting. The family has been found [or rather found me] and they can now take their share of a place in Australian history. I sincerely hope that all members of the Crawford clan step forward to place Barbara Crawford Thompson Adam's story up on history's pedestal. Thank you Glenys and Sherrin, thank you both very much for the many new hours of phone hopping excitement.

37/8930 – 23 September 1837

Sydney September 19th 1837

C. Crawford Stating Claim to Bedding as an Emigrant pr Ship John Barry

I beg leave most respectfully to inform you that when I engaged with Dr Boyter to come to this Colony, he informed me that I would not be permitted to take any beding with me, but that the Beding served out on board the Ship should be my own, This Promise induced me to part with all my beding previous to embarkation, and to take every precaution during the voyage for the preservation of that which I was served out with, after landing at Spring Cove I had every portion of it most carefully and perfectly cleaned in hopes indeed never doubting but I should have them according to Dr Boyters promise, But as Dr Thompson the Surgeon Superintendant issued Orders for all of it to be left behind us at Spring Cove, I of course complied with his Orders thinking they would be made good to me on my arrival here in this I am as yet disappointed, and as I am in expectation of an engagement, and will in consequence have to leave the Government Bazzar the first thing it will be necessary for me to provide will be Beding for my family, and having eight Children it will not be easy done as I find beding a very expensive article here – I therefor beg that you will take my case into considiration, and if posible get Government to give me some remuneration for (what my bargain with Dr Boyter intitles me to call) my loss

To the Hon. the Secretary of State

I Am Sir Your Most Obt Servt
Charles Crawford

Letter from Charles Crawford to Sydney officials. Sept. 1837

Charles in this letter is asking for remuneration on his family's bedding left at Spring Cove. Charles believed that he could keep the ship-issued bedding supplied to him aboard the John Barry but sadly the fever made it imperative that the bedding be left behind. A letter written in reply to Charles Crawford's allegations by Dr Thomson of the 'John Barry' stated that one Robert Hodge, whom he called a 'factious individual', probably wrote the letter for Charles. He also called Charles a 'worthless character', which seems a little petulant for one who has just lost many patients aboard the 'John Barry'. Robert Hodge could have been one of two men of that name. One of them was the sole survivor of Eliza Fraser's 'Stirling Castle' pinnace wreck. Like Eliza, Hodge spent time petitioning for financial compensation and he was a Sydney sider. While the other was a passenger on the 'John Barry' and would have known Charles and the doctor very well, the latter man is the more likely prospect of the two. The letter itself may not have been in Charles' own hand but his wife could certainly have written it. Still it is rather odd that so many small co-incidences seem to occur regarding the two shipwreck stories. During the 160 years that have passed since the events depicted in this work occurred, many writers have rewritten her story. All have relied upon the eyewitness accounts of her rescue given by Oswald Brierly, Thomas Huxley and John MacGillivray. These men were present shortly after she presented herself to the washing party from the British warship, HMS 'Rattlesnake'. Over the years, the story has been gradually embellished and many errors have crept into the many copies of copies of the tale.

Recent writers appear to have completely ignored the diaries of the men who were present at her rescue and contented themselves with imitating those who originally took the story from the works of the three scientists. This has led to books being published with much erroneous and exaggerated information. Why these modern writers have not gone back to the source is beyond comprehension, perhaps laziness or the 'sheep follow sheep' syndrome can be blamed for the lack of investigative work.

Major Information Sources:

Colonial Secretary letters, to Penal Colony Commandant at Moreton Bay 1835-1850, Queensland State Library.

Letters to the Colonial Secretary from the Commandant, Moreton Bay, 1835-1850. Queensland State Library.

Letters from the Colonial Secretary, to the Police Magistrate at Moreton Bay Penal Colony. 1842-1850. Queensland State Library.

Letters from the Police Magistrate to the Colonial Secretary in Sydney, 1842-1850. Queensland State Library.

Islanders and Aboriginals at Cape York David R Moore

Narration of the Voyage of the HMS 'Rattlesnake' John MacGillivray, 2 vols, Boone of London Queensland, University, St Lucia, Queensland

Ships passenger lists of the 'John Barry' voyage of 1837. Queensland State Library.

Convict lists for the ship 'Sophia' voyage of 1828/9. Queensland State Library

Kennet Report, 1869, Queensland State Library.

Isles of Despair, Ion Idriess.

Brisbane Town News 1842/1846, Thomas Dowse publisher. Queensland State Library

Brisbane Courier Mail 1850, Queensland State Library.

Sydney Herald newspaper 1836, 1837, 1842, 1843, 1850, 1853

Sydney Gazette 1842/50 Queensland State Library

Diary of Thomas Huxley, published by Julian Huxley, 1935, University of Queensland.

Biography of Captain Owen Stanley, Adelaide Lubbock

Diary of Dr John Thomson, surgeon, HMS 'Rattlesnake' Mitchell Library, Sydney.

Queensland University, St Lucia

All care has been taken to authenticate documents regarding the Crawford Birth, Death and Marriage certifications. Although errors do occur in old records, cross checking has been done on all of these files. An apology is offered to any surviving family where an unlikely error may have slipped by un-noticed.

Thank you to the staff at the State Library of Queensland for their patient assistance, with special thanks to Miles, Stephanie and Dennis.

The Queensland University supplied much information and graphics for this work and a special thank you to Rose at Friars.

Finally, thanks to all who assisted in this work with their helpful comments, research and unrewarded shoulders to lean on.

'Yawa ana Komilee, Yawa'
[Kaurarega]

About the Author;

Raymond John Warren was born at Broken Hill New South Wales on the 17th November 1944 and was schooled at Broken Hill High. After leaving high school as a non-graduate at fourteen, his working life began as roustabout on sheep stations near Tipbooburra, in the far northwest of New South Wales.

Work experience in the bush included Sawmilling, professional kangaroo shooting, rabbit trapping, Rail-line extra ganger, Jackaroo, Station Overseer and eventually Station Manager. He left the bush in Western Australia and progressed to ocean fishing on crayfish boats at Geraldton in Western Australia and longline shark fishing at Lakes Entrance in Victoria.

After relocating to the city of Adelaide, South Australia in 1969, he began a career with Encyclopaedia Britannica, starting as sales agent and progressing to Sales Manager. He travelled widely with that company, traversing both Australia and Papua New Guinea. He also entered the publishing world himself, producing a sporting newspaper, historic magazine and garden magazines. Later publications in Queensland included an historic tourist magazine. His obsession with Australian history and especially colonial 'Tall Ships', brought about an interest in shipwrecks and castaways. This eventually led to research on some of the many unsolved mysteries of the sea, including the Barbara Crawford Thompson story.

Upcoming books by the Author
Warrikame [White Fish from the Sea]
The Warren Encyclopaedic Register of Colonial Tallships